PRAISE FOR *A BROTHER'S INSIGHT*

"*A Brother's Insight* is both a compelling road map for eliminating racial violence toward people of color and a powerful story of love and perseverance. Dr. Joe-Joe invites you to witness his full life, infused with brotherly joy, yet peppered with racism, heartbreak, and pain. Dr. Joe-Joe provides new insights on how racism adversely impacts everyone, including white people."

—RHEEDA WALKER, PhD, author of
The Unapologetic Guide to Black Mental Health

"I highly recommend *A Brother's Insight* because it contains the common sense that the world needs a lot more of today."

—JANE ELLIOTT, internationally renowned educator, author of *A Collar In My Pocket: The Blue Eyes Brown Eyes Exercise*

"*A Brother's Insight* is the real deal. The book is challenging, informative, and action oriented. It is a must-have resource and guide for anyone serious about becoming antiracist and ending racism, white supremacy, and oppression."

—EDDIE MOORE JR., PhD, Founder and Program Director,
The White Privilege Conference

"Dr. McManus, with loving care and introspection, cracks open and lays bare his deeply personal and painful experiences with racism, sharing how they have shaped his antiracist living and practice in ways that can inspire us all. An undeniable invitation to do the same."

—JADE AGUA, EdD, Chief Learning Officer,
USC Race and Equity Center

"Drawing from his lived experiences and professional work, McManus challenges readers to engage in self-reflection, embrace solidarity, and take meaningful action against systemic oppression. *A Brother's Insight* is deeply reflective and is a clarion call to everyone committed to the fight for racial justice. Rooted in wisdom, courage, and love, it calls upon all of us to do our part in building a world where equality is no longer just a dream but a lived reality for all."

—KRISTAL MOORE CLEMONS, PhD,
National Director, Children's Defense Fund Freedom Schools

"This heartfelt, yet powerful and honest lifelong reflection at the core of navigating and negotiating white supremacist episteme offers exactly what antiracist practicing and aspiring souls require for this vital work. Joe-Joe's journey offers experiential and practical guidance filled with conviction, vulnerability, and expertise. His story models the love required of us to sustain the spirit and the humanity critical to transform both self and society. This book is an inspirational must-have for the antiracist toolkit."

—MICHAEL BENITEZ, PhD,
nationally acclaimed educator, Vice President for Diversity
and Inclusion, Metropolitan State University of Denver

"*A Brother's Insight* is a powerful and thought-provoking narrative that challenges readers to confront the realities of systemic racism while offering actionable steps toward lasting change. Dr. Joe-Joe's blend of personal stories and insightful guidance make this book a must-read for anyone committed to advancing racial justice and creating an anti-racist society."

—EDWARD C. BUSH, PhD, President,
Cosumnes River College, Cofounder/President-Elect, A²MEND

"If you're looking for a pragmatic, no-nonsense guide to becoming actively antiracist, no one does it better than Joe-Joe. *A Brother's Insight* combines personal reflections on a lifetime of unlearning and understanding the complexities of racism in America with research-based practices drawn from a career dedicated to these issues. This book is the essential how-to guide we've been missing for living an antiracist life. Equal parts heartwarming, thought-provoking, and educational, Joe-Joe breaks down a complex topic into digestible insights that anyone serious about antiracism can apply. I will be adding this to my list of recommendations for anyone looking to grow in their allyship and become an active participant in building a more just society."

—BOBBIE PORTER, EdD, Vice President and Chief
DEI Officer, California State University, Dominguez Hills

"Like its author, *A Brother's Insight* is high in integrity, deeply engaging, and unapologetically direct. I initially read it with great interest in Joe-Joe McManus's personal story of incessant striving toward the most impactful antiracist action, even in the face of difficulty and heartbreak. I will keep it handy and return to it for the loving, demanding, and profoundly informative reminders for why I must dig deeper, act with more consciousness, and transform, rather than tinker toward racial justice."

—PAUL GORSKI, PhD, Founder of the Equity Literacy Institute; coauthor of *Fix Injustice, Not Kids and Other Principles for Transformative Equity Leadership*

"*A Brother's Insight* is an important book for white people seeking a more just society and who realize that the rich and powerful are working to sow racial division among us. Drawing on his decades of personal and professional experience, McManus provides an understanding of how white supremacy works, as well as practical and strategic tools to help each of us become more effective allies for racial justice. *A Brother's Insight* will inform, inspire, and guide you in this essential work."

—PAUL KIVEL, social justice educator, activist, author of *Uprooting Racism: How White People Can Work for Racial Justice*

"In this highly personal, beautifully written account, Dr. Joe-Joe McManus bares his soul and shares the driving motivation for his years of dedication to combating racism and discrimination through education, training, and research. *A Brother's Insight* provides readers the perspective that touches hearts and the practical strategies necessary to transform willing souls from being apathetic to becoming active allies. It is a mandate to dismantle racism and achieve the inclusive, desired community we so long for and deserve."

—EURYDICE S. STANLEY, PhD, LTC, US Army, retired, coauthor of *The Worst First Day: Bullied While Desegregating Little Rock Central High*

"Dr. Joe-Joe McManus has woven a story and a message that deserves to be read by every person who wishes for this world to be better. Born out of personal pain and a lifelong, action-oriented commitment to antiracism, Dr. McManus has crafted a combination of memoir, handbook, and reflective mirror that provides an illuminating road map for personal transformation and long-term impact."

—SUMUN PENDAKUR, EdD, Founder, Sumun Pendakur Consulting

"Throughout his book, Dr. Joe-Joe weaves deeply personal stories that he has rarely told in an effort to not only show the trajectory of what it can look like to approach your growing edges with humility, but also how to align what matters to you within a greater historical context. *A Brother's Insight* moves beyond the rhetoric to real possibilities for sustained change, speaks to those of us who are 'done with ugly and still doing the hard work,' and shows us that we can indeed shift from problematizing to possibilities."

—CATHERINE WONG, renowned international speaker and consultant on inclusive education and community development

"Dr. McManus's remarkable description of a fundamental contradiction of the human condition is nothing short of powerful, poignant, and provocative. It reveals the heart of the man himself who has a remarkable revolutionary spirit stemming from his lived experience—his unrelenting quest for justice in a world where speaking truth to power remains challenging in the twenty-first century. Joe-Joe remains true to his mission of liberating hearts, minds, and souls in this exemplary literary work that is transformational and socially disruptive in equal measure."

—KIRINDI ODINDO, peace and decolonization educator, contributing author, *Decolonize Humxnize*

"When I was a young filmmaker exploring issues of racism and colorism through my film *A Girl Like Me*, Dr. McManus reached out to provide me with one of my first speaking and screening opportunities. This experience marked the beginning of my witnessing his unwavering commitment to confronting racism and fostering meaningful dialogue. . . . In *A Brother's Insight*, Dr. McManus brings that same unwavering commitment and authenticity to the page. This book is a deeply personal and unflinchingly honest exploration of what it means to lead an antiracist life, weaving together powerful stories and personal reflections that reveal the emotional depth and ongoing journey of confronting racism in all its forms. At a time when critical race theory is under attack, historical truths are being erased from classrooms, and essential books are being banned from school libraries, this work is more necessary than ever. Dr. McManus challenges readers to confront uncomfortable truths, recognize their own complicity, and take actionable steps toward dismantling racism and meaningfully contributing to the fight for equality. *A Brother's Insight* is not just an invaluable resource but a vital call to action, and I am confident it will be utilized as a tool for change for years to come."

—KIRI LAURELLE DAVIS, racial justice advocate, documentary filmmaker, *A Girl Like Me*

"In *A Brother's Insight*, Joe-Joe McManus opens his heart and shares a deeply personal story that speaks to the pain and resilience born from the harsh realities of racism. As someone who has walked a similar path of grief and healing after tragically losing my brother, Joe-Joe's journey resonates deeply with me. His words offer not only a source of inspiration but also a guiding light for all of us who seek to heal and grow in a world that often feels divided. This book is more than just a reflection of Joe-Joe's remarkable commitment to equity, inclusion, and justice—it is a powerful call for each of us to look within and embark on our own journeys toward understanding and transformation. . . . *A Brother's Insight* offers both wisdom and practical guidance. Joe-Joe's words encourage us to embrace our own growth and reflection, knowing that every small effort we make contributes to a larger movement of love and justice. This book is a heartfelt invitation to each of us to find our place in that movement and to help create a world where every individual can thrive in their full humanity."

—TASREEN KHAMISA, Executive Director, the Tariq Khamisa Foundation

"Dr. Joe-Joe McManus's book, *A Brother's Insight*, is a timely and powerful exploration of the deep-rooted issues of racism and how we can work to dismantle it in our society. Drawing from his personal experiences and professional career spanning over three decades, Dr. McManus provides readers with an intimate, honest, and deeply thoughtful narrative. What sets this book apart is the way Dr. McManus connects the personal to the systemic. He seamlessly weaves his own life story with broader lessons on how we can all play a part in advancing equity, inclusion, and justice. His ability to take complex issues and break them down into practical, everyday decisions—whether it's in how we shop, how we engage socially, or how we give—makes this book a must-read for anyone looking to live an actively antiracist life. The courage and conviction Dr. McManus shows in *A Brother's Insight* reminds us that the fight for racial justice is both personal and collective. His ability to challenge readers to examine their own actions while offering hope and a path forward is what makes this work truly exceptional."

—STUART C. LORD, DMin, CEO, Delta Developmental

A BROTHER'S INSIGHT

GUIDANCE ON DEFEATING RACISM and ADVANCING FREEDOM

Joe-Joe McManus, PhD
WITH FOREWORD BY RHEEDA WALKER, PhD

WONDERWELL
PRESS

This publication is designed to provide accurate and authoritative information in regard to the subject matter covered. It is sold with the understanding that the publisher and author are not engaged in rendering legal, accounting, or other professional services. Nothing herein shall create an attorney-client relationship, and nothing herein shall constitute legal advice or a solicitation to offer legal advice. If legal advice or other expert assistance is required, the services of a competent professional should be sought.

Published by Wonderwell Press
Austin, Texas
www.gbgpress.com

Copyright © 2025 Joe-Joe McManus, PhD

All rights reserved.

Thank you for purchasing an authorized edition of this book and for complying with copyright law. No part of this book may be reproduced, stored in a retrieval system, or transmitted by any means, electronic, mechanical, photocopying, recording, or otherwise, without written permission from the copyright holder.

This work is being published under the Wonderwell Press imprint by an exclusive arrangement with Wonderwell. Wonderwell, Wonderwell Press, and the Wonderwell logos are wholly-owned trademarks of Wonderwell.

Distributed by Greenleaf Book Group

For ordering information or special discounts for bulk purchases, please contact Greenleaf Book Group at PO Box 91869, Austin, TX 78709, 512.891.6100.

Design and composition by Greenleaf Book Group and Kim Lance
Cover design by Greenleaf Book Group and Kim Lance

Publisher's Cataloging-in-Publication data is available.

Print ISBN: 978-1-963827-11-8

eBook ISBN: 978-1-963827-12-5

To offset the number of trees consumed in the printing of our books, Greenleaf donates a portion of the proceeds from each printing to the Arbor Day Foundation. Greenleaf Book Group has replaced over 50,000 trees since 2007.

Printed in the United States of America on acid-free paper

25 26 27 28 29 30 31 32   10 9 8 7 6 5 4 3 2 1

First Edition

*With love and hope for Makaila,
my daughter and favorite person.*

*In loving memory of my brother Kacey
and our parents, Mike and Maxine.*

CONTENTS

FOREWORD
BY RHEEDA WALKER, PHD xiii

INTRODUCTION
KACEY'S BROTHER 1

1. THE LITTLE GIRL
How Racism Harms Us All, and What We Can Do About It 17

2. WHAT IF?
An Antiracist Vision of a Better World 47

3. LIES OUR TEACHERS TOLD US
How Schools are Weaponized to Divide Us 67

4. NOT RACIST IS NOT ENOUGH
Reimagining Education 95

5. THE PACKIE
Developing an Antiracist Lens 117

6. IT'S ME! IT'S MAKKIE!
The Critical Importance of Your Voice 135

7. SOMEONE FALLS IN A HOLE
The Power of Relationships, Community, and Solidarity 153

8. CHECK, PLEASE!
Racism as a Deal-Breaker 171

9. KILLED, FIRED, CANCELED
Being Prepared for Backlash 203

10. WANT THE BALL
Making Your Unique Contribution to Ending Racism 231

AFTERWORD
FOR ALL THE MARBLES
How We All Benefit from Choosing Solidarity 257

ACKNOWLEDGMENTS 273

NOTES 275

ABOUT THE AUTHOR 279

FOREWORD

A *BROTHER'S INSIGHT: Guidance on Defeating Racism and Advancing Freedom* is both a compelling road map for eliminating racial violence toward people of color and a powerful story of love and perseverance. Dr. Joe-Joe invites you to witness his full life, infused with brotherly joy, yet peppered with racism, heartbreak, and pain. His narrative reads not only as a guide but also as an open and vulnerable memoir, inclusive of his daughter's brave mandate to "do more" after the murder of George Floyd. This story has been a long time coming. Dr. Joe-Joe personally understands that individual, systemic, cultural, and other forms of racism and intersecting oppressions have persisted through time and across generations. *A Brother's Insight* is a must-read for every individual who cares to use their unique privileges to create a more racially just society.

There have been countless overtures to neutralize racism and microaggressive behavior. Why has so little changed? The systems are undefeated because those who possess white privilege actively and passively resist freedom *for all*. Every so often, usually after a shockingly violent event against a person of color, there is increased "sensitivity" to systemic racism. However, those who are most often victimized by these systems know that the sensitivity and subsequent "DEI statements" are superficial at best. Change is needed on a deeper and more *surgical* level. There can be no shortcuts.

A Brother's Insight is transformational and will, undoubtedly, motivate you to begin or continue on a devoted path toward living an antiracist life. As Dr. Joe-Joe points out, change can be uncomfortable and scary, but he asks and answers the bold question: *What if racism ceased to exist?* He navigates you through the "hows" and the "whys" of racism, as he comprehensively unpacks the layers of key related issues—from defining systemic racism to diagnosing its role in educational, legal, economic, and other powerful systems of injustice. For example, racism is, sadly, at the root of many mental and emotional health concerns in underserved and marginalized communities. Dr. Joe-Joe provides new insights on how racism adversely impacts everyone, including white people. He acknowledges that Black and Indigenous people are tired of carrying the burdens of racial oppression and the struggle against it. He makes it clear that it is time for those who benefit from systemic racism and white privilege to understand their role and change the narrative for future generations.

Not "being" racist is a mere starting point. Dr. Joe-Joe implores everyone to adopt racial justice as a core value, not a casual idea to be considered only now and again. He also acknowledges that antiracism doesn't look the same for everyone. Guided by a shared commitment to racial justice, each individual must navigate how best to use their own unique skill sets, experience, and access to actively promote change. Dr. Joe-Joe's message is that everyone must commit to personally engaging in what Congressman and Civil Rights trailblazer John Lewis termed "good trouble."

One aspect of *A Brother's Insight* that resonates and that cannot be overstated is the importance of using one's gifts and operating in one's own authenticity. There is something truly freeing about this disposition. There is no need for someone to take on more than they can. Instead, they must be courageous enough to be themselves, building confidence and finding potential along the way, to live out their core antiracist values. Dr. Joe-Joe has achieved this as a brother to Kacey, dad to Makkie, and trusted friend and colleague to those who have embraced him along the way.

A Brother's Insight is like no other antiracism or social justice text. It does not tiptoe around uncomfortable or difficult topics. There is no room for "white guilt" in this book. Dr. Joe-Joe notes that guilt may be part of the reason that some individuals subscribe prematurely, superficially, and temporarily to being "not-racist." Such guilt adds shame along with myriad other negative and unhelpful feelings, according to Dr. Joe-Joe. Fortunately, he also imparts tremendous insights for those who may feel powerless along the journey. Others may be unconvinced of the pervasive and systemic nature of racism, and there is wisdom in the text for them too.

Another invaluable dimension of this narrative and mandate is Dr. Joe-Joe's knack for anticipating every worry that could emerge for the apprehensive reader. He has clearly heard the fears and "justifications" for not embracing antiracism and gives the reader access to both his expertise and his tough skin. The book also provides specific guidance to manage the consequences of maintaining a genuine antiracist disposition and offers concrete strategies for navigating financial instability and avoiding other potential pitfalls of antiracism work.

A Brother's Insight provides enlightening information about people who prefer "strategic ignorance" or feign a lack of awareness of racism for the purpose of maintaining their innocence. Dr. Joe-Joe also exposes the tactics used to derail racial justice efforts—strategies that include asking questions meant to slow progress. These and other derailing strategies allow individuals to enable racism or simply stand by comfortably while it persists. His insights may also be freeing for those who too often feel stuck under the boot of oppression, wondering if they are losing their minds.

Dr. Joe-Joe has shares some of the most painful parts of his life's story to inform and to transform others, recognizing that there can be no freedom while racism exists. Throughout *A Brother's Insight* and in its conclusion, Dr. Joe-Joe acknowledges the difficulty of antiracist work, while inspiring confidence that even small numbers of folks who take big risks will ultimately persuade the masses. Everyone who reads this book will be encouraged to recognize the true divide between those who want to maintain systems of oppression and those who see both the beauty and necessity of justice, equity, and inclusion. The difference is in the willingness to act. Though history might tell us otherwise, the future is bright. This work is feasible because—as the Ethiopian proverb reminds us—when spiders unite, they can tie up a lion.

—**RHEEDA WALKER, PHD**
Author of *The Unapologetic Guide to Black Mental Health*

INTRODUCTION
Kacey's Brother

Action is the antidote to despair.

—JOAN BAEZ

MY COMMITMENT TO ANTIRACISM started early in life. It did not come about because I was a particularly enlightened child or because I had some intrinsic drive to educate myself on the evils of oppression. I learned about racism because I was Kacey's brother.

Kacey was brilliant, charismatic, and strong. He had the most beautiful smile, and he was the kindest person I've ever known. We were born only eleven months apart, and we did everything together as children. Mom even dressed us alike. She thought it was cute, plus she loved a good buy-one-get-one sale.

Nearly every memory from my youth includes Kacey. He called me his "little-big brother," because by the time we started school he was taller than me, even though I was the older brother. In many ways, along with our younger brother, B-J—the surprise—we were typical kids. We loved sports. We played and fought with each other. And we loved each other in that special way brothers do.

Our personalities and interests were different: Kacey was outgoing and loved to run and play football, while I was a shy kid obsessed with basketball. Kacey liked to go on long bike rides. I enjoyed reading. Our skin colors were different, too: Kacey was Black, and our little brother, B-J, and I were white.[1]

To be clear, having a brother who was Black did not make me or B-J antiracist. Adopting a Black child did not make my parents, or anyone else in the family for that matter, antiracist. Proximity to a person of color or having a Black friend, partner, or family member does not make you antiracist—it just doesn't. I've met too many white folks who claim that they "can't be racist" because of some connection, real or imagined, to a Black person, Black community, or some aspect of Black culture but who then proceed to say or do things that prove otherwise. Being antiracist is about beliefs, values, and behaviors. It can certainly be informed by connections to people, communities, and cultures that are different from your own, but proximity does not magically make anyone antiracist.

Our parents, Mike and Maxine, adopted Kacey into the family when he was about a month old. Mom and Dad shared an interest in adoption, but their initial intent was not necessarily to adopt a Black child. Adoption just felt like an important way that they could do something good in the world. So, they went through the lengthy process of applying to adopt a baby.

It was 1971, the year after I was born, and Mom and Dad were very excited to learn that their application had been accepted. When they arrived at the adoption agency, they were asked what type of baby they were looking for. Their response was that they would like to adopt a baby who might not otherwise be adopted. They were told that nobody wanted the Black children; only the adoption agent didn't say "Black children," she used the n-slur. Mom responded by scolding her about her bigoted language and saying, "Well, then we want to adopt a Black child."

Mom was a force of nature. It is easy to imagine how it went, because I saw her take on all sorts of folks over the years who dared spout their bigotry in front of her. I can picture it now: all five foot two and three-quarters of her, Boston accent blaring, going off, and Dad standing tall and proud right by her side.

After they received a less-than-sincere apology, Mom and Dad were escorted into a separate room that was filled with babies of color. The way our parents told the story, as soon as Mom saw Kacey she fell in love and said to Dad, "He's our child."

I imagine it was extraordinarily difficult for Kacey's birth parents, who at eighteen years old, must have struggled with the idea of letting go of their precious newborn child. Kacey and I talked about his birth parents sometimes. We didn't know much about them, but Kacey always said he wanted to meet them someday and that I had to go with him when he did. Kacey was curious about them and had lots of questions. Plus, I looked so much like Mom, and B-J so much like Dad, we were curious about which of his birth parents Kacey might resemble.

Our little family was pretty diverse. In addition to the racial difference, on Dad's side, Grampa was Irish Catholic and Grandma English Protestant, a match that was quite controversial in their day. Not to be outdone, I suppose, Dad then married Mom, who was Jewish. Growing up in such a diverse family was not easy, particularly in our small, white-flight town of Carver, Massachusetts. I remember a lot of great times as well, though. We lived in the attached apartment behind the Carver Package Store, or "the packie" in Massachusetts-speak—basically a liquor store. Our own little mom-and-pop shop. There was always something going on at the packie, and plenty of work to do. Never a dull moment!

Set at the convergence of several neighborhoods, the packie hosted a cross section of Carver's population every day. It may seem counterintuitive, but the packie was a safe space for us boys. For me, the basketball court that Dad built behind the packie, in the delivery area, was even more important. Dad and his buddy Roger, who owned a paving company, built it when I was around eight years old to provide a place for neighborhood kids to come together and play ball—and to keep us all out of trouble.

Some of the best memories of my childhood happened right there on the court behind the packie.

In the beginning, it was just Dad and his friends playing and coaching us kids. Before we knew it, other kids were coming to learn too. Soon, the court behind the packie became the place where all the best street ballers from the area came to play. It was no Rucker, the famed court in Harlem, but there was some talent in and around Carver at the time, and everyone came to play at the packie.

Everyone came through, but there were regulars on the court, just like in the packie. Interestingly, three brothers—Frank, David, and Joe—were among them; David was a white kid in an otherwise Black family. To this day, I am not sure what their story was. We never questioned it—it seemed normal to us at the time. In the summer, the court was always packed. That's when most of the players from farther away would come to play. Sometimes, Dad would find out about an open tournament and get a bunch of us together to enter as a team. The most memorable was the one we later called the Bad News Bears team, referring to the movie about a raggedy-looking baseball team. We were the only team without uniforms, and our sneakers were well worn, but we knew how to play together. To this day, I love to work in teams.

The court behind the packie was not just a safe space for us; it was also a space that provided us with a community—a mostly Black community—that other kids who looked like me did not have. Our school was predominantly white, and many of the white families in our town had moved there to avoid the desegregation of the Boston Public Schools, so they weren't exactly working to ensure their kids were part of a diverse community.

We didn't realize it until we were a little older, and not spending all of our time at the packie, but there was a great deal of racism in our small town. We always thought our parents and their friends were overly protective of us but, over time, we began to understand why. They were trying to protect their boys, most especially Kacey, from a world that was not even close to ready for us.

Racism in Real Time

Like everyone, Kacey was a multifaceted individual. Among many other things, he was a Black male, which meant people often viewed him as if he were a walking one-dimensional stereotype. That often meant that he was seen and treated as dangerous—even as a kid—and, outside of athletics, expectations of him were always low. Meanwhile, as a white kid, I was treated like a kid. Nobody feared me, and I was generally given the opportunity to demonstrate my character. People reserved judgment until I proved myself one way or the other. This incongruity was impossible to overlook, so I learned early on that, regardless of our innate human complexities—who we were, the different things we cared about, and all that we experienced—our skin color determined how most people treated us.

The year I was born, a documentary film called *The Eye of the Storm* showed how third-grade teacher Jane Elliott used eye color to give her students a small taste of what it feels like to be the target of discrimination. As part of that exercise, using academic tests to demonstrate the power of teacher expectations on student performance, she found that even very short-term low expectations damaged her students' self-confidence and produced lower test scores. Imagine the impact low expectations had over the long term on Black children like Kacey, or on other children of color, immigrant children, unhoused children, or girls in STEM. Seeing that documentary, as a teenager, years after it was produced, taught me that expectations matter and helped me see beyond interpersonal bigotry and begin to understand systemic oppression. It explained what I had witnessed happening to my brother in real time, for as long as I could remember.

> *I learned early on that, regardless of our innate human complexities—who we were, the different things we cared about, and all that we experienced—our skin color determined how most people treated us.*

Why so many people are capable of recognizing the distinct differences of individuals within their families and friend groups but simultaneously assume others to be monolithic stereotypes without any nuance or complexity is fascinating to me. Many would say that this is caused by a lack of "exposure" to other groups. That may be part of the answer and explain why relationships across racial lines do matter even if they do not override racism on their own. But the other part of the answer is that racism requires a suspension of critical thinking and even common sense. Those who benefit from racism choose to suspend their ability to think critically in order to justify and maintain their place in the racial hierarchy. They set aside their capacity to attend to obvious flaws in their views in order to avoid cognitive dissonance. This is how personal bias reinforces systemic oppression.

Before we go further, I want to point out that many people who understand white supremacist ideologies, stereotyping, hate speech, or discrimination at the interpersonal level get tripped up when the conversation shifts to systemic racism. It is, however, important that we understand our roles and influence at the systems level, because our responsibility goes beyond the interpersonal.

Those who benefit from racism choose to suspend their ability to think critically in order to justify and maintain their place in the racial hierarchy.

There is an easy way to understand systemic racism that I have heard described in a variety of ways over the years. Think about the systems in your home. Modern homes typically have multiple systems hidden behind the walls, such as electrical, plumbing, and HVAC. If, for example, your home has a dangerously outdated electrical system, or one that has been poorly installed, it would be a fire hazard. This is a serious problem and would require looking behind the walls to see what exactly is wrong and either fixing or replacing the system to ensure the safety of your family.

A system that is corrupted by racism, or that was designed with racist intent, is no different. In order to remedy the problem, we have to look behind the walls to see what is wrong with the system in order to determine how to fix the problem or whether it needs to be replaced with a better one. I have spent much of my adult life working behind the walls of our collective home, and I am letting you know that we have a problem. It is going to take real work to update our systems and to replace those that are beyond repair. Rather than electrical or plumbing, we're talking about educational, economic, and legal systems. And, in the same way that painting the walls and decorating won't solve a plumbing problem, we cannot expect to end racism by pretending it is not there.

As humans, we make choices all the time about whether to address problems or ignore them, sometimes consciously and sometimes unconsciously. Our choices matter, not just interpersonally but with respect to our contributions to the world around us. Ultimately, systemic racial oppression continues to work when people either choose to practice racism or to ignore it—either way, racism persists. This is true of all forms of oppression, I suppose. When I was a kid, it was the overt racism—when someone said or did something so racist that it was obvious—that stood out to me. It wasn't until much later that I understood the damage caused by the less obvious, less extreme events known as "racial microaggressions" and by all the people who stand back and do absolutely nothing about any of it. It wasn't until even later that I fully understood the systems of racism hidden behind the walls.

As a result, and regardless of whether a person deemed "white" invites it or not, whiteness comes with massive privilege, including, of course, the privilege of not being the target of racism, but also the privilege of choosing whether or not to acknowledge it or do anything about it. That doesn't mean that a white person cannot be oppressed. Most white people are oppressed to varying degrees based on their social class or socioeconomic status, gender identity, sexual orientation, or religion, to name a few major examples. They are not, however, oppressed because they are white.

As a young Irish Jew growing up in that small town south of Boston, I did not directly feel the pain caused by racial discrimination. But Kacey could not avoid the racial bigotry and systemic biases all around him, emanating from teachers, parents, the media, other kids—from what seemed like everyone, everywhere. As his big brother, I felt the pains of racism secondhand. The worst came from the fact that I could not protect him from all of the pain, self-doubt, and life consequences that racism caused, no matter how hard I tried.

If you are an older sibling, you understand my deep, instinctual need to protect my younger brothers. I would have done absolutely anything to prevent them from being hurt. Kacey was a tough kid—we all were—but no amount of toughness can alleviate the pain caused by experiencing acts of racist hatred, daily microaggressions, and the impact of systems of racial oppression they support.

Kacey used to say that we were "closer than blood" because of everything we went through together (a small sample of which is described in this book). Although both he and B-J grew up to be significantly bigger and stronger than me, I was able to protect them when we were young in many ways. There were times I was able to protect them from bullies or teach them something useful, and I felt like a good big brother, like someone they could look up to. But there were far too many times I could not, primarily because I couldn't figure out how to protect Kacey from racism.

Losing Kacey

Over the years, no matter how resilient Kacey was or how hard our whole family fought to shield him from racism, the cumulative effect of that fight took its toll. In me, anger and a deep sense of inadequacy grew from my inability to protect Kacey from the myriad racist attacks coming from so many directions. On top of that, the perpetrators almost always denied these attacks were even happening. Sometimes the gaslighting made me think I was crazy. It was all real, though, and it did real damage.

Kacey was just a kid trying to live his life, and I was just trying to be a good big brother. We were both looking to the future, planning to become first-generation college students. Back then, you couldn't google universities for the one that fit your particular goals and needs; you had to pore through catalogs and huge resource books that listed basic facts about various colleges and universities. While some would-be students could rely on word of mouth, we didn't know many people who had gone to college. Finding the right university wasn't easy, especially for Kacey, who was looking for a very specific combination: a culinary arts program, an approach designed to support students with learning differences, and a good football program.

Kacey was a sight to see on the football field. In high school, he played middle linebacker—an important and complex role, like the quarterback for the defense—and occasionally fullback. Although we did not know much about his biological parents, for some reason, his adoption papers included a note that they liked sports and that his father particularly liked football. I wish his birth parents had been there to see the time he broke through the line and shook off the entire opposing team to score a sixty-yard touchdown. I lost my voice cheering him on! It was one of those moments you never forget.

As we continued our college search, Kacey decided to visit a university down south that seemed perfect for him: The sports program needed a middle linebacker, and the school had the culinary program he was interested in, along with what he needed to succeed academically. Excited about the possibilities, Kacey and Mom went on a campus visit. After the tour, Kacey sat with the coaches, watched a football practice, and spent some time with the team. Both Kacey and Mom liked the campus, and the coaches seemed interested in Kacey as a player. But when Kacey came home, he didn't seem excited anymore.

I didn't understand what was wrong. I found out later, from a friend, that some of the players had told Kacey that the head coach was a racist who wanted a white player for Kacey's position. He thought white players were smarter and more suited to lead the defense.

Some time passed, and Kacey began to believe that he might have a spot on the team after all. He was holding on to that hope when things started to go wrong. His SAT scores were not what he had hoped. Like many adolescents, he was having issues with his girlfriend that seemed insurmountable. And then a letter arrived from the university football coach, saying they had found another player for the position and had decided not to offer Kacey a spot on the team.

Mom and Dad asked me to break the news to Kacey. I showed him the letter that night, and as we talked about his options, he came up with what I thought were unrealistic ideas. I shot them all down. Surely, there was a way he could still go to college and play football—but how? We were both frustrated, and I was not helpful.

The next morning, Kacey was not in his room. His favorite red coat was left on his bed. That was strange, so I went straight to school to see if he had gone early to work out.

When I couldn't find him at school, I rushed back home. Mom and Dad were out: I learned later that they were looking at a pizzeria that they hoped to buy—a surprise backup plan for Kacey. He loved pizza and could already cook his butt off. Whether he studied culinary arts at a university or culinary institute or learned on the job, they figured, one way or another he would become a chef someday.

Up in Kacey's room, the red coat was still on his bed. I looked everywhere before finally going down into the basement. There, in dead silence, I found my brother's body.

I am not capable of adequately describing how I felt, or the horror that followed. I don't know how to articulate that much pain.

After rushing to call 911 and then holding Kacey for I don't know how long, reality sank in: He was gone. I could think of nothing but joining him.

I charged up the stairs, my mind in total chaos. Who knows what might have happened if I hadn't literally run into Clive, one of my teammates who was staying with us. I will always be grateful to Clive for protecting me from myself that day.

I cannot imagine what my parents felt as they returned home to see our home surrounded by emergency vehicles, lights flashing, and me standing in the middle of all the traffic, screaming. That was the scene as Mom and Dad learned that we had lost Kacey.

No research or expert can fully explain why some individuals take their own lives while others (sometimes facing circumstances that seem much worse) never even consider it. Perhaps some of us are predisposed to suicide, as we are to addiction or a particular disease. But Dr. Rheeda Walker, psychology professor and nationally recognized expert on suicide within the Black community, speaks about the role of "psychological fortitude," which depends on the "combination of how much exposure you have to life stress, discrimination, and relationship problems and your internal mind and body states."[2] Like any young Black man in America, Kacey experienced racial hatred and discrimination. Over time, it wore down his ability to endure and recover from difficult situations; it diminished his psychological fortitude. Racism may not be the only cause for why my brother became a victim of suicide, but it *was* a factor.

It has been more than thirty-five years since Kacey passed. He had so much going for him, and a bright future ahead that never happened. When he died, those of us who knew and loved him lost something irreplaceable. Everyone who would have met him in the future lost something too. Even if you never would have met him, you still missed out on at least one thing: the opportunity to read a better story, written by Kacey instead of his grieving brother.

Losing Kacey took a piece of me that I cannot explain or ever replace. Like others who have lost a loved one to suicide or racism (or both) and experienced this type of anguish, regret, and guilt, I blame myself. The guilt haunts me. More than anything, I simply wish I could change what happened to my brother—not just how his life ended, but all the pain he felt that pushed him there. While the pain lingers, I have found purpose in it: a drive to do all that I can to end the scourge of racism and white supremacy that has taken so many lives and oppressed countless more.

My brother, like so many others we have lost, should be here today. Kacey's death was another in the long and

I cannot go back and prevent the outcome, but I can honor Kacey's memory by living my best antiracist life and helping others do the same.

shameful line of deaths caused, at least in part, by anti-Black racism. I cannot go back and prevent the outcome, but I *can* honor Kacey's memory by living my best antiracist life and helping others do the same. I can continue to seek inspiration in all the people who are doing their part to end racism as well. Sometimes, I don't have to look far at all, because that inspiration comes from my own child.

Makkie's Challenge

It was June 2020, and our little girl, Makaila ("Mak" or "Makkie"), had just completed the fourth grade. Due to COVID-19, like millions of other students across the nation, her last few months of the school year had taken place online. Our socially outgoing child had found remote learning particularly frustrating, but she had adapted and kept hoping for news that the stay-at-home orders would be over soon. In addition to the pandemic, however, the news also focused on the murder of George Floyd and the worldwide protests against racist police violence.

"Can we talk about Mr. Floyd?" Makkie asked one evening as we sat chatting on the couch together. She was confused: Some of her friends were saying Mr. Floyd did something wrong, but none of them knew what. Others were saying the police did not think Black lives mattered, and so they killed him.

As little Makkie talked, I realized that her friends were simply giving voice to their interpretations of what they were hearing at home. Sometimes, as parents, we forget that our children are always learning from what we say and the examples we set. This is one way we pass racism—or antiracism—to the next generation.

As I contemplated showing my ten-year-old child what had happened to George Floyd, I thought about all the parents who had no choice, no way to shield their children from seeing or experiencing racialized violence. In fact, the brave young woman who recorded the video, seventeen-year-old Darnella Frazier, had been there with her nine-year-old cousin, and both had witnessed the murder of George Floyd in person. If not for Darnella having the presence of mind to record what happened, and the courage to make it public, the false police report would probably never have been challenged, and the man who murdered George Floyd would not be in prison today.

As with every parent, my instinct is always to protect my child, but I understand that there is a difference between protecting and trying to shelter with my privilege. I also wanted Makaila to understand the decision she faced: to learn the reality of what had happened or just listen to rumors and other kids' opinions.

"There is a video of what happened to Mr. Floyd. Do you think seeing it could help you understand better?" I asked her. "It will be difficult to watch, but we can stop at any time."

Mak nodded hesitantly. She wanted to see what had happened and make up her own mind, but it was clear that she was nervous. So, I pulled my little one close and brought up the footage. We sat quietly together and watched the entire video of a white police officer murdering a Black man while other police officers kept anyone else from intervening.

Sometimes, as parents, we forget that our children are always learning from what we say and the examples we set. This is one way we pass racism—or antiracism—to the next generation.

Witnessing my little girl's reaction was painful and disheartening. Little Makkie was leaning forward, tears streaming down her face, eyes intently focused, forehead tensed, lips pursed. I had never seen that look on her face before. Again and again, I wanted to stop the video, but I chose not to. When it finally ended, Makkie was quiet for a moment. She looked deflated. When her questions and comments started coming, they conveyed anger, sadness, and a deep concern.

"What about Mr. Floyd's family and friends?" she wondered, with a child's compassion and genuineness. Her ten-year-old mind could not fathom the hatred and the disregard for human life that she had just witnessed. Not fully aware of the long history of white supremacy leading to that moment, she didn't know that most adults—primarily those who share a skin color with her dad—choose to ignore the history and ongoing normalcy of this type of behavior. So much so that their first question after seeing George Floyd murdered right in front of them was, "What did he do wrong?"

Makkie, however, never asked about Mr. Floyd's behavior. Instead, she expressed an innate understanding that this was a heinous crime that should never have happened. "Why didn't anybody stop him from being murdered?" she asked angrily. She paused. "Isn't this why you do your work?"

"Yes," I replied. "Me, and your mom, and Uncle Stuart, Auntie Cathy, Granny Jane, Uncle Eddie, Tio—"

"You have to work harder, Dad," Makkie said, cutting me off before I could list all the names of our extended family members who do anti-racist work.

"Yeah," I replied, not knowing what else to say.

"Sorry, but it isn't working," Makkie insisted, looking me in the eye with such determination. "What if this happens again?"

Feeling my innocent child's distress and disappointment, I did not have the heart to tell her that George Floyd's death was just the most recent in a long line of lynchings—and that it would almost certainly happen again. And of course, it *has* happened again and again since then. Our discussions about racism and justice continue.

Both my personal and professional lives have been guided by my commitment to fighting racism since I was a child myself. So, it didn't feel great to hear that my work and that of so many others was not enough, but it certainly was not news. At the same time, I also heard my child's directive: that I must examine my life's work and strive to have greater impact. So, after considerable introspection and many conversations with family, friends, and colleagues—and in response to Makkie's challenge—one decision I made was to write this book.

Introduction

I have been encouraged for many years to write about my life experiences, my professional work, and my insights on living an antiracist life. I resisted doing so because I believed that white folks should work behind the scenes in the struggle against racist oppression. We simply need to do our part, not seek the spotlight. I also avoided telling my story because it is painful and imperfect, and because telling it invites harsh, reactive criticism. It has also drawn hateful attacks that take a toll not only on me, but on my loved ones as well.

The problem with my stance was that other white people need to see examples of white antiracists at work in order to see their own potential. They need to hear from practitioners, not only the pundits. They need to hear that it is possible to raise children with a critical antiracist lens. They need to hear the uncomfortable truths from white people who were raised to actively oppose racism, not only those who came to oppose racism later in life. They need to hear about the risks and realities of opposing racism in personal, professional, and social contexts. White people need to hear that standing on the sidelines claiming to not be racist only supports racism and that they have a responsibility to do their part to end racial oppression—and oppression in general. It was time for me to push past my excuses—and to help people who want to live an antiracist life push past theirs.

Having lived a life in the antiracist tradition, I remain dedicated to doing my part by raising my voice to promote racial equity, inclusion, and justice. For me, this wasn't exactly a choice, at least in the beginning. It was my parents' choice, something akin to raising a child in a religious tradition. My story starts with the family they created, and it includes great joy, heartbreaking tragedy, and lessons learned from a purpose-driven life.

Whether opposing racism is a new consideration for you, or you already consider yourself actively antiracist, this book is an invitation to live in the powerful history and tradition of antiracism in your own uniquely impactful way.

1

THE LITTLE GIRL
How Racism Harms Us All, and What We Can Do About It

Antiracism is the commitment to fight racism wherever you find it, including in yourself. And it's the only way forward.

—IJEOMA OLUO

WHEN BARACK OBAMA WAS elected president of the United States, I was excited. So were many other people who care about equity and inclusion. Eager for the opportunity to witness the swearing in of our first Black president, I went to the presidential inauguration in Washington, DC, and stood in the freezing cold for ten hours with Stuart Lord (one of my closest friends) and Makaila's mother, and it was worth every moment. To be there with loved ones and my extraordinary colleagues from the City University of New York (CUNY) Leadership Academy, who brought a busload of our students, was a blessing. We met people who had gathered at the historic March on Washington, in 1963, and heard the Reverend Dr. Martin Luther King Jr.'s iconic "I Have a Dream" speech, and many others who were born much later. It was a beautiful experience and a historic moment.

Many people—almost exclusively white folks—rushed to declare the United States "post-racial" the moment Barack Obama took office. But the 2008 election of President Obama was not the end of racism in our country by any stretch of the imagination. The backlash that has followed highlights the depth of division on racial equity, inclusion, and justice in the United States. We were not post-racial then, and we are not post-racial now.

Celebrating steps forward, like President Obama's inauguration, is important for morale and to mark cultural progress. However, victory over racism will take much deeper and broader change. Whether we want to admit it or not, we're not there yet. Racism is still harming us all. And it starts far earlier than many people realize. From early childhood, all children are faced with racial pollution in the media, in their community, and in many, if not most, homes.

Some white families worry that elementary school is too early for their children to learn about the evils of racism. Naturally, any parent wants to protect their child's innocence. What about the innocence of children of color? Should we continue to accept that children of color experience racism, while protesting that even speaking with white children about racism is too difficult? This disparate treatment of our children preserves a racist hierarchy and further advances the idea that only white people are fully human and deserving of consideration. Far too many white parents do not seem to recognize (or mind) that Black children are regularly assaulted with racism—through both interpersonal bigotry and the impacts of racist systems on their lives. The unacceptable truth is that white kids are learning racism—and kids of color are experiencing racism—from day one.

My brother B-J and I learned about racism differently, and at a much earlier age, than most white kids. It was in the countless moments when our brother, Kacey, was prejudged and treated differently because of his skin color that our education began. Our parents learned that when your child is Black, you don't get to choose when to start addressing racism. I am aware that some white adoptive parents of Black children, and other children of color, address racism by pretending it is not there. Our parents took a direct approach, like they did on most things. Our parents were values-driven and expected us to live our values out loud. They taught us that racism was evil and should be actively opposed. They also taught us that family was the most important bond and that it was our responsibility to stand up for one another—to protect the family.

As a result, I suppose, my first fight was on the school bus, on my second day of kindergarten, when another white kid said something racist about my family. I knew that it was my responsibility to stand up for us, and I did. That decision, made among those green vinyl seats on that loud yellow school bus, was the first time I remember consciously choosing to oppose bigotry. I think some people consider whether to stand up each time they notice racism or some other form of oppression. For me, I made that decision once, in kindergarten, and I have been living by it every day since. That doesn't mean that I've always known what to do, just that there was no longer a question as to whether I would do something.

Over the years, there were more fights, although they rarely accomplished much and usually got me in trouble. Some stemmed from anti-Semitism directed toward my family, some were rooted in classism, based on where we lived, but usually it was about racism. Racism, anti-Semitism, classism—none of it was good, and it all took a toll. But in our experience, nothing was more ever-present than the racism directed at Kacey, both in and out of school.

One particular experience in high school stands out. I was sitting in English class, trying my best to pay attention, when Kacey walked in. He stood just inside the door at the front of the class and said "C'mon," motioning to me to come with him.

I stood up and walked toward the door. Of course, the teacher asked what was going on.

"I just need my brother," Kacey said, and we kept it moving.

I'm sure there were consequences for our behavior, but I don't remember what they were. Walking down the hall, I asked Kacey what was up.

He told me that another student had called him the n-slur.

My blood began to boil as Kacey shared the details. By this point, it wasn't exactly a new experience but if anything, that made it more infuriating. Then he said something different: "So, I think you should make him cry."

That made me laugh a little at first, but Kacey looked serious and said, "Do you remember the little girl?" Of course I did, and I knew exactly what he meant.

We were quiet the rest of the walk across campus toward the cafeteria where the kid was waiting for Kacey to return. My brother could be intimidating when he wanted to be—add to that the stereotypes that kid likely believed about young Black men—and there was no doubt he would be right where Kacey had left him.

I thought about what had happened when Kacey and I were about nine and ten years old. We were in Boston for a doctor's appointment with Mom. As she went to the reception desk, she told us to go sit quietly in the waiting area. As we did what we were told, Kacey noticed a little girl playing with some blocks. An outgoing and friendly child (unlike his older brother), Kacey dragged me toward her, saying, "Let's go play with the little girl."

The girl was younger than us, maybe around four years old, white, with blond hair and blue eyes. She greeted us with a big smile. Kacey said what he always said: "Hi, I'm Kacey. This is my brother, Joe-Joe."

The girl looked up and said, "Hi."

"Can we play with you?" Kacey asked.

The little girl's smile disappeared. "No, I can't play with you, cuz you're a . . ." She then proceeded to use the n-slur.

I was pissed, but I knew I was not supposed to hit a girl, no matter what. I could not let her get away with hurting my brother, though. So, I did the only thing I could think of: I cursed her out, using every bad word I'd ever heard in my whole young life.

Next thing I knew, Mom was grabbing me by the arm and pulling me away. I think the girl had started crying, but I was focused on explaining to Mom that this girl had been wrong, that I was doing the right thing. Mom wasn't hearing a word of it and insisted that I apologize.

I complied, and then sat down with my arms crossed, bright red in my anger. Kacey sat quietly next to me, waiting for me to calm down. Finally, he stood up and said, "Let's go play with the little girl again."

"What?" I muttered. "Are you crazy? No!"

"Okay," Kacey replied. Then he walked back over and started to play with the girl again, as if nothing at all had happened.

The girl stopped crying, and they began playing together. I just sat there, dumbfounded, trying to figure out if my brother had lost his damn mind.

I don't know where she had been before but after a while, the girl's mother stomped over and yanked her daughter away from Kacey as if he were a monster trying to eat her kid. And then *she* called Kacey the n-slur.

That was it. *She* was the monster, and no one had ever told me that I couldn't hit a grown woman. So that's what I did: I ran over and attacked her, beating on her leg like I was really doing something. I'm sure it looked ridiculous, and probably only lasted a couple of seconds, but I wanted to hurt her, because I knew that her words hurt my brother.

In different ways, her racism hurt all of us. It obviously directly hurt Kacey, whose kindness was met with hate—even if the little girl didn't know what she was saying. It hurt my heart, indirectly, knowing that my brother had been pained by her words. Similarly, it hurt Mom once she found out what had happened. It even hurt her daughter, the little girl, who was subjected to learning racism from her mom, limiting her in ways she couldn't, as a child, have known. That woman's bigotry had harmed us all, much like racism writ large hurts all of us collectively—assaulting our souls, limiting our connections to one another, and diminishing our humanity.

Several years later, when Kacey asked me to make that kid cry in high school, and reminded me of the little girl, he kick-started my life as an antiracist educator. Kacey realized that people could unlearn racism—and that we could help them. That lesson stuck with me.

Taking Responsibility

Parents often look forward to teaching their children about a favorite sport, reading a special book to them for the first time, or cooking a particular dish with them that has been passed down through the generations. These joyous moments are priceless. Those who care for young people also need to share things that are difficult to talk about, but necessary. Although "the talk" about racism happens differently for people who are racially oppressed than for those who are racially privileged, I don't think anyone looks forward to their first time explaining racism to a child. I think it is embarrassing, on a deep level, to have to explain that this is part of the reality that awaits them. Some avoid this talk, and some even try to ban it from being taught in school, maybe due to a feeling of embarrassment that they are part of the problem. Parents of children of color have little choice but to have the talk about race and racism to try to ensure the safety of their children in a world that remains hostile toward them. And for those of us who aim to actively oppose racism, it is our responsibility to talk to our children about racism and the importance of working together to end it.

My child had just turned ten years old when we watched the video of George Floyd's murder together. Makkie's reaction was what I imagine mine might have been the first time I saw an extreme racial injustice. But the truth is, I cannot remember the first time. I have witnessed violent racism throughout my entire life. I'm in my fifties now, and I have been angry about racism for as long as I can remember.

To complicate matters even more, racism is not a Black–white binary, and it never has been. The experiences of individuals within racialized groups are not all the same either. People experience racism and white supremacy on a spectrum, based on their racialized identity—and their perceived racial identity—and where they fall in the racist hierarchy, among other factors. What has been constant is the purpose of white supremacist ideology and racist systems, which is to benefit white people, most especially those with wealth and power.

This necessitates addressing racism over time, in multiple conversations, rather than with a singular talk. Part of the absurdity of it all, at least for those willing to have the conversation, is explaining to our children that we already know how to end racism and oppression of all kinds—that we know how to dismantle it and build equitable and inclusive systems instead, but for a variety of ugly reasons we have chosen not to. And for those of us who are white, it has been primarily the people who look like us who have done everything in their power to resist change. This should be disturbing to us all.

Have you found yourself wondering what you can do to help end racism? Do you sense that this is the time to step up, if you only knew how? More and more people around the world have begun to acknowledge the terrible, ongoing harms of racism and to ask these types of vital questions. This is especially true following the convergence of Trumpism; the COVID-19 pandemic, which revealed deadly racial disparities; the Black Lives Matter (BLM) movement, which formed after Trayvon Martin's killer was acquitted in 2012 and then grew nationally in response to the murders of George Floyd, Breonna Taylor, and Ahmaud Arbery; and more recently in response to the attempt at genocide of Palestinians in Gaza by the Israeli government. For example, many people, particularly those who are white, turned to their Black and Brown friends, acquaintances, or colleagues for answers when BLM protests were in the news: *I believe that Black lives matter, but what can I do?*

Asking questions like this is well intentioned, but they often have unintended consequences. Using the BLM example, here's why: Black folks are already coping with a lifetime of some level of systemic oppression and interpersonal racism. Meanwhile, absorbing the news of the most recent extrajudicial killings of Black people takes a toll. All while dealing with widespread threats to diversity, equity, and inclusion (DEI) work that was designed to combat (or at least mitigate) historical and ongoing racism and other types of oppression.

Does this sound like a lot? That's because it is—and for people of color, it occurs on top of the daily stressors we all have. So, being expected to provide white friends and colleagues with answers on how to fix racism—preferably in a few easy steps that will not inconvenience them too much, take too long, or have any potentially negative consequences—may simply be too much to ask.

Of course, by asking Black and Brown folks how you can help fight racism, the intent is not to offend or overwhelm. But, too often, that is how such questions land. For most, being tasked with providing a concise checklist for how to learn about, dismantle, and solve racism is, I would imagine, quite stressful.

As if that were not enough, people of color are also expected to respond with kindness while navigating white tears, hearing confessions of bigotries past and present, and providing comfort for how difficult this is for white people. And could you hurry up and answer before our interest fades—and then quickly get over it already.

Predictably, this takes both a personal toll and a toll on relationships. While these inquiries may be well intentioned, they are also pathological manifestations of white privilege, which can be exhausting for those expected to respond. In other words, this approach is not helpful. In fact, it can be quite counterproductive. Whether it is the first, tenth, or hundredth inquiry, everyone has a breaking point. So, when possible, these inquiries are often redirected to white folks who are not new to opposing racism—people like me.

These questions are not simple, but they do have answers. We do know how to end racism and other forms of oppression—we really do. We just need to have the collective will to do our part and hold others accountable for doing their part as well. Having served as an activist, an advocate, an educator, a senior diversity officer, and now an executive advisor around these issues, I've learned that ending racism and other forms of oppression is going to take far more than the changes we can make as professionals in the field—meaning we cannot do it alone. It will require a critical mass of individuals willing to take responsibility for change—to raise their voices in solidarity across various anti-oppression movements. We will have to use our skills, share our knowledge, and pool our resources to effect change.

Personally, I have lost count of how many texts, emails, and voicemails I have received from friends of color that have started out something like this:

> *Your people keep asking me how they can solve racism by Thursday. Call me before I hurt somebody's feelings!*

> *I had no idea I had so many white friends. Why do they think I know how to magically end racism? If I knew, wouldn't I have done that a long time ago?*

So, in the quest to plug yourself in to real change, you may have found that you are left with a handful of offended Black friends and a bunch of books about our racist history, but with no clear path forward.

Hundreds of years of intransigent racism is not going to be dismantled, replaced, and forgotten easily or overnight. Racism is not simply an interpersonal issue in your community or mine. Racism is a global plague, created by Europeans to justify colonization, slavery, and predatory capitalism. These and other systems of oppression have gone largely unchecked for centuries, and when change has come, reparations for the damage done have rarely followed, leaving open sores that continue to fester in our society and open lanes for oppression to continue.

There's no point looking for a concise list of to-dos or a simple game plan for how to end racism in a week. If you want the unvarnished truth about how you can contribute to real change, pushing past checklists and ineffectual quick fixes—and if you are committed to doing your part—then I encourage you to keep reading.

As with any other massive endeavor, the end of racism will come when we take one step at a time in the direction of progress. The more of us who take these steps together, the more effective our efforts will be, and the sooner we will experience that illusive *liberty and justice for all* that, to date, has been little more than US American mythology.

Privilege Scraps

During my second year of high school, I was hanging out at a friend's house on a pretty unremarkable day. This was before cell phones, so when the phone rang, he went to answer it in the kitchen. I didn't know who was on the line, but I could hear him say he was hanging out with me and then describe me as "cool for a white guy."

That pissed me off. I appreciated that my Black friend did not see me as the same old privilege-flaunting white guy that was likely his norm, but it felt like a backhanded compliment. Why did I have to be "cool for a white guy"? Why couldn't I just be cool?

I felt like my friend was judging me as "less than," saying I was not fully cool—just cool in the context of suspect white folks. But as that friend, now Dr. DeReef Jamison, a professor of psychology and African American studies, reminded me recently: We were fifteen years old. We had not yet learned about all the social forces that were at play, and my reaction was based on the little I understood at the time.

I heard my friend's compliment as an insult because I wanted to be seen as somehow outside of the racist reality that we had inherited. But, obviously, we cannot separate ourselves from the reality we live in. I could not be just *cool*, because our context was—and is—a society with very real racial divisions, discrimination, and disparities. Within that context, I was cool for a white guy, and I could learn a great deal more if I reserved my judgment and pushed pause on my anger until I understood my friend's perspective.

Expecting to be held up as an exception highlighted my privilege and our problematic reality. Because of my story and the way that I live my life, I have subsequently been embraced by some communities of color. Some Black folks, who have gotten to know me, have insisted that

I am "not white" or even claim me as Black. On some level, I am good with that, and of course I appreciate when I am invited to the proverbial cookout. On the flip side, however, I have also been seen as an outsider, called a "race traitor," and had my "white card" revoked in many white communities and workplaces.

White people often use what is unique about my experience to make me the exception to some "rule" of racial division, saying "You practically grew up Black" or (one of my favorites) "That's not the way normal white people act." Some people use my story as an excuse for why they do nothing in the face of racism: By seeing my life as the exception, they give themselves permission not to learn or make different choices in their own lives. Dismissing me as an outlier can give white folks an excuse to feign ignorance and to continue colluding with racism. I have learned that it is important for me to take away this excuse for white apathy and inaction. I have found it to be important to own who I am, to resist being made the exception, in order to set an example for other white folks.

The US American brand of racism, which in many ways has spread across the world, requires conformity to racial division. Systemic racism separates us and isolates those who oppose white supremacy. Over time, initially by law and later by cultural norm, mechanisms have been established to keep us divided. This is not happenstance; it is by design.

While we often think of race and racism within the context of our modern experience, it is an old and tired concept. The use of the term *race*, at least as far back as fifteenth-century France, came about after centuries of racialization and discrimination against Jews and Muslims.[1]

The use of race during the Spanish Inquisition is often marked as an early escalation of systemic racism. In *The Myth of Race*, Sussman states, "Unlike earlier inquisitions, the Spanish Inquisition did not focus on religion alone but expanded to include ethnicity or race, introducing the notion of *limpieza de sangre*, or 'impurity of blood.'"[2]

The concept of race was later promoted by Europeans as a "scientific" hierarchy of humanity, with themselves conveniently at the top. It was cloaked as anthropological, but racialized divisions were actually developed in line with European biases, not science, and used to further justify ongoing colonization, enslavement, and oppression of those not classified as "white."[3]

That race is not a real thing is well documented, though. It is clear, through scientific study, that there is one human race. Currently a very fractured race, but one race nonetheless.

It is equally important to note that for as long as racism has existed there have been people who have fought against it—including those who were newly categorized as "white." I note this because they are the white folks I think we should celebrate, not those who promoted this garbage and used it to justify their racist behavior—including many US presidents and others who we glorify in our history books.

From this opposition rose the abolitionist tradition, which emerged in the late 1600s. A well-known demonstration of this resistance happened when a multiracial group of oppressed people came together in colonial Virginia and began to revolt in solidarity against those who were profiting from brutally enforced slave and indentured labor. Commonly referred to as Bacon's Rebellion, the revolt's causes were not that simple, of course. As author and advocate Heather C. McGhee explains, "Bacon had started his rebellion as an anti-Native crusade, but the multiracial alliance of landless freedmen, servants, and slaves who carried it on had their minds set on freedom."[4]

The ruling white elite had other ideas. They employed the ever-effective divide-and-conquer approach, passing laws to legally distinguish between races—most specifically Black and white people—with the goal of quashing further unity and rebellion. McGhee informs us, "The law separated the members of the lowest class by color and lifted one higher than the other. The goal, as it has been ever since, was to offer just enough racial privileges for white workers to identify with their color instead of their class."[5] That's not to say throwing this bone of white privilege was insignificant—but it certainly had little impact on the ruling white elite or the inequities of the socioeconomic status quo.

The white folks who chose these privilege scraps over solidarity with their comrades of color were the original US American sellouts. This move helped solidify the racialized class structure that we live under today. Although our laws have changed, the cultural norms that developed over hundreds of years stemming from these early, divisive regulations have not changed enough to end the racial discrimination and disparities that persist across nearly every measure of success. We still segregate and discriminate based on race and in service to wealthy and almost exclusively white parasites who sit atop our predatory socioeconomic system. In fact, the economic gap between those at the top and the rest of us has actually become more extreme.

Yet far too many white people continue to sell out by doing the bidding of the small group of wealthy and powerful (who are still predominantly white), trading their integrity for an updated set of privilege scraps not much different from those that tempted the original white sellouts centuries ago. These scraps offer a level of privilege to white folks that is inconsequential to the wealthy elite, offering just enough to divide white folks from people of color.

> *The white folks who chose these privilege scraps over solidarity with their comrades of color were the original US American sellouts.*

This has negative impacts not only on those who face discrimination but on those with racial privilege too. Although white people are generally aware of racism, most still do not acknowledge the benefits they receive in the form of white privilege. They also avoid recognition that living a life in collusion with racism comes with significant costs, such as limited opportunities for learning, building relationships, and advancing what you care about. But the most obvious are the psychological and moral costs of racism.

White people, by perpetuating or pretending not to see the racism around them, suffer the psychological consequences of knowing that they are part of the problem. They lose credibility with many people of color and white antiracists, but also with themselves whenever they take stock of which side of history they are standing on. McGhee points out, "We all like to see ourselves as on the side of the heroes in a story. But for white US Americans today who are awake to the reality of US American racism, that's nearly impossible. That's a moral cost of racism that millions of white people bear and that those of us who've borne every other cost of racism simply don't."[6]

The consequences of racism for white people are worse for those who choose to do nothing to oppose it. The moral conflict between what you want to believe about yourself (that you are on the side of good) and the reality (that you are fighting to maintain what you know to be a moral wrong) impacts one's self-image and sanity. Knowing that you are on the side of the villains in this story—that you are contributing to the oppression of other human beings—can take a significant toll. This ethical crisis "can cause contradictions and justifications, feelings of guilt, shame, projection, resentment, and denial," McGhee continues. "Ultimately, though, we are all paying for the moral conflict of white Americans."[7]

> *The consequences of racism for white people are worse for those who choose to do nothing to oppose it.*

My experience may be atypical, but that does not remove me from our shared context or absolve any of us from the responsibility to continue learning and doing better. We can learn to oppose racism just as well as we can learn to support it, and this can happen at any time in our lives. The racism or antiracism we learned as children may be determined more by the choices of others—parents, teachers, and others in our daily lives—but at some point, our learning, experiences, and behaviors are guided by our own choices.

Today's white folks who choose racism, including those who know better but do nothing, are no different from those white folks who chose whiteness over solidarity with people of color more than 300 years ago following Bacon's Rebellion—accepting racial privileges and division in exchange for their integrity. But oppression is not a simple binary choice. There is actually a web of intersecting oppressions, which are used to fracture any solidarity between those of us who are working in opposition to any specific form of oppression.

Intersecting Oppressions

The term *intersectionality* was introduced by the Black feminist legal scholar Kimberlé Crenshaw, who was addressing the disparate impact, specifically for Black women, at the intersection of racism and sexism in the workplace.[8] She and others have built upon this concept to help us understand that oppression is not a simple binary; it has evolved into a matrix.

In this matrix, racism intersects with sexism and other oppressive forces. Our access to privilege is manipulated to pit us against one another based on sexual orientation and expression, religion, citizenship, socioeconomic status, and so on. The goal: to set antiracists against those fighting for women's rights against those advocating for transgender rights against those struggling to achieve immigration rights . . . The list goes on. This strategy has been remarkably successful.

An "intersectional privilege matrix" may sound complex. In simpler terms, the folks in power keep the rest of us judging, hating, and fighting one another while they enjoy the fruits of our labor. The solution is equally simple: Recognize that all oppression is unacceptable, and work together to dismantle systems of oppression regardless of their target. That means, to be antiracist, we must oppose the oppression of anyone, anywhere, by anyone. If we can find solidarity across anti-oppression movements, our numbers become untenable for those hoping to maintain their unearned and unjust power.

McGhee puts it this way: "Today, as in colonial Virginia, the wealthy and powerful maintain an unequal society with the complicity of white people who share color with them but class with almost everybody else."⁹ From my perspective, understanding this reality should help fuel our desire to work toward a new solidarity in the fight for freedom and equity for us all. We are more than capable of dismantling existing systems of oppression and providing equitable access to resources, education, and opportunities for us all.

We are the unfortunate beneficiaries of the reinforced divisions that followed Bacon's Rebellion: a racialized class structure as the backbone of modern systemic oppression and the US economy. A straight line can be drawn connecting the intentional acts of racialization perpetrated by those who benefited directly from the genocide of Native Americans and the enslavement of Africans in America by Europeans hundreds of years ago to the sociopolitical and racial divides we continue to struggle with today. These divisions impact our current relationships because they do not exist in a vacuum; they exist within the socioeconomic realities that have been forged over the centuries. Until we interrupt these intersecting systems of privilege and oppression, we cannot expect the interpersonal divisions between us to disappear on their own.

> *Until we interrupt these intersecting systems of privilege and oppression, we cannot expect the interpersonal divisions between us to disappear on their own.*

The actions of those wealthy white elites, and the white folks who chose to sell out everyone else for scraps of white privilege, matter today because not enough of us have chosen to follow a different path. To make matters worse, those with wealth are now assumed to be leaders—to be exceptional beyond their ability to exploit people and the system. But wealth is not a measure of who is the best or smartest of us, and certainly not a measure of who is best able to regulate justice. Wealth makes people powerful in a capitalist system, but allowing ourselves to be manipulated into thinking it makes the wealthy most worthy to lead is something we must overcome if we hope to make social progress of any sort.

Following in the tradition of abolitionists could provide a path that would promote different values and different measures of worth and success. Since the malignant inception of race and racism, there has been opposition. From Frederick Douglass to Jane Elliott, from John Brown to Angela Davis, from Grace Lee Boggs to Alicia Garza, Patrisse Cullors, and Opal Tometi—the list is long and impressive. At least as important are the multitude of antiracists whose names we may never know but who together have brought progress and hope for those of us who follow.

Unfortunately, from the very start of our nation, we have chosen instead to follow white supremacists, including many of those we think of as the founding fathers of our nation. As a result, we are ruled by plutocrats who built their wealth on the back of others' labor, seek only more wealth and power, and actively block liberty and justice for the rest of us.

Changing direction is absolutely possible. However, we cannot expect to make progress if we pretend that we can erase hundreds of years of oppression overnight, that it did not happen, or that there are not consequences today, even between friends.

I understand that there are many who don't want to "dwell" on the negative aspects of our history. The problem is, without facing the worst of our history—understanding how recent it was and the ways it has morphed into our current systems—we will remain unable to understand it well enough to create sustainable change. While we are capable of becoming the free and just people we aspire to be, pretending that we are already there does not make it so.

Living an Antiracist Life

What does it mean, exactly, to live an antiracist life? It means that your opposition to racism is a core value that actively influences your decisions and your behavior—in all aspects of your life. Someone can claim to believe in racial justice but have no investment in it and do nothing to promote it. While believing in racial justice is a good first step, to live an antiracist life means that you demonstrate your commitment to racial justice. This may sound ominous, but it is what we do every day—we live the values we genuinely hold.

Our values are often derived from our beliefs, but they go further by serving as guides for our behavior. The difference is evident in a story about a young white woman I knew in high school and her first interracial dating experience. She was fifteen years old when a young man from school—someone she had been crushing on—finally asked her out. She had been on dates before, so she knew the routine: Her date would have to meet her parents and answer some basic, but potentially embarrassing, questions before that first date.

When her crush arrived to pick her up, though, her parents started acting strangely. Leaving her alone with her date, they stepped into another room to talk. When they returned, they explained that something had come up, and the date was going to have to wait until another time. She asked what was wrong, but her parents claimed it was a family matter and abruptly ushered her date out the door. After he left, her parents danced around the issue for a while, until she realized the problem: Her date was Black.

Later, I heard this story from Kacey's perspective. He was the crush who had been sent away.

Kacey understood what had happened all too well, and that there would be no rain check for the date. "Her parents are racist," he told me very matter-of-factly when we went out for pizza that night. My first reaction was anger at the young woman and her parents, mostly because I did not know how to express the pain I felt for my younger brother. Kacey let me curse and rant for a while, but he refused to place blame on the young woman. He was clear: This was about her parents.

"I think they accidentally taught her not to be racist," he explained, "and they only realized their mistake when they met me." It was almost funny.

Kacey was right, though. It was accidental. By saying they were opposed to racism, knowing that's what they were supposed to say, these parents had unwittingly taught their daughter to be opposed to racism. They never made racist statements, and by claiming to believe in racial justice, they had instilled that belief in their daughter. They would often refer to Martin Luther King Jr.'s statement about judging people by the content of their character, not the color of their skin. They were good "nonracists." They had forgotten to inform their daughter that their opposition to racism was just for show, and certainly did not apply when it came to the possibility of a young Black man dating their daughter.

Kacey decided to remain friendly with her, and eventually had a conversation with her about that night. She shared that she had argued with her parents after Kacey left that night, and what they said caused her not to speak to them for months. While he appreciated why she chose to give them the silent treatment, Kacey encouraged her to try and teach them better. From his perspective, she was in the best position to influence their thinking, and she became determined to do so. Antiracism had become one of her core values.

Any of our core values are more than something we say we believe in. They guide our thinking, decision-making, and how we behave. When racial justice is a core value, it is no different. Your antiracism is not limited to compliance with equity and inclusion policy at work or following a checklist of antiracist behavior in public. When racial justice is held as a core value, it manifests in those you surround yourself with, how you hold one another accountable, and how you treat people personally and professionally. It becomes a normal consideration as you go through your daily life.

Think about it this way: Let's say you are someone who truly values the environment. The well-being of our planet will be a natural consideration whenever you make decisions. You do not need reminding that the environment matters in your decision-making process; it just matters to you all the time. It is likely that you vote for politicians who understand climate change. You try to influence your friends to adjust wasteful behaviors. You teach your children to recycle, and you encourage sustainable practices at your workplace. It matters to you, and you act accordingly. Likewise, when you embrace antiracism, it is natural to just oppose racism and oppression when you encounter it and to be proactive about promoting equity and inclusion. When you recognize racial disparities at work or bias coming from a friend, you respond accordingly. And if, for example, you are white and your daughter is interested in dating an extraordinary young man, it wouldn't cross your mind to stand in the way simply because he is Black.

Our credibility as antiracists, or as antiracist environmentalists, is inextricably linked to our actions. We all have opportunities each and every day to demonstrate our values. Whatever is truly important to us is always relevant. No matter the circumstances, whether we're eating, shopping, interacting with colleagues, providing a service, going on a date, or socializing with friends, there are moments when our antiracist values come to the forefront. It matters when we read books, listen to music, and travel. It matters when we choose where to go to college, where to live and work, and where to send our kids to school. From family and friends to politics and the economy, we must realize that racism simply is unacceptable and allow our antiracist values to guide us toward the change we all deserve.

Bridging the Empathy Gap

My choice to live my life as part of the antiracist tradition does not make me special. It is what I was taught to do. I had different experiences, and different guidance, from most white people and chose my path accordingly. I don't consider my story to be exceptional; I think of it as an invitation for others to develop an informed antiracist lens—and to use it. Living your best antiracist life simply requires that you make the decision I made on that school bus on the second day of kindergarten: to do what you can to oppose racism.

Sometimes, that means simply opening your eyes to see humanity beyond the myth of race. Sybrina Fulton, Trayvon Martin's mother, appeared along with the mothers of Ahmaud Arbery, Breonna Taylor, Botham Jean, Eric Garner, Tamir Rice, and Antwon Rose on *Good Morning, America* to share a message with the nation: "I want to encourage people to take a look at these tragedies. Think to yourself, 'What if that was my son?'"[10]

I have spent a lifetime studying racism, so I understand how powerful it is, how it distorts the way people see the world. Still, I cannot comprehend how anyone could hear Ms. Fulton's words and feel anything but deep empathy for her loss—feel the pain of knowing a loved one was terrorized and murdered, as her son was. Yet many of our fellow humans are unable to feel that empathy, because they are unable to bridge the racial constructs that divide us. They cannot allow themselves to imagine their son in the place of Ms. Fulton's Black child. Instead, they perform sympathy while seeking fault in Trayvon and every other victim of racist violence and oppression. They defy all logic and understanding to delete the realities of race and racism from the situation. They twist themselves up doing mental gymnastics to absolve the perpetrators and to free themselves of any guilt for making no effort to oppose the hate that leads again and again to the deaths of other people's children—simply because they are holding tight to the ideas that whiteness equates with innocence and goodness and that Black bodies are "less than" and a threat.

Even a passing glance at history makes it evident that white supremacy has taken countless lives and oppressed countless more. From colonization and genocide to the slave trade to the Holocaust—from the murders of Freedom Riders to the murders of Black folks and other folks of color for driving, bird-watching, or just walking home with Skittles—the history is well documented and available. Yet, somehow, far too many people who look like me see white folks as the heroes in the human story and have managed to cast Black, Indigenous, and other people of color as the problem. Choosing not to apply critical thinking to this viewpoint makes it difficult to engage with empathy, even in the face of tragedy.

In today's sociopolitical landscape, even the simple statement that Black lives matter triggers immediate deflection, and often rageful resistance, from those so deeply invested in their whiteness that they cannot see straight. It requires a seriously distorted perspective to witness the barbaric murder of George Floyd and not feel the natural compassion for him and his loved ones that Makkie demonstrated when we sat together and watched the video. To instead defend the police officer who took his life and those who assisted by standing guard seems not only absurd to me but heartless. But that is where we are. I don't doubt that Ms. Fulton's plea for us to ask ourselves *What if that was my son?* has caused some introspection and changed some hearts and minds, but far fewer than it should have.

For me, hearing Bridgett and Philonise Floyd lamenting the loss of their brother at the hands of racist police officers, I recognized that pain. The circumstances differed from what happened to Kacey, but I still feel a connection to those family members who have lost loved ones to the evils of racism. I recognize the difference in our experiences: Those family members are not only dealing with their tragic losses; they must also continue to deal with the same types of racial microaggressions, oppression, and violence that took their loved ones from them. Because I am white, I do not have that added burden.

The ongoing effort to promote white supremacy, including the dehumanization of Black people, has been far more successful than most of us want to accept. The evidence is overwhelming: Systems infected by racism continue to work and adapt exactly as they were designed to by protecting white power, property, and privilege. This includes policing people of color and anyone else who threatens the status quo.

Despite the claims that every racist act is an isolated incident and that each of the cops who are caught terrorizing communities of color or murdering unarmed Black folks are the exception and not the rule, we all know better. Truly good cops are those who stand up and speak out against racism within the police force. Good cops exist but, evidently, they are few and far between. Most do not cross the "blue line." They do not stop colleagues from committing acts of racism or speak up when they witness racial harassment and violence. To say that most cops are "good" when it comes to racism in policing would mean that most cops actively oppose racism. I see no evidence of that.

It seems to me that if Breonna Taylor and her partner had been white, the same people who defend the cops who killed her would be up in arms about an unlawful warrant. They would say that her boyfriend was standing his ground and had every right to defend himself from unidentified intruders. They would be able to empathize with Ms. Taylor's loved ones as they mourn. They would see the extreme disparities in how people are treated by the police, and the disparities in general in our world today. They would recognize that the facts do not fit the racialized narratives they are hearing. Instead, racism—likely unconscious—has poisoned their perception and their ability to empathize.

In these examples of how collusion enables racial injustice, we're focused on the police force. But similar, though generally less murderous, examples exist across sectors, workplaces, and communities.

Finding ways to bridge the empathy gap across racial and other socially constructed divides is an important step in our collective work to end racism and white supremacy. Whether we are talking about police officers or anyone else, if the skin color of a person determines whether you care if they live or die, then racism has distorted your humanity. When folks begin to recognize this in themselves, that white guilt tends to hit like a ton of bricks.

Finding ways to bridge the empathy gap across racial and other socially constructed divides is an important step in our collective work to end racism and white supremacy.

Beyond White Guilt

Many white people feel a heavy sense of guilt as they begin to learn about and engage in antiracism: guilt for what people who look like us have done historically, guilt for actions in their own past that have supported systemic racism, guilt for their failure to actively oppose racism within their spheres of influence. This feeling is natural, and having a conscience is a good sign. However, white guilt is toxic.

Though guilt can be a normal part of the process of awakening to the racism that surrounds us, it can also be a trap that blocks us from contributing to progress. Guilt does not feel good. It can bring up issues of shame. It can trigger denial or other defense mechanisms. It can also cause folks to engage prematurely, before they are well informed or prepared. Working through all that can take time, but it does not have to prevent you from being engaged in a constructive way.

My awakening to racism came early in comparison to most white people, but it was also immature and incomplete. I experienced racism as Kacey's brother, experiencing his pain secondhand, or when people would project their racist beliefs and hate onto me because of their reactions to Kacey being Black. Kacey, on the other hand, had to deal with it head-on. I could see what was happening to Kacey, but I could rarely do anything to protect him. As a child, my understanding of racism was limited to the interpersonal, and my response was just as limited, usually just coming out as anger. I did not yet appreciate the scope of racial injustice or how I benefited from white supremacy—whether I supported it or not—and I certainly did not know how to effectively do my part to oppose racism and white supremacy.

As I began to grasp the concept of white privilege, the guilt never outweighed my well-established anger or my nascent but unwavering commitment to antiracism. Guilt had to take a back seat as I prepared to combat aspects of racism that I had not previously recognized. Knowing that I benefited from white supremacy—something that I loathed and raged against—felt bad, but I somehow understood that it was important not to allow feelings of guilt to keep me from doing something about it.

This guilt often results in white people centering their need for answers, forgiveness, or appreciation from people of color. This only adds to "Black fatigue": the physically, mentally, and emotionally draining impact of coping with a host of daily inequities.[11] When you are already exhausted from dealing with racism on a daily basis, the additional burden of newly "woke" white folks asking a million questions, looking for forgiveness, and wanting credit for seeing the obvious is not helpful, to say the least.

Here's what *is* helpful: taking responsibility, educating yourself about the history and causes of racism, broadening your experiences, and working to become an effective change agent. For someone new to antiracism, overcoming white guilt and working toward a more useful stance can be a very real challenge; it requires a great deal of humility and the ability to keep an open mind. In my experience as an educator, I have found that focusing first on learning can be empowering.

Learning about antiracist history and the work being done today can help, for example, by providing examples of white abolitionists and antiracists. This can not only offset the glorification of racist explorers, settlers, and supposed leaders that we have all been exposed to but also introduce you to a supportive tradition of antiracism. Additionally, conversations within circles of white friends and family and learning from antiracist educators and advocates can provide guidance as you work through white guilt. By focusing on learning and seeking well-informed guidance, many find constructive direction, illuminating a path through guilt and toward action.

The onset of some degree of white guilt is natural, but it serves no one if it's keeping you from doing better going forward. Educating yourself, serving as a partner, and taking action to oppose racism can make a real difference and have a positive ripple effect that you may never fully comprehend. While some feelings of guilt may remain, particularly around your own past behavior, beyond that guilt is the promise of your own potential impact on ending racism and white supremacy. As antiracism becomes a core value for you, the feelings of guilt will just as naturally take a back seat to your new focus on living an antiracist present and working toward the most free, equitable, and inclusive world you can imagine for the future.

Choosing to Educate

Sometimes wisdom comes from the open minds and unencumbered hearts of children. Kacey possessed wisdom that came through in how he lived his tragically short life. The way he sought to teach that little girl at the doctor's office was beyond me at the time. At that young age, Kacey's spirit had not yet been worn down by years of facing hate and discrimination. He was not yet aware of the long history of racism or the systems in place to oppress people like him. Those evils were coming, but at the time, he still felt the hope and optimism of a child.

I don't remember what happened after Mom pulled me away from that little girl's mother and apologized for my behavior, but I'll never forget what happened as they were about to leave: Before walking out the door, the girl slipped her hand from her mother's and ran over to Kacey, who was sitting in the chair next to me. Jumping into his lap and throwing her arms around him, she gave him a big hug and a kiss on the cheek. Then she said something I would have never expected: "I love you, Kacey. Don't tell my mom!"

Nine-year-old Kacey responded by saying, "Never forget that I love you too."

I was confused. *What the hell just happened?*

My brother saw the look on my face. "I don't know," he said to me, shrugging his shoulders. "Maybe she learned something."

We were all just kids: Kacey, me, and that little girl. She was already being taught that people who looked like Kacey were somehow "less than" and that she should not play with them. And Kacey was already experienced enough at dealing with racism that he could see this girl was just learning and doing as she was told—and that maybe she could learn to do better.

In the years to come, Kacey spent a lot of time teaching people who I would have just cursed out and walked away from. That was a burden he shouldn't have had to bear, and the fact that I would have just dismissed them demonstrated white privilege that I had yet to recognize or understand. The same was true of how Mom reacted. When we told Mom what she had missed, she cried and then apologized to us. She wished she had demonstrated how to handle bigots in that moment, and more importantly, that she had attended to the harm that had come to her boys, especially Kacey.

My younger self didn't understand that whenever I just dismissed someone who said or did something racist, it was like saying my time was more important to me than preventing the future damage their racist behavior would do. I eventually learned that I have a responsibility to teach, even when it is frustrating, because it could make a difference. Those moments are opportunities to help someone unlearn racism and potentially prevent harm.

So, when I sat down at a cafeteria table across from the boy who had called my brother the n-slur—the most vile word in the English language from my perspective—Kacey didn't want me to hurt him. He wanted me to teach this kid by telling stories about what racism does to people, until he cried. He figured that the kid's tears would indicate that he understood and that he might remember the experience and, hopefully, change his ways.

With Kacey by my side, I proceeded to tell this random kid about the little girl and a few of the other racist experiences Kacey had lived through—painful experiences that had hurt him and ultimately everyone who loved him. I didn't stop until the kid was bawling. We sat for a moment until the kid looked up at Kacey and apologized. Shaking and sobbing, he promised to never use the n-slur again.

Kacey shocked me by giving him a hug and telling him that he hoped he meant it.

I don't know whatever happened to that young man, but I'll bet anything that he remembers that day.

"You okay?" I asked as we walked away.

"Yeah," Kacey replied, but we both knew that wasn't true. I noticed a difference in how he looked: tired, without the hope in his eyes that he had when we met that little girl years earlier. His natural optimism, and his psychological fortitude, had been diminished.

Kacey had been dealing with this type of racist vitriol his entire life. But he reminded me that day, and over many other experiences, to be open to the idea that people can learn, that we all make mistakes, and that we all have the capacity to do better. In our youth, we are in something akin to a perpetual learning mode; as adults, we often need to make a conscious choice to educate ourselves—and others.

I learned a great deal at my brother's side, and I continue to learn as I hold my child's hand through these early years of her life. I honor Kacey's memory today by accepting Makkie's challenge to do more. From Black Lives Matter protests to the efforts of the water protectors to the most recent demands to end the attempt at genocide in Palestine, there have been many calls for change of late. These messages, like those that have come before, are all connected, rooted in the innate human desire for freedom. It is critical to understand that work needs to be done not only in the political realm but also in our families, communities, schools, workplaces, and communities of faith, across all of the socially constructed divides meant to keep us from coming together in solidarity. The good news is, each of us is uniquely positioned to make a difference because our voices hold weight in all sorts of different places and spaces, in every nook and cranny of the globe.

The good news is, each of us is uniquely positioned to make a difference because our voices hold weight in all sorts of different places and spaces, in every nook and cranny of the globe.

Considering the impact racism had on my brother and so many other loved ones, and given what I have learned over the past few decades as an educator, I know we cannot afford to underestimate the scope of white supremacy and systemic racism. I am equally convinced that we have the power to make meaningful and sustainable change. It is time for each of us to address this problem more directly and consistently. We must imagine a world free from racism and hold one another accountable for doing our part to help get us there. We must find our voices and do more than just claim to be opposed to racism: We must live our racial justice values out loud, consistently, not just when it is convenient, popular, or comes with no risk.

It is time for all of us to rise to Makkie's challenge and step up our efforts for the sake of all of our children and all of their friends.

2

WHAT IF?
An Antiracist Vision of a Better World

We don't have to engage in grand, heroic actions to participate in the process of change. Small acts, when multiplied by millions of people, can transform the world.

— HOWARD ZINN

BEFORE I CENTERED MY career on antiracism, equity, and inclusion, I dreamed of becoming an astronaut. Following my second year majoring in space sciences at the Florida Institute of Technology, I was selected to be a junior research scientist at the Special Astrophysical Observatory in what is now the Russian Academy of Science. It was August 1991, amid the fall of the Soviet Union, and I was truly honored to be the first US American employee of the Observatory and to serve as a People to People Student Ambassador, a program established by the Eisenhower administration to enhance international relations. I was also looking forward to traveling outside the United States for the first time, meeting new people, and broadening my views on both science and culture.

In my capacity as a student ambassador, I was asked to share my "American perspective" as a speaker at events throughout the collapsing Soviet

Union. I had been doing speaking engagements at home for a few years on topics related to racial and social justice, and I was interested in engaging in dialogue around similar issues in Russia and other former Soviet nations. The first few events were more challenging than I expected, mostly because they were focused on topics I was not particularly interested in, and it also took some time to find my speaking rhythm while using a translator.

Fortunately, a university asked me to speak about US holiday celebrations. I was able to use that topic to focus on social justice. I chose to speak about the mythology of Thanksgiving, the importance of Juneteenth—even though, at the time, most US Americans didn't even know what it was—the divisiveness of Independence Day and intersections of whiteness and patriotism, and how Martin Luther King Jr. Day had yet to be adopted as a holiday nationwide. Discussing "beloved" US national holidays in the context of racism led to a raucous dialogue with the large audience—mostly college students and professors—that was split between those who saw the US as an idyllic nation built on unshakable values and those who saw an evil empire built on greed.

There was no shortage of voices or opinions on a wide range of national, revolutionary, and anti-oppression leaders and issues. We spoke about racism, sexism, and anti-Semitism, as well as the propaganda of capitalism and communism versus the realities we understood from experience. The dialogue was encouraging, not only because I hoped for this type of opportunity to learn and engage but also because there was hope in the discourse. Even though there were many divergent perspectives, we were listening to one another and responding thoughtfully, not just waiting for our turn to say whatever we came to the event to say. It was a constructive dialogue about the potential for a future free from poverty, war, and oppression, and it was a powerful experience for me.

Through my travels for scientific and speaking obligations in Russia, and while breaking bread with people I met along the way, I learned about the oppression of Jews in the former Soviet Union through awful stories of anti-Semitism that sounded all too familiar to the stories I heard from Mom about our history. I learned how Ukrainians were tyrannized by the Soviet government and how just speaking Ukrainian could provoke fury among Russian neighbors and entanglements with law enforcement. I learned about the oppression of Muslims in the local region, where so many were persecuted simply for trying to practice Islam. And I witnessed racism firsthand, too.

At one stop on my speaking tour, the Pedagogical Institute for Foreign Languages in Pyatigorsk (now Pyatigorsk State University), the audience was enormous and far more diverse than at earlier events, where the faces had all been shades of what US Americans would call "white." The Institute attracted students from nearly one hundred countries around the world. Taking the opportunity to stay and engage for a week or so after the event, I was able to connect with folks from nations in Africa, South Asia, and South America. One friend, Felisberta ("Lela"), from Guinea-Bissau, took me on a tour of the local area. On the bus ride back to campus, as we were laughing about something, several young men on the bus started speaking toward us, not with us, in Russian. Whatever they were saying turned the happiness on Lela's face into a mix of anger and fear.

Lela assured me that everything was fine, but something was obviously not right. It was not like me to shy away from a conflict, but I was confused about what was happening. I stood between Lela and the young men until we got off at the next stop. There, we met another friend, Sheikh from Sierra Leone. He spoke with Lela in Portuguese and Russian. Then, furious, he explained to me what had happened: The young Russians had used a racist slur that means "monkey," a sort of Russian equivalent for the n-slur. This was nothing new for Lela or Sheikh. I listened as they recounted the pain, anger, and frustration caused by multiple incidents of overt racism during their time in Russia. Their experiences sounded a lot like what I had known back home in the United States.

I had not expected racism in Russia, a nation that wasn't involved in the initial colonization of Africa or the slave trade—a nation whose propaganda railed against US American racism. But there it was: racism, just like at home. The intersecting oppressions of racism, sexism, homophobia, anti-Semitism, and other forms of subjugation worked together to maintain a hierarchy in Russia that was not all that different from in the United States. Those young Russian men on the bus might as well have been waving Confederate flags. In fact, I learned later that white supremacists worldwide often use the flag of the losing side of the US Civil War to express their racial bigotry.

Amid a great deal of learning, academically and socially, I made some lifelong friends and memories that year that I still treasure. I learned a lot about the many peoples of Russia, who previously were only partially sketched in my mind based on the half-truths I had been taught in school and through US American media. I also began to comprehend the global reach of white supremacist ideology and the ominous scope of systemic racism and intersecting oppressions. I understood that oppression takes many forms, but I learned that it adapts to different cultures, and that the use of intersecting oppressions to divide and oppress is a global strategy. I also learned a lot about myself and what I wanted to do with my life.

My first international experience under my belt, I began thinking more about the world outside of the US and how our issues fit into the broader global context. Back at Florida Tech, I thought about leaving the sciences, and sought out faculty who were engaged in social, cross-cultural, and multicultural psychology, each of which offered opportunities for engaging around racism and other forms of oppression. Eventually, I decided to abandon my dream of becoming an astronaut and instead focus my professional life on the pursuit of social change, peace, and social justice.

As always, Kacey was on my mind, and I thought often about how we used to imagine what our dream world would be like.

Shared Dreams

Before setting out on a new journey, it is always good to understand where you are trying to go. So, before we focus more specifically on how to engage in antiracism, let's imagine what it would be like to live in a world free from racism and intersecting oppressions.

For Kacey and me, the idea of imagining our own dream world came from Dr. King's famous "I Have a Dream" speech. The core of our shared vision was that no one would be super rich, and racism would not exist. Our experiences had taught us that money and racial hierarchy were corrupting influences that manifested in people who were unkind to us or those we loved. Inspired by Dr. King's words, we imagined, in some detail, a world without those types of oppression. In our dream world, freedom from elitism and racism brought on advances in every possible way.

As kids, my brothers and I loved to watch *Star Trek* because it allowed our imagination to run wild about advanced technology and the possibilities of other, better worlds, but our parents were a little more jaded. Dad used to complain about how, as a kid, he was promised a future full of flying cars, where everyone would be able to travel into space.

"Where's my flying car?" he would say in exasperation. "And why can't we take a vacation on the moon?"

In the world Kacey and I dreamed up, that was all reality. And years later, when I took Makkie to see *Black Panther*, I found myself crying when T'Challa and Nakia returned home in a super-advanced flying vehicle. As the invisibility cloak parted to reveal the wonders of Wakanda, I saw the dream world that Dad had been waiting for and that Kacey and I had dreamed up together.

Wakanda is a vision dreamed up and given life in comic books and on the big screen, a fictional country in sub-Saharan Africa known for its rich resources and as a global symbol of African excellence and culture. But not everyone had the same reaction to the film that I did. Even before we could collectively take in the possibilities of this dream world, as if on cue, the haters were there to throw shade.

In our dream world, freedom from elitism and racism brought on advances in every possible way.

Resistance to the idea of Wakanda originated from those who viewed the film with a defensive and fundamentally racist perspective. Many called it "anti-white racism" or "reverse racism," terms that reveal a reactionary response to a perceived threat to white supremacy and the privilege scraps so many of my fellow white folks hold so dear. Such defenses of privilege serve only as an attempt to disguise racism. They cannot stand up to any scrutiny, but then again, they are not meant to. Instead, they are meant to comfort the privileged and excuse their failure to critically examine their own perspective or consider anyone else's.

Inspired by prolific writer and activist James Baldwin, contemporary thinker Robert Jones Jr. said, "We can disagree and still love each other, unless your disagreement is rooted in my oppression and denial of my humanity and right to exist."[1] So, if someone didn't enjoy *Black Panther*, that's fine, unless the reason they disliked it is rooted in white supremacy. If that is the case, I'd say their white fragility is showing.

We should not confuse the perceived mistreatment of white folks with actual racism. The only "mistreatment" in the dream world of Wakanda was that, in this story, white folks were not the center of attention, the holders of power, or the primary heroes. From a white supremacist standpoint, a world where a Black superhero leads a highly advanced African nation to prosperity without relying on the "great white West" is contrary to what they believe to be the proper order of things. Offending their racist sensibilities, this seems to be taken as an invitation to blather on about nonsense like reverse racism to avoid considering why they were having such a visceral response in the first place.

To be fair, other resistance stemmed from this fictional vision being set in an imperfect world. Wakanda is a monarchy—not exactly the ideal government from the perspective of those who believe in democracy. But to consider the possibilities of this dream world with an antiracist lens requires setting aside reactionary judgment. The first step in reaching a freer, more equitable society is to allow ourselves to imagine it together, without immediately pointing out whatever is missing or imperfect. Only then can we actively consider the various aspects of a better way of governing and living together. Unlocking the possibilities sometimes requires knowing that people with a different perspective from your own may have ideas that could benefit us all.

Imagining a world free from racism requires a mental shift—from the defensive posture often adopted by those protecting their privilege to an inviting posture that welcomes the unfamiliar and explores the uncomfortable. This may simply mean suspending judgment for a moment, taking a breath, and actively listening to understand, learn, and even find ways to collaborate. Imagine what we could come up with if we all put our heads together.

The first step in reaching a freer, more equitable society is to allow ourselves to imagine it together, without immediately pointing out whatever is missing or imperfect.

Think about it: Is our US American democracy perfect? Certainly not. What about our brand of capitalism? Not even close. Sometimes, it seems we are living in more of a nightmare than a dream, in a world where bigots with gun fetishes blindly follow fascists who could not care less about them. In the US, we are falling toward a complete plutocracy, where literal slavery has morphed into a modern form of stratified mass servitude. Our world feeds us lies about each other based on race, ethnicity, nationality, and other irrelevant social constructs so that we will fight one another for status and stuff. The current real world supports systems where we work our lives away so that a small group of excessively wealthy people can enjoy the fruits of our labor—many of whom have never done a hard day's work in their lives.

But despite the imperfections, some of our systems are founded on valuable concepts that are worth considering as we work to form what the US Constitution calls "a more perfect union." And globally, there are other systems and ideas that can help us all find peace and allow us to expect justice. As we reach toward a dream world, one free of oppression, we do not need to immediately develop systems that are flawless in order to see change as worthy. Other nations, cultures, and systems don't need to be perfect for us to learn from them or to find ways to work in solidarity toward a world that we dream together.

I cannot count how many times I've wished Kacey were here for special moments, even small events like seeing *Black Panther*. We would have talked through the night after seeing the vision of Wakanda—a world we could only dream of—on the big screen. I wonder how his view of the world may have changed if he'd had the chance to travel the way I have. I wonder where he might have chosen to travel and what experiences might have shaped his worldview as an adult.

After seeing the movie, I had a conversation in my mind with Kacey about this Wakandan dream world—about whether *our* dream world would ever become real beyond our small gatherings of friends or the imaginations of filmmakers and other dreamers. As I laid in bed that night, it was hard not to imagine Kacey asking, "What if . . . ?"

What If We Do Better?

Kacey was fond of asking "what if" questions. Whether we were doing homework, getting ready for bed, or just sitting in our room together, he would break the silence with "What if we were three sisters instead of three brothers?" or "What if we had superpowers?" or "What if we were aliens from another planet, and we came to Earth on vacation and just stayed?" Kacey's "what ifs" always sparked our imagination and started conversations full of energy. We took those conversations seriously, and they could get heated or funny or deeply contemplative. Those memories remind me of the joy we shared and keep me inspired to continue asking questions that engage and challenge.

And our current social, economic, and political landscape is certainly challenging.

Kacey and I were born into Generation X, in the early 1970s, toward the end of an era shaped in large part by the Civil Rights Movement, when there was a great deal of hope in the struggle to end racism. My lifetime has seen extraordinary backlash to that movement, however, and a significant weakening of many of the gains of that era. Desegregation did not bring about equity and inclusion. The "savage inequalities" described in Jonathan Kozol's 1991 book of that name persist in our education system and far beyond.[2] Voting rights have been diminished, and gerrymandering has ensured the underrepresentation of people of color in the US Congress and, indirectly, in the judiciary. Housing remains segregated, and predatory mortgages and rent increases have disproportionately impacted people of color and poor white folks.

Yet many people believe that, in spite of overwhelming evidence, racism and other forms of oppression are simply not real. They feed this denial, often to their own detriment, by claiming that oppression is "fake news" used by the political left to demonize the right. We can certainly disagree on language and politics, but despite the disturbing proliferation of "alternative facts," there are actual objective, nonpartisan facts that should concern anyone interested in racial justice—or living in an even remotely just world.

This denial flies in the face of hard data that clearly illustrates the persistence of racial disparities—video evidence of racist police violence and murder, and a nationally televised insurrection by people openly displaying racist symbols, fueled by the rhetoric of national leaders at the highest social and political levels. For anyone who denies that racial oppression exists, I ask you to explain the racial disparities that are well documented in everything from household income to infant mortality. There are only two answers: Either racial discrimination and injustice exist, or you believe the white supremacist propaganda touting the superiority of white folks—and the inferiority of everyone else—is correct.

Sophisticated efforts to obfuscate, deny, or lie about racial oppression have deepened the divide between those who seek equity and social justice and those who seek superior status, personal advancement, and political gain. Over my lifetime, this national and global divide has become more pronounced. Again and again, I feel the need to warn that we could be headed for a second civil war in the United States, which could even end up becoming a third world war.

While some progress in racial justice has occurred since Kacey and I entered the world, there has also been further entrenchment of white supremacy and the bigots and bystanders who keep it alive. The convergence of white supremacists, armed militia, and a national political party openly espousing racist rhetoric is cause for grave concern. My intention in sounding the alarm is not to promote civil war, but to prevent it. For the most part, I maintain a fragile hope for my country and for humanity. On the individual level, I believe anyone is capable of overcoming the racist ideologies that they have been taught.

I believe this because I have seen it happen.

I have seen awakenings—moments when it all begins to click—in young people and elders alike. It is a lot like when a child recognizes words that rhyme or when a student first grasps the idea of algebraic variables. Remember in *A Christmas Carol* when Scrooge has an epiphany after seeing the abhorrent behavior of his past, present, and potential future selves? I saw that spark years ago in the eyes of that little girl at the doctor's office, and even in the kid hugging Kacey in the high school cafeteria and promising to do better. I have seen change in students, colleagues, and strangers—in people who have become friends and those who have contributed to progress.

Mere anecdotes do not amount to large-scale change, and individual epiphanies cannot bridge nationwide or worldwide divides. No national or international figure, powerful speech, or motivational book alone can shift global culture. Sustainable change will happen one little girl, one neighbor, one teacher, one customer at the local packie at a time.

I continuously imagine a world as diverse and inclusive as my own circle of family, friends, and colleagues. This hope fuels my work and keeps me engaged, even when our wheels seem to be spinning in mud. Like my professional peers, I pose questions to students, clients, and colleagues, encouraging them to imagine what could be possible. Asking "what if" questions can challenge people to envision new approaches, consider different perspectives, and drive innovative thinking.

I think a lot about our education systems. What if our school systems served all our children by teaching a curriculum inclusive of all of our experiences and histories and demonstrating the values of equity through their educational practices? What if every student had access to a team of appropriately paid and resourced educators who reflect the full diversity of humanity? What if every school could create a variety of opportunities that inspire all of our children?

Higher education, where I have spent the majority of my professional life, tends to extend and even exacerbate the inequities of our elementary and secondary school systems. Curricula are sometimes used as a tool to indoctrinate students with racist, sexist, and otherwise corrupted mythologies. While extraordinary student and educator activism has introduced greater diversity in the courses taught, there is still a long way to go.

What if higher education served as a resource to improve prekindergarten through twelfth-grade education in the ways noted above? What if education was recognized as a right, free at all levels? What if the curricula and faculty were sourced globally, providing access to diverse perspectives across fields? What if students were afforded a broader range of opportunities based on their interests and aptitudes? What if every curriculum was based in facts and inclusive of multiple perspectives? What if we stopped believing the lie that we cannot afford all of this, or great health care for everyone, or to ensure housing for all? It is all possible. It is simply a question of priorities and ensuring that everyone pays their fair share, even billionaires and corporations.

Systemic racism works across sectors, from housing and community development to banking and finance, corporate business, health care, and media. The so-called captains of industry meet with their counterparts in government, education, and other sectors to ensure only the results they want to see, largely by maintaining and expanding on the oppressive systems that brought them to power in the first place. Their money and influence then translate to the adoption of their self-serving perspectives in law, policy, and practice.

What if antiracist leaders, professionals, and community members across all sectors worked more closely together to address intersectional oppressions at scale? What would a coordinated, strategic approach to dismantling and replacing racist and intersecting oppressive systems look like?

These are necessarily big questions, because racism is like a global pandemic—and we have failed to employ a vaccine, despite having the knowledge and ability to do so, for hundreds of years. Racism has spread across fields, sectors, and national borders, mutating over time to thwart all efforts to eradicate it. And as we experienced with the COVID-19 pandemic, coordination across fields, sectors, and borders is critical in the search for effective solutions.

What would a coordinated, strategic approach to dismantling and replacing racist and intersecting oppressive systems look like?

Our tragic, complicated experience with the COVID-19 virus also revealed that beyond government and industry leaders, and beyond those involved in research and policy work, the rest of us—those on the front lines—have a critical role to play. When the coronavirus was burning through the world like wildfire, many of us did our individual part by wearing masks, social distancing, and getting vaccinated, and that made all the difference. Where people did not educate themselves and take action, or were unable to, the virus took advantage and continued spreading.

I cannot think of a better metaphor for racism.

But what if we choose to do better?

Racism was employed during the COVID-19 pandemic to blame Chinese people, the Chinese American community, and (since US Americans tend to clump all Asian people together) Asian folks in general. This strain of bigotry was used by the Trump administration to shift public attention from their dismal performance in addressing the virus and its deadly costs—a clear example of the deadly consequences of racism.

What if we each did our part to shift our perspective and refused to engage in reactionary racism? What if we resisted the urge to unjustly scapegoat people of other racial backgrounds and ethnic heritages? What if we did not allow the racism of politicians, pundits, and talking heads to influence us to serve their dubious political purposes? If we allow our better angels to guide our responses to such questions, we could find a clear path toward a world worth dreaming about.

Glimpses of a Brighter Future

To this day, I feel Kacey leaning on my shoulder, asking, "What if . . . ?", as though he were still guiding me to see the possibilities ahead.

After he passed, memorial services held for him looked like the United Nations, just as the gatherings at Kacey's lunch table at school had. Back in school, it was as if every group had sent a representative: Kacey ran track and played football, so there were usually some athletes, but he welcomed every other kind of kid, too—the popular and those who were typically ostracized by the popular, kids who were into drama, kids in student government, the pretty people, and all the rest of us. It seemed everyone wanted to be in Kacey's orbit.

Kacey had a huge impact on people, and we all came together to remember him, share stories, and be part of Kacey's world one last time. Memorials were held in the three states where we had lived: Massachusetts, Maryland, and Maine. As we came together to remember and celebrate Kacey, the services were a continuation of what he had always brought to life in the communities around him. At all three events, I saw the pain on so many faces, young and old, from so many backgrounds. Everyone consoled one another, reaching across all the social constructs that normally keep people apart. Each celebration of his life was another window into the dream world we had talked about so many times.

Under all the loss and sadness, I found solace and a bit of inspiration in witnessing these manifestations of what could be. It motivated me to learn more, and to find my best way of effecting change in the world. I wanted to build on what Kacey had started. Now, at get-togethers with family and extended family, and when I am in the company of antiracist communities of activists, advocates, and educators, I am reinspired. Those moments are more than just reminders of our dream world; they are glimpses of what I know is possible.

I have been blessed with glimpses of our dream world many times over the years: in the global community in Pyatigorsk that I returned to frequently during my time in Russia, as we broke bread or came together to debate topics of the day; between sessions at professional conferences, when friends and colleagues of all backgrounds gather; and when my community came together to welcome baby Makkie into the world. I also saw our dream world in the Black Lives Matter movement, in student encampments promoting peace in Palestine, and I see it whenever my daughter gathers her circle of friends. These glimpses of diverse groups of people meeting up to enjoy one another, celebrate life, and promote justice allow me to believe that the future has dream-world potential.

As a goal-oriented realist, however, I believe we need to reimagine our future first. We need to envision what is possible for our world if we hope to ever find our way there. I am not a can't-we-all-just-get-along, kumbaya-singing kind of guy. Far from fearing conflict, I often invite it as a useful tool for learning. So, when I talk about a dream world, I am not imagining that we will get there overnight, that it will come without struggle, or that it will ever be perfect.

A pragmatic approach requires accepting that we are not all going to agree on one vision of an ideal world community. Preferring different forms of government or economic systems is not a problem. We can disagree on how much to spend on infrastructure or the military or space travel. Reasonable people can disagree about many things and still demonstrate respect for one another. But we must acknowledge and honor each other's humanity if we ever hope to live in a just and peaceful world.

The world is far more complex than Kacey and I understood in our youth, and the forces behind systems of oppression and exploitation are far more entrenched and powerful than we ever imagined. Even for the most resolute antiracist, the task at hand can be overwhelming. This reminds me of the adage, "There is only one way to eat an elephant: a bite at a time."[3] For many years I tried to eat as much of that metaphorical elephant as I could, until I realized that a lot more progress is made when we all come together to feast. Massive change requires the might of the masses.

Although sometimes I have to dig deep, I find hope in the work of peace- and justice-seeking people, near and far, who remind me that if we work in solidarity, we can change our nation and the world for the better. I used to think being an antiracist meant abandoning all other work to focus on the most important fight of all. That's why I left the sciences: I thought I could not pursue my dream of becoming an astronaut and also contribute in a meaningful way to the struggle against racism. Experience has taught me that I was wrong. I don't regret my decision, but I feel like it is important to encourage others to pursue their passions, whatever they may be, and bring their antiracist lens with them.

Massive change requires the might of the masses.

We need antiracist astronauts, and scientists in every field, willing to see how racism and other forms of oppression are entangled in scientific communities, organizations, and approaches. We need for them to do better, to bring the Medici Effect to life through the power of diverse perspectives to illuminate innovation.[4]

We need antiracist economists to uncover and lead efforts to enhance economic systems to make them inclusive and equitable.

We need educators to upend and replace the hidden (and not-so-hidden) racist curricula in our schools and to teach the brilliance of all peoples to inspire greatness in generations to come.

We need everyone to help oppose racism and demand inclusive practices and equitable treatment in their fields of expertise, spheres of influence, and circles of friends.

When antiracists with different professional knowledge and personal experience work in solidarity, it becomes possible to improve complex systems in ways that benefit us all. We do not all need to become DEI professionals in order to live impactful antiracist lives. The world will change when people in every field, all sorts of careers, and in every community live their own unique antiracist lives in solidarity with one another.

Our full diversity, in solidarity, is our greatest strength.

Strength Through Solidarity

I arrived in sunny Phoenix, Arizona, in the autumn of 2006 to serve on a keynote panel at a national education conference. Our assignment: to articulate the concerns and new ideas of the next generation of multicultural educators. Each member of the panel, which included extraordinary educators Paul Gorski, Carli Kyles, Mahjabeen Rafiuddin, and Tania Chance, gave a mini-keynote address that articulated an inspired vision for the future of their chosen field.

I decided to take a bit of a different route.

As a part of my statement—the only part anyone likely remembers—I chose to offer questions in critique of the current reform movements in the field of education at the time, pointing out the various strains of bigotry that were evidently acceptable within each. Why was homophobia tolerated within multicultural education leadership? Why was racism accepted within critical pedagogy circles? Why was sexism evident among some key antiracist educators? From my perspective, we were failing, as critical educators, to address these obvious problems. I had hoped for this to serve as a rallying call to address these problems and promote solidarity. But it went down like a lead balloon.

I have had the honor of serving on more panels than I can recall over the years, but that particular panel stands out in my memory. Maybe my delivery could have been more inviting; maybe my words were too cutting for people to hear what I was trying to say. It is difficult for me to say, but others who heard me speak that day have said that the people in the room were not ready, simply too divided to receive the message I was trying to convey.

Historically, even the most powerful movements for civil and human rights in the United States have been slowed by division. Profound racism hampered the progress of the women's suffrage and women's rights movements. Sexism and homophobia undermined the Civil Rights and Chicano movements. But history also teaches us that when the masses join together in opposition to any iteration of oppression, progress is inevitable.

We are currently experiencing another one of those pivotal moments of change, and this time things could be different. Within the past decade, anti-oppression movements in education and other fields, as well as large-scale movements, have hit a major turning point: the rise of intersectional leadership.

Despite being coined more than three decades ago, the term *intersectionality* has been embraced more recently by the next generation of activists and advocates, inspiring deeper understandings of identity and the impact of various types of oppression. As the concept gains traction in the public forum, we are beginning to collectively understand that discrimination is often based on the combination of multiple oppressions, ultimately serving to oppress the majority of us. The clear solution is to unite, working together to combat oppression of any stripe.

If we do the simple math, the people who experience some degree of discrimination—racism, sexism, classism, heterosexism, and so on—far outnumber those who do not. So, why is it that, in a supposed democracy, the majority of the population continues to be oppressed? The answer, as we have already discussed, is that notorious strategy known as "divide and conquer." Imagine if women, people of color, people who identify as LGBTQIA+, people who are not Christian, and white people living in poverty, or just struggling financially, recognized their common ground and found a way to work and vote in any way resembling solidarity. Our elected officials would be forced to change oppressive laws and systems if they cared about reelection—and they clearly do—because gerrymandering and all the tainted money in politics wouldn't matter.

These various groups are not coming together yet because we have all been taught to hate and oppose one another, and to fight for any scraps of privilege we can muster. We are taught that our problems are because of each other, when the truth is that they're manufactured by the folks who benefit from our division and from our collective labor. Going along with the status quo is easier, but what if we allowed ourselves to see how we are getting played? What if we hit a tipping point, where enough of us refused to allow ourselves to be pitted against one another anymore?

I have been imagining this better world for a long time and working to understand how we might get there. Solidarity is part of the answer; I have no doubt about that.

It will take courage and humility to adjust how we see ourselves in the world—to allow ourselves to see how our perspectives have been manipulated to a skewed understanding of the world. Just as it has been for civil and social movements historically, facing the truth—that our behavior may be contributing to the oppression of others—is truly a challenge for each of us today.

The Black Lives Matter movement has demonstrated the power of intersectional activism on a large scale better than any other movement to date. When three Black women who understood intersectionality—Alicia Garza, Patrisse Cullors, and Ay (formerly Opal) Tometi—used their voices to launch #BlackLivesMatter, their advocacy sparked a network that has embraced the idea that fighting racism requires inclusion and active opposition of all forms of oppression. The BLM website has operationalized an intersectional approach, explaining: "To maximize our movement muscle, and to be intentional about not replicating harmful practices that excluded so many in past movements for liberation, we made a commitment to placing those at the margins closer to the center."[5]

At Black Lives Matter marches and protests, we saw diverse Black leaders along with activists from many other backgrounds working in solidarity to oppose anti-Black racism in the justice system and beyond. The global reach and impact of BLM is evident in the vitriolic and often violent reaction from those who fear change and oppose racial justice. This is a critical shift, and we have seen successful glimpses of it whenever the goals of multiple social movements have overlapped. When allies join in struggle despite not feeling the direct impact of the specific social injustice being addressed, solidarity strengthens the movement in the way rising tides lift all boats.

As Chief Diversity Officer at California State University San Marcos, I had the opportunity to lead the Office of Inclusive Excellence. I am usually not one to focus on big events in my work. I prefer to spend time, energy, and resources on infrastructure, professional development (PD), and systemic change. However, I have learned that there is a critical place for events that serve to inspire, educate, and challenge participants, particularly on a university campus. One event that ticked all those boxes was in 2017 when the university invited Alicia Garza to campus. She spoke about her role in the birth of the Black Lives Matter movement and gave us a glimpse of her own personal experience. What was most impressive, though, was her strategic focus on inclusion. Her words and

> *Black Lives Matter is one example of a next-generation social movement, one fueled by explicit solidarity.*

her interactions with students, faculty, and administration set an example of what solidarity looks like.

Black Lives Matter is one example of a next-generation social movement, one fueled by explicit solidarity. This is our future—the path toward realizing our hopes for a better, more inclusive, and just world. Imagine what future generations will dream up, unfettered by all that holds us back today.

3

LIES OUR TEACHERS TOLD US
How Schools Are Weaponized to Divide Us

There's no such thing as neutral education. Education either functions as an instrument to bring about conformity or freedom.

—RICHARD SHAULL

For most of my adult life, I have heard that racism is inescapable. That you inevitably absorb it because racism is everywhere, and it becomes a part of you, and that white people cannot avoid growing up racist. Very well-meaning white people have told me this. But I have always known it to be untrue.

Racism has been so embedded in our culture for so long that it might *feel* inevitable. But in fact, white supremacy and racism, and all other forms of bigotry, are learned beliefs and behaviors. They are not hardwired from birth. No one is born somehow already believing in the mythology of race. If you are raised in racism, or if your home is silent about race—the nonracist approach—then you will be highly susceptible to the racism taught both explicitly and implicitly in school, in the media, and so on.

But there is another, rather obvious, possibility. Just as racism is learned, antiracism can be as well. We can be taught to view the world through an antiracist lens, to develop a mindset in opposition to oppression.

This is how my brothers and I were raised. It took a long time for me to understand why people kept saying that learning to be racist is inescapable for people who look like me, and to be able to articulate why this assessment is incorrect and slows progress.

The perspective that learning to be racist is unavoidable stems from what I call "good white people syndrome." White folks, like everyone else, I suppose, want to believe that they and their loved ones are good people. I think it is safe to say that "good white people" agree that racism is bad. Given that, how can white people hold on to white supremacist ideas and perpetuate racism and still see themselves as good? The fallacy that racism is inevitable and racial bias is a natural thing promotes the idea that white people are not *choosing* to be racist, which leaves them blameless for any racist beliefs and behaviors. Very convenient, but no less false.

If you are questioning my assertion that there is an alternative to growing up racist in a racist society, and maybe feeling a little defensive about how you grew up, then your good white people training may be kicking in. The good news is that if you are able to recognize that defensive feeling, you are self-aware enough to see this as a learning opportunity. Having been indoctrinated into a racist mindset is not a life sentence. We are all capable of intellectual growth.

I learned antiracism in my childhood, as part of how my parents taught us to see the world and oppose oppression and hate. If whoever raised you did not do that, I'm not saying they are bad people; I am saying that we can do better moving forward. The worldview that my parents promoted helped me develop an antiracist lens, which has served me well. That does not mean I have always gotten it right or that my antiracism has been flawless. It just means that I learned to see the world through an antiracist lens rather than a white supremacist lens. That is part of the reason I got in so much trouble in school: I resisted the racism in my education because I had been taught to recognize and oppose it—and the system responded accordingly to protect itself.

The schools I attended were generally designed to promote white supremacy and suppress antiracist resistance. Our teachers (with too few exceptions) told us many lies, left out a lot, and taught us to accept white supremacy as factual and racism as normal. It is what they were taught, and I doubt that most even recognized their complicity. They were following the official curriculum defined by the state and the schools. And anytime I challenged racism in that curriculum, I was called disrespectful, punished in how I was graded, removed from class, or given detention. When I was in college, as ridiculous as it sounds, one of my professors even took a swing at me when I called out the white supremacist ideology embedded in what he was teaching.

Schools today (public, private, parochial, charter, or independent) are only marginally improved, and most only superficially. I mention this because I wouldn't want you to think that my experience was so long ago that this couldn't happen today. In fact, resistance to those educators who were trying to advance our educational systems to be antiracist, equitable, and inclusive has taken the biased teaching and racist curriculum of the past and codified it into law. The current legislation in multiple states includes the banning of books that address racism and white supremacy (as well as other social justice topics), further entrenching systemic racism and intersecting oppressions.[1] They have not banned, however, the teaching of white supremacist concepts, such as "manifest destiny."

Children who develop an antiracist lens early on are able to build resistance to racist teachings, whether those teachings emanate from school, friends, the media or elsewhere. Does it mean nothing will ever get through? No, but it does equip them with the tools to recognize bigotry, stereotyping, and injustice. An antiracist lens also allows them to more easily recognize and learn to oppose other forms of discrimination and hate as well. For me, I learned a great deal about race and racism, but less, for example, about the oppressions faced by LGBTQIA+ folks. But when informed about the struggles they face, I did not feel any need to resist or doubt. I was open to learning and recognized my responsibility to oppose oppression even when it looked different from the racism, classism, and anti-Semitism that I had learned about and had more experience with.

The racist and otherwise bigoted backlash against advances in equity and inclusion in education that we are currently experiencing have highlighted how racist systems resist change. We are seeing it on display in real time. Specifically, it has put a spotlight on how individuals support racism not only by actively engaging in it, but also as bystanders watching it happen and pretending not to know what is happening on their watch.

The Heroification of White Supremacists

Mom and Dad were imperfect humans, much like the rest of us. At times they did not know what to say about what was going on or what we experienced, so they would just listen. At times they did not know the answers to questions that we had, so they would try to figure things out with us. At times they got stuff wrong as well, and when they realized this, they would take responsibility and do their best to fix it.

One thing they got right was teaching us that if we were smart enough to recognize that something was wrong, we should see it as our responsibility to try to correct it. Mom and Dad had very little tolerance for complaints, even when we were very young. Their response was always "Okay, so what are you going to do about it?" Children or not, they expected us to take action.

They wanted us to understand what was wrong in the world because they believed that we could do better—that we could, and should, actually change the world. They taught us truths about our nation's past that our schooling left out or distorted: that slavery was part of US American history, as was the genocide of Native American peoples, and that the US chose not to get involved in fighting Nazi Germany until long after the government knew what was happening to Jews in Europe. That sounds like a lot for young children to handle, and we certainly did not grasp the entirety of any of those atrocities. But we understood that slavery and genocide were horrifically wrong and that good people fought against those wrongs. We were taught to respect those people—the ones who fought against injustice, not the ones who were leading the injustices or those who just stood by and watched them happen.

One of the specifics we learned about slavery was that some of the early US American presidents owned plantations and enslaved African people. This fact seemed obviously important. So, in fourth grade, when my homework assignment was to memorize "important facts" about the first dozen US presidents, I wanted to know why my teacher thought that it didn't matter enough to include in our assignment.

Part of how my brothers and I had learned about slavery, a few years earlier, was by watching and discussing the seminal television miniseries *Roots*, based on Alex Haley's epic book of the same name.[2] Despite our youth, Kacey and I were engrossed in the story. Curled up with my brothers in the "warm spot" behind Dad's bent legs as he lay on the couch, I realized for the first time that racism and oppression were not just about white people being mean to Black people. Racism was bigger than I had understood and had a much deeper and uglier history.

Our parents took this opportunity to explain that slavery was actually even worse than what they could show on television and that the impact of it was still causing problems today. I felt angry and upset, because people who looked like me were murdering and enslaving people who looked like Kacey. But Mom and Dad also explained about the women and men who fought against slavery—how they looked like all of us and how there was a place for us in this ongoing abolitionist tradition of opposing white supremacy and racism.

"Whenever we speak up against racism, we are like them," Mom and Dad would say. For me, having abolitionists to look up to provided me with some hope and direction.

So how could my fourth-grade teacher choose to glorify white people who chose to enslave other human beings as heroes instead of the real heroes, the people who fought against them? In my young mind, it was like we were being taught to root for the bad guys.

Despite typically being too afraid to raise my hand or speak up in class, even when I knew the answer—and always dreading that the teacher might call on me to read a passage out loud—I was a pretty good student. So, I took the assignment home, on that freshly mimeographed page (with that great smell!), and began studying what they said about these early US presidents. The "facts" were simplistic: George Washington was the father of the nation and had lived in a beautiful home, Mount Vernon; Thomas Jefferson wrote most of the Declaration of Independence; and Andrew Jackson championed the common man (white men only, of course). What struck me was that there was no mention of slavery, just a simplified glorification of these so-called leaders.

This was long before Google or Wikipedia, so I hit the family encyclopedia for answers: Which of these twelve presidents had enslaved people? Who held the racist belief that people who looked like my own brother were less than human? Most of them, I learned.

The next day in school, my teacher asked who was ready to stand up in front of the class and recite the facts about these great men who had served as US presidents. It was the word *great* that set me off. It was as clear to me then as it is today that parasitic enslavers like Washington, Jefferson, and Jackson were not "great."

Suddenly, my fear of speaking in class vanished. Before the teacher even called on anyone, I stood up and began speaking.

"You're wrong," I told the teacher. I can't remember my exact words, but I do recall focusing on the idea that most of these guys were sorry people who thought they could own other people. That they made African people work for them for free, and beat and raped them, all so they could get rich. I also reminded my classmates, who seemed surprised that I was even speaking, about *Roots*, which I knew most of them had seen. I remember finishing my nervous statement by saying that these people that we were supposed to see as heroes were "just plain evil."

I had thought a lot about what I was going to say, and I felt that I was pretty articulate in my argument, but my teacher did not react well to my monologue. In an effort to dismiss what I'd said, she doubled down on her claim that these were some of the greatest men in history. "They just lived at a time when slavery was normal, but that did not make them bad people," she insisted, a line I have heard repeated many times since by those trying to excuse the horrific sins of people they want to admire.

I was angry about that assignment, and that drove me to overcome my fear and speak up to an authority figure. Rather than allowing for discussion, my teacher sent me to the vice principal's office. That was the day I lost trust in my teachers and what was being taught to me in school. It was also the day I began to find my voice.

This first attempt at activism (although I did not understand it as such at the time) opened the floodgates. I became the outspoken brother. This did not come naturally but, as a child of Mike and Maxine and especially as Kacey's big brother, it felt necessary. My parents soon became well acquainted with the principal and vice principal. But whenever I got in trouble for speaking up against racism or injustice, Mom and Dad had my back. They took me seriously and, while they often talked to me about how I might take up my cause in a more constructive way, they never tried to minimize my efforts or the problems I was trying to address. That meant everything to me. It let me know that they believed in me, that they understood I was speaking up for what I believed to be right and not just "misbehaving." I was actually doing exactly what they had taught us kids: to not just complain that something was wrong but to "do something about it."

I can still see Mom's face, so determined as she marched into the school offices to defend me. And whenever I got kicked out of school for the day for "disrespecting a teacher," Dad would find time to take me to get an ice-cream cone or visit my grandparents. More than once, I overheard him proudly telling Grandma and Grandpa about what I had done. If my parents had chosen to discipline me for my behavior rather than encouraging me as they did, my activist spirit may have been crushed. Instead, they let me know that they were proud of me. Their support gave me confidence and helped sustain me through the many challenges, missteps, and setbacks that I have experienced over the years, which could have discouraged me from continuing to try and make a difference.

I have often wondered whether I would have reacted that way to the teacher's attempt to erase the horrors of slavery if Kacey had not been my brother. I would like to think so, but I can't be sure of that. I've heard plenty of people say that they would have been on the right side of history but then seen them stand firmly on the wrong side while saying it. I might have cared, considering what our parents taught us, or I might have remained too scared to speak up and sat there doing nothing, like my classmates. I do know that I took it personally because I was Kacey's brother.

I never told Kacey what happened in class that day. I had hoped that if I could just convince this teacher that she was wrong, Kacey would not have to hear her say that those racist white people were great when he was in her class the next year. I did not know exactly how that would feel for him, but I knew it would hurt. I also didn't realize that the problem was so much bigger than that assignment or that particular teacher.

Looking back, I doubt that my words mattered much to my teacher, and it hurts to think about what the racism Kacey faced in school did to his spirit over the years. I have no doubt that the damage done to my brother's heart in school contributed to why he is not with us today.

The *Yankee Doodle Dandy* don't-mind-the-racism narrative of how we are taught US history is harmful to all of us, but particularly those targeted by the oppression being left out or lied about. We don't need to glorify white racists for white people to see themselves as part of a great history, though. There are better heroes, many of whom were white, and amazing truths for us to study: Those who opposed white supremacy, who fought against colonialism, genocide, and slavery, and whose legacy is the progress that we have made provide a rich history and examples for us to follow. But that is not the story that would allow for today's racist systems to persist.

An accurate history is far more diverse than what many people learn in school, because amazing people, events, and advancements emerge from every nook and cranny of humanity. The truth about the US American story is far more complex and compelling than the watered-down, whitewashed version nearly all of us are fed in school. We have a great deal to learn from our collective experience—if we are willing to learn the whole story.

The potential for learning that could come from studying our collective history, from multiple perspectives, and providing the next generations with the tools to build better systems gives me hope. Of course, this will require a major shift away from the white supremacist (and otherwise biased) mis-education that is the norm. But we can do hard things. In fact, we take pride in the challenges we have overcome as a nation—the Great Depression comes to mind as a good example. What if we successfully overcame racism? That would certainly give us all reason to be proud.

> *We don't need to glorify white racists for white people to see themselves as a part of a great history.*

Strategic White Ignorance

White people have been taught that feigning ignorance of all things racial excuses us from any reasonable expectation that we take action to oppose racism, or even acknowledge its existence. We learn this in school, and it is reinforced at home, in communities, and through media. But acting oblivious does not absolve us of our responsibility to be honest about the past and do better for the future.

Charles W. Mills goes into great depth about "white ignorance," which includes the purposeful lack of knowledge about issues of white supremacy and racism.[3] In a more generalized way, Ralph Hertwig and Christoph Engel discuss the conscious choice not to seek knowledge, which they call "deliberate ignorance."[4] Together, these terms speak to what I think of as "strategic white ignorance": the intentional performance of naivete by white folks who seek to be excused from any responsibility for opposing racism due to their supposedly unavoidable ignorance.

I have spent countless hours working with white people who are otherwise intelligent but claim total ignorance when it comes to issues of race. Through these experiences, I have learned that this stance is not actually based on naivete; it is practiced and disingenuous. It is a strategic approach, allowing the individual to maintain the illusion of innocence while actually supporting racism through inaction.

This feigning of ignorance when cornered about racism is a defensive measure to deflect responsibility. White people are taught to claim that they were innocently unaware of whatever racist reality is being addressed. What's more, we also place the burden of teaching about racism on others—mostly people of color—because, as discussed earlier, we are taught that our whiteness makes it impossible for us to be truly aware of racism. This is why a white person with an experience like mine is said to be an exception, not the norm: to maintain the myth of white innocence and justify ignorance.

The manifestations of this performative ignorance can take many forms, including attempts to revisit basic definitions in an attempt to run out the clock on our attention span for race-related issues. "Can we go back and define *diversity* before we continue?" or "Shouldn't we take some time to discuss what *racism* actually is so that we are all on the same page?" are examples of questions intended to derail critical conversations and stall progress. They rely on strategic white ignorance to protect them from being challenged as they seek to redefine language to serve their narrative or to simply avoid the difficult discussions necessary to advance learning or make real change happen.

In education, strategic white ignorance can, for example, be seen in how teachers teach white supremacist curricula without question, feigning ignorance if they are challenged. White supremacy and racism are evidenced in curricula by minimizing genocide, heroifying enslavers, or being hypercritical of leaders of color. A curriculum is as much about what's left out as it is about what's included. Beginning the history of the Americas when Europeans showed up to "discover" everything, for example, leaves out the history of the Indigenous peoples who had already lived there for millennia. This promotes white supremacy because it advances the idea that nothing mattered until the white folks showed up and civilized everyone—which is absolute mythology.

> *A curriculum is as much about what's left out as it is about what's included.*

When I was younger, I fell for this strategy of playing ignorant many times. By the time I was in front of university presidents and other organizational leaders, however, I understood the strategy and knew how to expose it. When unmasked, some people just blow it off, moving on to their next strategy for avoiding progress. Those who genuinely do not want to promote racism, however, have often taken the step to recognize the problem with their unconscious behavior and move forward with new understanding. Others have become defensive, calling me disrespectful or even racist against white people (or self-hating) for not buying their nonsense. I refuse to believe that so many otherwise brilliant folks are somehow profoundly dimwitted about anything to do with race and racism.

Strategic white ignorance allows white people to benefit fully from white privilege while maintaining a self-image, and reputation, of not being racist. Claiming to be "nonracist," just like alleging to be "color-blind" or saying "I don't have a racist bone in my body," is a linguistic red flag signaling the use of strategic white ignorance. These assertions are all attempts to maintain blamelessness and an image of good intent, when in fact this bystander position serves as critical support for ongoing racism. Without so many bystanders, there is no way that racism could persist.

Despite many people working hard to remove white supremacy and racism from curricula, the US American classroom far too often serves as a primary source of racist mythologies. The mythology that spreads throughout the education system tells us that white people are inherently good, absolving them of responsibility for historical atrocities and ongoing oppression perpetuated primarily by white people. It exculpates white individuals and historical figures from the moral and ethical standards rigorously applied to people of color, who are most often juxtaposed as inherently bad, evil, and unworthy. This approach is necessary to maintain the mythology of white supremacy.

Strategic white ignorance allows white people to benefit fully from white privilege while maintaining a self-image, and reputation, of not being racist.

Tactics of strategic white ignorance, promulgated by parents, teachers, school curricula, the media, and so forth, are critical for maintaining a posture of innocence for those enabling systemic racism. On the individual level, this posture of innocence helps white people avoid feelings of guilt and responsibility, and the need to support change. Only when this veil of ignorance is removed can an individual effectively engage in the personal growth necessary to contribute to our collective progress toward equity and inclusion socially and systemically.

Strategic White Centering

The first time I heard the term "white tears" was at an education conference, where it was happening right in front of me: A white participant said something racially offensive. When called out on it, they tried to plead ignorance.

When that was challenged, they just cried. As I tried to contain my frustration with everyone who was catering to this phony emotional performance, another participant said, "Here we go with the white tears again."

Giving that behavior a name provided an opportunity for a productive discussion. Other participants explained what was happening, challenging the white participant's behavior and enlightening everyone about this common tactic. This quick, brilliant lesson caused the white tears to dry up quickly. More importantly, it got us all back on topic.

When white folks are called out for their behavior around racial issues or actions that have a racist impact, many resort to centering their own experience and feelings. Like strategic white ignorance, white tears are a strategic and often defensive tool meant to elicit sympathy, maintain a positive image, and again, deflect responsibility. This turns attention away from the issue of racism, and the harm to people of color, and focuses instead on tending to the imaginary wounds of the white person. This disingenuous move is like a ball player faking an injury to avoid embarrassment and responsibility when an opposing player blows by them and scores. It is pathetic, but also strategic. This is particularly concerning in this case, at a conference on education, because of what this educator, who was trying to avoid responsibility for racist remarks, may have been teaching their students.

Unfortunately, most people still respond to these dubious tactics by trying to provide comfort. A common example in higher education is when a white person objects to an antiracist initiative being discussed by decision-makers. Offering no evidence or justification for their objection, they assert that they feel the initiative could make white students feel excluded. Instead of discussing the merits of the concern, colleagues too often go immediately into negotiation mode until the person who raised the concern and whoever is supporting their objection are made comfortable. The result ends up being a weakened initiative, which was their *strategic* objective all along. We can be compassionate without allowing strategic racism to guide decision-making.

Racist Gaslighting

The use of these and other strategic methods to derail antiracism is not new. One of the most egregious examples of gaslighting in human history, for example, is the promotion of the white supremacist mythology of race itself as scientific fact.

We usually think of gaslighting as a form of psychological abuse within interpersonal relationships, but it happens on the sociological level as well. The active promotion of white supremacy as science to the masses is an example of gaslighting at scale, manipulating our understanding of humanity, history, and reality. The idea that people were color coded by intelligence and worth should have immediately been recognized as obviously false. However, manipulating people using gaslighting tactics caused a critical mass of white people to buy into the false narrative of white superiority— primarily out of misguided self-interest.

We know that the invention of race was no benign scientific discovery (as discussed earlier). It was a nonscientific social construct developed with the express purpose of promoting a completely made-up hierarchy of peoples, with those deemed "white" at the top and everyone else below. Simply put, whiteness was invented to justify colonization, subjugation, and oppression, and the resulting stereotypes persist to this day, propped up by the continued teaching of white supremacy in schools and the desire of white folks to hold on to their privilege scraps.

Racist gaslighting is the cornerstone of the US American brand of white supremacy. It was literally built into the founding documents, systems, and economic strategies of the country— all that stuff behind the wall. To this day, we are taught mythological narratives in school, through the media, and by our "leaders," who deny and defy reality all the time. Genocide in what is now the United States was made acceptable because First Nations peoples were deemed "non-white";

> *Racist gaslighting is the cornerstone of the US American brand of white supremacy.*

this gave us the false narratives of discovery, explorers, and settlers. Likewise, the enslavement of African people was made palatable to Europeans and European Americans by the promotion of the lie that African people were racially inferior.

Today, few would disagree that the original US American sins of slavery and genocide were objectively horrible and worthy of condemnation. However, ongoing gaslighting continues to prevent those in power in the United States from taking responsibility for—or even teaching our children honestly about—the slavery and genocide that marked the birth of our nation and the source of its enormous wealth. Spoiler alert: The wealthiest didn't get there through hard work, at least not their own.

These national gaslighting narratives were not, and are not, accidental. They have been deliberately included and doggedly preserved in our schoolbooks and national consciousness because they are the foundation of the US American story that those in power need to tell to stay in power. Like most untruths, attempts to whitewash US history and current events continue to grow and become more bizarre and outlandish over time. To maintain the systems built upon this mythic foundation, the gaslighting has become more extreme and the lies have grown more absurd. That's why so many people today recognize hyperpatriotism as a racist dog whistle.

Here's the kicker: Anyone who dares challenge this set of false narratives is then marginalized and treated as an extremist or accused of pushing revisionist history to promote a radical agenda. More gaslighting.

Doling out consequences for stepping out of line, which we will discuss in detail later, is how the powerful protect ongoing systems of racist oppression. If privilege scraps are the proverbial carrot, the consequences of opposing racism are the stick. The reaction to attempts at truth-telling is so embedded in our national culture that when people protest racism, the natural inclination of many white folks is to condemn the protests as anti-American or unpatriotic. How distracted, pacified, or gaslit do we have to be to not see a problem with this?

The racist, sexist, and classist defining of "all men" who were said to be "created equal" laid the groundwork for where we are today. We are a nation that cannot even agree that the lives of Black people matter. Take that in for a moment: We, the people of the United States of America, cannot agree that Black people's lives even *matter*. I don't know about you, but this hardly makes me want to wave the old Stars and Stripes.

If you perform an online search for "American values," you will find a plethora of lists. At least three values are common to nearly all of them: freedom, equality, and the idea that hard work will result in prosperity. Yet none of these values have truly been the reality for most US Americans. This unavoidable truth is at the crux of our national dilemma.

Trying to make our nation's history conform to the values we claim to hold dear has served only to promote a false sense of national pride propped up by a fictional narrative. We pretend that domestic terrorism has not been a constant reality for people of color since Columbus sailed the ocean blue. We routinely leave out or minimize this reality in our retelling of our history, from the triangular trade to the Ku Klux Klan and lynching to Trump's insurrection. The values we espouse as a nation sound wonderful, but our ways often do not reflect our ideals. This contradiction between what we say we believe and how we behave has created a culture in deep denial. This is the sociological equivalent of "good white people" syndrome. Just as individuals do mental gymnastics to absolve themselves of fault in order to see themselves as good, as US Americans we do the same thing to see our collective selves as the "good guys," regardless of our history and behavior as a nation.

Take your pick from among the many ways our behavior is in direct conflict with our espoused values. Let's start with the fact that as a supposedly peace-loving people, we have been at war somewhere in the world almost every day since we became a nation. How about the militarization of our police forces and their objectively racist practices: Is that concerning? Then there is the fact that we lock up a higher percentage of our citizens than any other nation on Earth—not to mention that wealth determines who can afford cash bail and access to excellent representation, or the reality that racism is a major factor in who ends up in prison. How do these truths match up with all the freedom and justice for all that we claim as national values?

White supremacy, along with predatory capitalism, is among the United States' most powerful exports. Over the centuries, our nation has built on the racism that Europe spread around the world through colonialism, by exporting white supremacy in a neocolonial manner using our economic, military, and cultural muscle. Adherence to the US American mythology has prevented us from coming to terms with our history, making amends, and moving forward in a manner worthy of our deepest, most honorable national aspirations.

We continue to try and justify our behavior as a nation, domestically and internationally, but far too often, our actions contradict what we claim to be our values. So, what do we do? We simply lie—to ourselves and everyone else. We lie to ourselves because that is what we have been trained to do since childhood: *Slavery was not all bad. The Civil War was about states' rights. Justice is blind.* There is no evidence to support any of these assertions—and plenty of evidence exists to the contrary—yet every US American student has heard them declared as statements of fact.

Teaching White Supremacy

An important part of the strategy to maintain systemic racism in the US is to teach white supremacy to each generation of children. As an educator, I recognize that racist mythology and strategies of white ignorance are forms of psychological and sociological violence. Every lie that serves to demean, discourage, and mislead students does damage to the spirit of every student in the room, most especially those being targeted. It takes a toll on children of color, and it prepares white children to grow up and do the same while still seeing themselves as good white folks like George

Washington and Thomas Jefferson. It also promotes physical violence in defense of white supremacy.

Because they lay the foundation for what Isabel Wilkerson brilliantly describes as the US American caste system, our schools are a critical battleground.[5] Laws are passed across the nation to ban classes that teach about the cultures, accomplishments, and brilliance of people of color. States ban books that offer a critical view of US history, and so on. These legal maneuvers have a direct impact on students, and not just in "red states" or conservative districts.

One of my child's assignments as a middle schooler in Southern California was to write an essay in response to a question where enslaved African people were referred to as "workers" and equated with white migrant workers who chose to leave their hometown to go work at a factory of their own free will. This is a perfect example of how educators teach racism and why we need teachers to employ a critical antiracist lens to the curriculum and in their teaching strategies.

Makkie's teacher presented racist gaslighting as fact and then asked her to expound upon it. Presenting enslaved people as comparable to those who made an economic life choice of their own free will, no matter how difficult that may have been, fails to tell the truth about either group's experience. It also minimizes the wrongs done by enslavers—including so many of our founding fathers and mothers.

Rather than just doing the assignment, Makkie gave it to me and explained her concerns. I let her know that I was proud that she recognized what was wrong, and then I did my part by advocating for my child and her classmates. In this case, advocating meant pointing out to the teacher, administration, and district diversity officer that this curriculum was racist, explaining how it supported white supremacist ideology, and promoting curricular change as well as professional development (PD) and disciplinary measures for the teacher. The small order of success that we had in that particular case cannot protect Makkie or her classmates from all of the bias and bigotry that schooling will push, but every effort matters. Not just because a bit of change occurred, but even more so because Makkie felt supported in her budding advocacy for change, like I was by my parents, and she saw me do something. If I had told her not to worry about it and done nothing, that would have sent a very different message.

It is important to educate preservice teachers and provide training for in-service teachers in ways that prepare them to examine the curriculum and either enhance or change it to ensure that it is accurate and inclusive of multiple relevant perspectives, and actively promotes the development of an antiracist/anti-oppression mindset. This type of teaching is not the indoctrination that those who prefer to hide history and promote white supremacy claim it to be. In fact, the point is to stop indoctrinating our children into the cult of white supremacy, which has been the hallmark of a US American education to date, and to teach them to think critically about our past in order to learn from it and do better.

We must prepare educators with the tools to undo whitewashing, replace racist mythologies with accurate accounts of history through multiple perspectives, and ensure that all our children can see themselves in their teachers and the curriculum. This requires teacher educators to adopt an antiracist lens similar to that employed by critical race theory (CRT)—a well-established concept that exposes and counters systemic racism embedded in our laws and legal systems. In the most basic terms, CRT is simply an approach that reminds us to consider the impact of racism as we analyze historic and current events.

Of course, CRT has become one of the more recent boogeymen used by conservative politicians to redirect the anger of struggling white folks away from those actually causing their

> *CRT has become one of the more recent boogeymen used by conservative politicians to redirect the anger of struggling white folks away from those actually causing their struggles and toward people of color and progressives working to promote remedies.*

struggles and toward people of color and progressives working to promote remedies. This misdirection campaign is meant to hijack CRT, redefining it as "anti-white," which is objectively and demonstrably not true—so, the gaslighting continues.

Without looking through a CRT lens, we are taught, for example, that women fought for and won the right to vote through the Nineteenth Amendment in 1920. But this is only part of the women's suffrage story, excluding the racist collusion within the movement. To say that women won the right to vote in 1920 assumes that the only women who matter are white women. A more accurate statement is that white women in the United States won the right to vote in 1920, but it was not until the Voting Rights Act of 1965 that women of color won the right to vote, and even then, they were discouraged and disenfranchised for many more years after that. The fact that efforts to disenfranchise people of color from voting are happening today is a testament to what happens when we lie to ourselves about our history—it makes it easier to repeat past injustices.

Today, although many schools adopt inclusive and sometimes even antiracist mission statements, and occasionally include revolutionary perspectives in a few courses, they also actively model white supremacy in nearly every possible way. This is done not only through inaccurate curricula and biased teaching practices but also in the administration of the schools themselves. We may want to believe we are sending our children to schools that are not teaching racism, but do not be fooled by the "inclusion delusion"—the superficial public relations efforts on websites and in mission statements that make schools and other organizations look far more diverse and inclusive than they actually are. The disparities in discipline, graduation rates, grading, college counseling, and educator hiring and promotion, along with the inequitable public school funding and highly problematic private school admissions, tell a different story—exposing all the public relations efforts as little more than lipstick on a racist pig.

Far too often, US American students are taught that Black lives, Indigenous lives, and the lives of people of color in general do not matter as much as white lives. This white supremacist teaching is achieved subtly in today's classroom. We have become more sophisticated in our bigotry, employing hidden curricula and communicating bias by modeling that white lives are the most precious—in assignments like Mak's teacher gave, which minimized the violent realities of slavery.

If we assume that the multicultural mission statements are true, we might not question students being taught that Thomas Jefferson, a founding father, opposed slavery and freed his slaves when he died. Employing a critical antiracist lens exposes a lot wrong with that very common teaching. First of all, if you oppose slavery, why would you enslave anyone? And how is "freeing" people you enslave after your death supposed to be seen as benevolent? In fact, Jefferson enslaved more than 600 people during his lifetime, including Sally Hemings, with whom he fathered six children—I can't imagine that she had any choice in the matter—but this has somehow been whitewashed into a love story. And he only freed five people upon his death; the rest, including Sally Hemings, became the property of his widow.

Downplaying the injustices perpetuated by white people who enslaved other human beings, and all the atrocities that went along with that, promotes a white supremacist narrative. Excluding or excusing such behavior by white people lays the groundwork for future bigotry, discrimination, and violence of all kinds, including the racist police violence that has become normalized today—and the excusing of it all.

Nationwide, our education systems support a curriculum that glorifies white people who participated in genocide, perpetrated colonization, enslaved people, and openly espoused racist ideologies. This is done to promote the mythology that white people are morally and intellectually superior, that they were the good guys who built the United States on an exceptional moral foundation. Elementary and secondary students learn that those racist atrocities (if they are taught about them at all) were not entirely bad, that those who committed them were good people just doing what was done at that time, and that European colonizers brought good

Christian culture to savage Africans and Indigenous people—none of which is based in fact.

Stereotypes are introduced and reality is twisted to fit a narrative that teaches us all to believe that European cultures—better yet, US American white culture—are in all ways superior to everyone else. Our children absorb this perspective, which encourages them to become comfortable with excusing racist behavior.

At the same time, every possible flaw tends to be noted about the incredibly few leaders of color who are even mentioned in the curriculum. For example, schools teach a watered-down version of who the Reverend Dr. Martin Luther King Jr. was and minimize the depth of his message, offering a few palatable lines from his works while leaving out the parts that make white people uncomfortable—but they always find a way to teach that he cheated on his wife. Didn't Jefferson cheat on his wife, or is raping a woman you enslave not considered cheating? This double standard teaches students to accept that people of color are bad, inferior, and even at fault for how they are mistreated.

The histories of entire peoples are relegated to elective courses or heritage months, if they are included at all. Every group of people that is not deemed "white" is subtly (or not so subtly) demeaned, transformed into something that fits the mythology, or simply left out of the curriculum. Outside of my home, I never learned about the histories of nations anywhere in the world beyond Europe until they were colonized by Europeans, as if these cultures were irrelevant until white folks "discovered" them.

In school, my classmates and I learned that Europeans invented everything and wrote everything worth reading and that the rest of the world's people (who were not deemed "white") were more primitive, especially the "natives" who had been colonized. I was introduced to Plato's *The Allegory of the Cave* at least seven times during my formal education but learned next to nothing about the brilliant thinkers, authors, artists, and innovators around the world who were not European or European American. I did learn a bit about a few abolitionists in US American history, but they were presented as problematic rather than heroic.

Does this sound like a system that teaches its rising citizens to apply critical thinking skills to matters of race? By the time we graduate into adulthood, the vast majority of us have been provided with an almost exclusively Eurocentric curriculum in explicit support of a white supremacist worldview. We are taught to reject any assertion that the "good white people" of America today would discriminate against people of color. This training rejects any accountability for hundreds of years of wrongdoing, or any ongoing impact. So, why consider reparations? Obviously, this inability to acknowledge generations of human rights violations slows progress toward the equity and freedom so many of us claim that we already practice.

I genuinely believe that we want to be the nation we claim to be. To date, however, we have not reached a critical mass of those willing to make the sacrifices or do the hard work necessary to get there. Those who have benefited most from systemic oppression in the United States continue to use their obscene wealth and enormous power to influence political, economic, and educational systems in order to maintain what has worked so well for them. Unfortunately, anti-Blackness and anti-Indigenous racism, and broader racism against all people of color, while less blatant than in the past, remain the norm in the classroom. Not enough has changed since they tried to teach me these things decades ago. I was fortunate that my parents had provided me with an antiracist lens that helped me, at least sometimes, to see the hypocrisy, contradictions, and white supremacist lies for what they are. More of us need to do this for our children.

College-Level Racism

Entering college, for some reason, I expected that racism would not be as prevalent. While meeting a white person who turned out to be racist had become almost routine, I thought college would be different. These were supposed to be the smart folks! Unfortunately, too often—and in spite of the ramblings of right-wing pundits—higher education is an extension of the biases, inequities, and miseducation that we experience in our prekindergarten through twelfth grade (P–12) education.

My fantasy of an antiracist higher education was quickly squashed during my orientation tour of the Florida Tech campus. Our student guide talked to us about all the great facilities, professors, and opportunities around campus, and about the great diversity of students—just before they warned us not to go into "Brown Town." Yes, that is how they referred to the Black community in Melbourne, Florida. I had questions, and the guide's answers were predictable. After pointing out the racism in our guide's statement, I left the tour early. As I walked away, the tour continued as if I had said nothing and all was normal—because it was.

Although I was a complete fish out of water as a first-generation college student, I was not new to being upset by normalized racism. It was no different from what I had already experienced in school up to that point. I continued to do whatever I could think of to oppose the bigotry all around me: I complained to the dean of students about the racist statement that was part of the campus tour. I wrote a letter to the editor of the student newspaper about the Confederate flag hanging in the window across from my dorm room. At the annual speech contest, I gave a speech about racism on campus. I was active in the local community and started a student organization called the Cultural Awareness Council, which focused on combating racism on campus and ultimately resulted in the addition of a staff position focused on campus equity and inclusion. I was disappointed but remained active.

The fact is, the demographics of tenured faculty and administration do not reflect the diversity of college campuses, never mind the nation or the world. Our elite colleges and universities discriminate in admissions by giving advantage to children of alumni and wealthy donors. On top of that, the cost of a higher education has risen exponentially while incomes have remained stagnant except for those of the extremely wealthy, putting college hopes out of reach or promising extreme debt for many students of color and white students who do not come from wealth. Our higher education system perpetuates systemic racism and classism and, more often than not, serves as another primary source for white supremacist ideologies, segregation, and more discrimination. And even the progress that we have made (though there is still a long way to go) is under fire as we face legislation that ends programs designed to address systemic inequities, removes positions focused on equity and inclusion, closes centers that counter social exclusion, and dismantles scholarships meant to address generational oppression.

These measures were only starting to make a dent in the systems of oppression that have existed since the founding of higher education institutions in the US. The progress made for students of color and many first-generation white students, not to mention immigrant students, LGBTQIA+ students, and other marginalized students was just too much to allow for those who expect the full benefits of their white privilege.

Back to my undergraduate experience: I recall looking forward to taking a particular course with a popular professor. The course description claimed we would explore the philosophical and theoretical histories of the sciences. I had heard that this professor was smart and engaging and really made the class interesting. He was, but my enthusiasm began to fade quickly. The syllabus included assigned readings exclusively about European or European American scientists and philosophers, most of whom I had already learned about in high school. From lectures at the planetarium by Dr. W. Russell Blake, my first mentor, I had already learned that the origins of astronomy and astrophysics were rooted in Chinese, Egyptian, Indian, Mesopotamian, Mayan, Aztec, and Greek cultures, so I was unimpressed and disappointed when nearly all but the Greeks' contributions were omitted from the syllabus.

As the semester went on, I began to ask questions that the professor did not appreciate. I would look up the roots of some philosophical or scientific thought and then challenge him on giving exclusive credit to

European thinkers. "What about the African influences on Greek philosophy?" I asked. "Why is it so out of the question that Greek philosophers could have learned from Egyptians, an advanced society so close in geographic proximity?"

After class, in his office, with a friend of mine, the professor acknowledged that the Greeks may have learned from the Egyptians but found a way to point out that Egyptians were "not Black." When I noted that Egyptian culture was not homogenous and questioned his need to bring modern notions of race into the discussion, he accused me of calling him a racist.

After reciting random facts intended to prove this to me, he capped it off with a predictable statement: "I am not a racist."

"I learned a long time ago that only racist people feel the need to say they are not racist," I replied.

His response was an attempt to physically assault me.

Think about it: A white professor got so rattled when confronted with his own racism that he actually swung at a student who refused to buy into his white supremacist teachings. His intelligence was trumped by his need to maintain those racist beliefs. His brain short-circuited when faced with the possibility that brilliant Black people could teach or influence brilliant white people.

As an antiracist educator, and as a professional who advises leaders and consults with organizations on DEI work, I often run across people who believe that only stupid people are racist. Sure, there are certainly plenty of stupid racists. We see them being interviewed by comedians at Trump rallies and getting caught on video yelling "Go back to Mexico!" at any random person with brown skin. Stupid racists might be more visible, but they are just a subset of the larger group. There are far more racists who are plenty smart enough to know better. They are smart enough to know that the Confederate flag is not about culture, that antifascism is not an organization, that opposing fascism is a good thing, and that the well-documented racism spewed by Trump and his enablers is wrong.

I have met university presidents and CEOs who are as racist as the loudest Make America Great Again (MAGA) rally participant swearing that President Obama founded ISIS. I met anti-Semitic people in Russia who were some of the smartest astrophysicists in the world. It is not about intelligence at all; plenty of people hold racist beliefs and a college degree simultaneously. I have met racist people who demonstrate brilliance in science, finance, philanthropy, law, medicine, and pretty much any other field you can think of, and almost none of them were unintelligent people. Racism is not limited to people who are uneducated, live in specific parts of the US, are working class, or belong to a certain political party. It is not something that people are tricked into believing because they're not very bright. It is something that we are all taught from birth, and that many actively choose to believe in spite of evidence that it's nothing but a collection of lies to justify oppression.

In fact, it often takes significant mental gymnastics to maintain racist beliefs when confronted with all manner of contradictory evidence. And people reliably expend that much effort to hold on to racist beliefs unless there is a benefit to changing their perspective.

White people, and some others, have bought into racist nonsense because it feeds their ego, as with the professor whose self-worth was wrapped up in seeing himself reflected in the whiteness of great philosophers. Racism feeds their greed for power and admiration, like in the many cases of politicians who use racist dog whistles to ensure support from bigots who vote. It feeds the personal narrative of those who have achieved financial success and who look around at all their white colleagues—in the C-suite, in their exclusive neighborhood, in their child's legacy admissions into their alma mater—and need to believe that discrimination had nothing to do with how they got there.

For those who have not been particularly successful, part of what makes racism so attractive is that it also provides ready scapegoats. As much as a successful white person wants to believe that discrimination against people of color had nothing to do with their success, a white person who has struggled wants to believe that their failures were because of unfair advantages given to someone else. It does not matter if their failure is as an athlete, in their education, in a career, or in life in general—this magical thinking can apply at any level. Racism feeds their fears and delusions, allowing them to justify the disparate treatment of people of color while simultaneously blaming them for any of their own misfortunes.

For both the successful and the struggling, the evidence does not support their racist beliefs. However, the comfort gained by viewing their experience through a white supremacist lens takes precedent over any interest in the truth. Unfortunately, higher education is not immune to any of this, which broke my heart as a first-generation college student walking onto campus, hopeful for something different. Still, I fell in love with higher education, and since my undergraduate days, higher education has made some real progress. Today we are suffering a backlash from those solidly entrenched on the wrong side of history. As this is expected, we continue to do the work, and we will ultimately reach the inclusive excellence in education that I had hoped to find years ago as a first-year student.

4

NOT RACIST IS NOT ENOUGH
Reimagining Education

> *In a racist society, it is not enough to be nonracist—*
> *we must be antiracist.*
>
> —ANGELA DAVIS

EIGHTY-ONE PERCENT OF US Americans believe racial and ethnic discrimination is a problem.[1] That number varies by race and over time, but across racial categories and over at least the past five years, the majority of us acknowledge that racism exists as a challenge in today's world. The next eleven steps in our twelve-step program to recover from racism, however, are still being written. Without a doubt, though, educators have a major part to play.

Since our formal education systems continue to be a major contributor to systemic racism, any discussion of dismantling systems of oppression must include early childhood education, elementary and secondary schools, and higher education institutions. As students, parents, community members, and colleagues, we can all do our part to support these institutions and educators, particularly when white folks (including politicians) resist change in order to preserve unearned privileges for themselves and their white constituents. Each of us can take action to help shift our schools from being super-spreaders of racism to examples of constructive change toward equity and inclusion.

Extraordinary antiracist teachers lead the charge, lining up on the front lines of education reform. They have an unquantifiable impact on their students, and they work hard to address institutional and systemic racism in their schools, school systems, communities, and in the field of education. While these antiracist educators are still too few and far between in the lives of most students, their impact is growing, and they are advancing to higher levels of influence. This increasing influence has touched a nerve for those deeply invested in white supremacy. This is evident in the political efforts to ban books, courses, and initiatives that promote inclusion.

Today's antiracist educators work in the tradition of those who have employed education as a means of emancipation and liberation throughout history. Learning about this history was important for me because it provided me with strategies and hope in my early years as an educator. The first book to open my eyes to this tradition was *Pedagogy of the Oppressed*, by Brazilian educator Paulo Freire.

That book led me to study Septima Clark, a Black educator who formed Citizenship Schools, which were critical in the fight for voting rights. Clark worked with Myles Horton to lead the Highlander Folk School (known now as the Highlander Research and Education Center), which served as a meeting place and training center for leaders like Rosa Parks, Martin Luther King Jr., Ralph Abernathy, John Lewis, and many other leaders from a variety of social justice movements. The antiracist tradition is rich, with many individuals, organizations, and movements to learn and draw inspiration from. Yet most of us were never taught about the Citizenship Schools or Highlander in our schooling. Were you?

Teaching in an antiracist tradition requires more than simply presenting a more accurate and inclusive curriculum. It also includes teaching how to employ critical thinking skills to recognize and remedy the misinformation taught by others; understanding the white supremacist roots of racist mythology and miseducation; and implementing strategies for living an antiracist life with intentional and strategic impact.

Racism is not stagnant nor relegated to the past. It is fluid and adaptive because those who benefit from it continue to actively promote and protect racist institutions, mythologies, and systems. To counteract this, we must work continuously to reimagine and make real an education system that refuses to perpetuate racist ideology.

Consider, for instance, the challenges of dealing with people who falsely claim that the Confederate flag and statues of Confederate leaders are about "heritage, not hate." Confronting these claims requires more than accurate historical information, because to those who are determined to maintain their white supremacist beliefs and benefits, the truth does not matter. They have learned to employ the tactics of strategic white ignorance and racist gaslighting, giving themselves permission to dismiss as fake news or revisionist history anything that contradicts their racist perspective.

Whenever we're up against manifestations of institutional and systemic racism—whether in corporate policy or policing or teaching—we must understand the roots of racist practices as well as the skills necessary to dismantle and replace them. This is a heavy lift, and it cannot be fully achieved by exposure to only a few classes throughout our educational experience that contradict the racist norm. Making the equitable, inclusive, and sustainable change that we all deserve requires us to change education systems from early childhood through graduate studies. And it starts with reeducating our nation's teachers.

Teacher Preparation

Beyond reenvisioning curriculum development, pedagogical strategies, and classroom management through an antiracist lens, teachers also need to be reeducated regarding white supremacy, racism, and racial justice—within a larger understanding of social justice.

We already demand a lot of teachers—more now than ever. We required them to figure out overnight how to teach online during the pandemic. We expect them to protect our children from gun violence on school grounds. We demand that they show every child all the attention they need, in spite of large class sizes. Oh, and all too often, to teach an unsustainable class schedule. So, how could we possibly expect more? My answer is not more, just better.

First, we need to lighten the load, pay teachers better, and provide professional development that is engaging and promotes student engagement and success. The good news is that there is no shortage of excellent antiracist/antibias curricula available to educators for every subject area, which provide multiple perspectives and develop critical thinking skills.

The curricular change is not as difficult as the professional development necessary to remove racist and otherwise biased teaching from the classroom. While some teacher education programs have made excellent progress, most teachers were not taught in an antiracist tradition when they were children themselves, and their teacher education programs did not provide the necessary training to help them develop an antiracist lens through which to do their work. Reeducating our teachers, therefore, is the heavier task. For those who are already well prepared but face resistance to their antiracist teaching, removing those barriers will allow for change. But for those who are not prepared, professional development will be necessary for them to be able to deliver a more inclusive and antiracist curriculum.

Teacher education programs across the nation have been required for some time to incorporate some level of diversity and inclusion into how they educate preservice teachers. Unfortunately, these accreditation processes often fail to uphold or enforce their own standards. In other words, we have to begin by enforcing the existing requirements of teacher education programs, which call for graduates being prepared to teach in an equitable, inclusive, and therefore more accurate manner.

While this is a shift, it is necessary if our schools are going to transform from being a serious part of the problem to a powerful part of the solution. Think about it this way: Imagine if an aerospace engineering student was taught that the Earth is flat—and believed it. Would they be prepared to do their job well? Of course not. So, is it enough to tell the aerospace engineering student that the planet is not flat? Or do we teach them that it is an imperfect sphere, offering as much detail as possible about our planet and the forces that have shaped it and encouraging them to continue to think critically about the subject?

For teachers to be well prepared to educate our children in an inclusive, equitable, and antiracist manner, teacher education programs will need to provide courses that include factual information; promote critical thinking; and develop antiracist, pro–equity and inclusion mindsets. This is often where those who oppose equity and inclusion will say that this is forcing a political agenda on preservice teachers, and ultimately students. Let's address this accusation directly.

First, it is important to understand that education is guided by perspectives, including political perspectives. Differences in access, resources, and educational opportunities are largely determined by political decisions. Additionally, the decisions about what to teach, what not to teach and, of course, whether or not to tell the truth about what we choose to teach are also influenced by politics.

Ultimately, we are faced with two fundamental questions. First, should we do our best to provide an excellent education to everyone? To oppose equity is to answer no to this question, and sadly this has been the answer to date. To answer this question in the affirmative requires political action to change the systems that have maintained racial and class disparities in educational access, resources, and opportunities.

The second question is: Should we teach the truth to the best of our ability? To oppose inclusion is to answer no to this question as well. Teaching myths about our history, excluding voices of minoritized peoples, and limiting access to critical perspectives is a choice to miseducate with the purpose of maintaining oppressive systems—to lie. To teach demonstrable facts, multiple perspectives, and critical thinking skills is to say yes, we will tell the truth as we understand it.

Providing educators with training in equitable teaching, assessment, and classroom-management strategies is critical to their success in providing an excellent education for all students. In order to advance equity and inclusion, they will also need to teach about how racism, consciously or unconsciously, works on the interpersonal, institutional, and system levels and about how to promote positive change. Simply put, in order to produce graduates who are prepared to provide all of our children with an excellent education, many if not most teacher education programs need a major overhaul.

Part of the problem is also that we rarely incorporate any mandatory training for incoming faculty at the college or university level. So, most faculty in higher education have never learned how to teach or how to review or develop a curriculum. As a result, most teach what—and how—*they* were taught. Again, there is good news. There are model programs that can be learned from that have excellent teacher education curricula and practices.

Another factor is the work done by researchers and writers in education whose work does not comply with biased norms, including those in teacher education, who continue to be opposed by those who sit on the wrong side of history—and who do not want that history to be told. These attempts to block progress add to the enormous challenge of countering and replacing the racially biased curricula, policies, and practices that have been the norm in our educational systems from the first days of formal public schooling in what is now the United States.

Touted as the oldest school in what is now the United States, Boston Latin School was founded back in 1635 to offer free education to white boys, regardless of financial status. More than 380 years later, in 2016, Boston Latin was in the news when #BlackAtBLS went viral, exposing the reality that racism was still the norm at Boston Latin. As part of the team called in to work with the city's school principals to address this issue at the system level, I was not surprised when the Boston Public Schools' superintendent chose to take very little of our collective advice. Efforts persist by antiracist educators who continue working to make a difference in the city's schools, but change does not come quickly or easily when oppression has been built directly into the foundation.

Success in antiracist education has come mostly in fits and starts, resisted at every turn by educators, parents, and politicians too stuck in their ways—or too stuck in their racism—to accept change. The adaptive nature of racism has limited most progress to a finite period of time, whether in a classroom, a department, or an entire school. While the trend is toward equity and inclusion, large-scale or long-term successes tend to be few and far between, and few accolades are showered on those educators who have spent a lifetime providing an equitable, inclusive, and responsive education to students within systems not built to support that work. Today, to add insult to injury, those educators' efforts are even being criminalized through anti-DEI legislation.[2]

Embracing change wholeheartedly and living up to our progressive reputation as educators is possible, but it will take leadership across teacher education programs, accrediting bodies, school districts, and colleges and universities. It will also take political cover from elected officials and support from a critical mass of students, parents, alumni, and community members—all of us can play a role.

This may seem daunting, but what is encouraging is that the work to transform our teacher education programs has already started. Every aspect of teacher education has been considered and redeveloped with an antiracist lens—focused on equity and inclusion across the full spectrum of diversity. Any teacher education program that is ready to make the shift needs only to access existing resources and adapt them to the program in question. Teachers and programs committed to supporting antiracism, equity, and inclusion can choose from a variety of excellent texts on intersectional antiracist curriculum development, teaching, and educational leadership. Countless articles and specialists address equity and inclusion across all aspects of the teacher education process, and we can all learn from the existing exemplary programs. We know how to make this important shift; instituting it is simply a matter of will. In addition, there are multiple teacher education programs that have embraced antiracism and social justice that can serve as models.

Meanwhile, highly problematic trends are pushing back on efforts to ensure equity and inclusion for all students. Too many of today's corporate charters promise a better option while treating already underserved students as commodities and providing oppressive military-style or factory-model schooling. Teacher training quickies like Teach for America install underprepared teachers in underserved schools, furthering the myth that if you are smart you can teach without substantive training as an educator, and perpetuating the unspoken attitude that students of color and low-income students do not deserve well-prepared educators. These and other approaches to maintaining the educational oppression of marginalized populations are nothing new; they have just been repackaged. We all need to learn how to better recognize these predators disguised as saviors and refuse shortcuts that promise—but fundamentally cannot provide—long-term, comprehensive solutions.

There is no doubt that transforming our schools and universities is a massive task, and much of that hard work will need to happen behind the scenes. But again, we can do hard things, we just need to decide that it is worth doing. Is it worth taking this on to make real the idea of a nation characterized by equity, inclusion, and justice? Considering the impact our schools have on us, I say absolutely.

Inclusive Excellence

Looking toward the long term does not mean, however, that we can wait for official curricula to be revamped or for the next generation of antiracist teachers to reach critical mass. Just as any education advocate can access all the curricula, research, training, and professional support necessary to transform any course, school, or system, current teachers and professors can take matters into their own hands by leveraging numerous books, articles, conferences, and other educational opportunities that describe how to teach through a multicultural, antibias, or antiracist lens: Isabel Wilkerson's *Caste: The Origins of Our Discontents* and Robert Sussman's *The Myth of Race* provide background on the social construct of race. *How to Be an Antiracist* by Ibram X. Kendi; *Uprooting Racism* by Paul Kivel; and *Everyday White People Confront Racial and Social Injustice*, edited by Eddie Moore Jr., Marguerite W. Penick-Parks, and Ali Michael, all provide personal narratives and guidance for aspiring antiracists. James Loewen's *Teaching What Really Happened* and *Teaching for Black Lives*, edited by Dyan Watson, Jesse Hagopian, and Wayne Au, provide specific classroom guidance.

There are more diverse teaching materials, made available through nonprofit organizations like Rethinking Schools and others, that represent diverse perspectives and provide more guidance on inclusive teaching than ever before. Source materials are also far more easily accessed online through the Library of Congress, National Archives, multiple university archives, and other resources, and they are far more interesting than the bland, whitewashed descriptions in history textbooks of the past. Students can read firsthand accounts rather than interpretations, which are often biased. Like other antiracist educators, I do my best to provide links to the latest materials and opportunities on my website (drjoejoe.com). There really is no excuse for any educator today to claim ignorance or blame anyone else for the biased curriculum that is too often the norm in our classrooms.

Classroom teachers in our schools are not the only educators responsible for righting the proverbial ship. In addition to parents and other community members, school support staff and administration, school boards, and alumni representatives are all able to make a difference. In most cases, that may require continuing education, and this is where rigorous PD is important. PD in schools often gets a bad rap, and we often hear that teachers and other educators dread their PD days. It has been my experience that this is fully dependent on the quality and applicability of the PD being provided, and whether the administration will support implementation over time.

DEI in colleges and universities is often referred to as "inclusive excellence." Coined by the American Association of Colleges and Universities (AAC&U), inclusive excellence refers to efforts to expand DEI practices to all aspects of the institution. The idea is to take a holistic approach, leaving no corner of the institution unexamined. From hiring and promotion to vendor contracting, the curriculum and pedagogy to student life and living learning, "town and gown" relations, and of course, all things budget and finance, there is no aspect of the institution where inclusive excellence is not relevant.

Having spent the majority of my career in higher education, I hold this subject close to my heart. I have worked at an historically Black college or university (HBCU), a Hispanic-serving institution, an Ivy League institution, and an international university, as well as at a religiously affiliated college and at the public university system level. I have taught, I have served as staff, and eventually I became an administrator. I have also consulted extensively with presidents and senior diversity officers on everything from curriculum development and program evaluation to strategic planning and leadership. No matter the role, my work has always centered on antiracism, equity, and inclusion. As a result, I have learned a great deal over these past few decades about inclusive excellence.

Higher education is, at the same time, an awesome resource for countering white supremacy and racism in education and, like primary and secondary education, still far too often a source of racist ideology and practices. Most campuses have policies and practitioners who are still working to maintain the status quo as well as those focused on creating change. This is to be expected as higher education undergoes a transition from being a fundamental part of the problem to becoming an important part of the solution. Understandably, since not everyone is on board with this transition, it has and will continue to be challenging.

Still, there is great promise in higher education. Imagine if we were to teach students not only how they can make a difference today but also how they can become change agents in their respective fields as professionals. Ultimately, schools and universities have the power to help students learn how to think critically and use their skills, knowledge, and experience to create positive change. Imagining the progress that will be made by future generations brings me joy and encourages me to continue doing the work.

Most higher education institutions have hired (or are in the process of hiring) a high-level diversity officer—at least this was true prior to the rash of anti-DEI legislation. Where these positions do exist, they are still too often under-resourced, especially given that the scope of work for collegiate executive diversity officers extends across all aspects of the institution and into the local community. The position requires a broad skill set and, like other cabinet positions, appropriate budget and staffing to ensure success. I should also note that the role of an executive diversity officer, like other executives, is to lead and provide guidance and resources, not to be the only one working to create change. Beyond the usual executive skills and presence, these positions also require a thick skin and significant political savvy, as they remain under attack by right-wing politicians legislating to outlaw efforts to ensure equity and inclusion altogether.

Higher education administrations have a long list of reasons why they need an institutional diversity officer, and they often claim an equally long list of reasons why they cannot afford to provide the resources necessary to accomplish the many worthy goals outlined in the job description. Where success is the goal—and not just appearances—it's reasonable to assume that significant resources are necessary. What the role requires is nothing short of leading the transformation of the culture, climate, policies, and practices of an entire institution—all while facing massive resistance to systemic change. This requires serious preparation and support.

I like to note the good news as well, and here it is: Buried under that resistance, these types of positions are now finding traction, and the professionals taking on these roles are increasingly well prepared to lead. In many cases now, diversity officers have become presidents, bringing with them well-developed equity mindsets and inclusive approaches to leadership. Prominent professional associations, such as the National Association of Diversity Officers in Higher Education (NADOHE), exist to support efforts toward inclusive excellence. A wide range of conferences, too, address DEI in education, including the National Conference on Race and Ethnicity in American Higher Education (NCORE), the AAC&U Conference on Diversity, Equity, and Student Success, and the National Association for Multicultural Education (NAME) Conference, among others.

We are not starting from scratch. The research has depth, excellent teaching materials are available, and new approaches and frameworks have been proven effective. Antiracist leaders are stepping up in every aspect of education, ready to advise and guide a real and sustainable shift toward intersectional antiracism. This is why white supremacists, and their political representatives, are scared and acting accordingly.

Of course, taking on all of this work and dealing with the resistance and backlash is a heavy lift. However, all of the lifting is not on any one of us. As more of us do our part—in most cases simply by being actively supportive of those doing the work—the load on each of us becomes lighter.

Antiracist leaders are stepping up in every aspect of education, ready to advise and guide a real and sustainable shift toward intersectional antiracism.

While our education system has been a major source of racist indoctrination, it is not the only source. We also learn from our parents, our peers, the media (including social media), and our own outside reading and experiences. At some point, we become responsible for our own education and how we process information from all of these sources.

Antiracist Literacy

From the time when I stood up in class to challenge my elementary school teacher for perpetuating the heroification of former US presidents who enslaved African people, I began to take control of my own education. My parents encouraged me to be inquisitive about everything and apply my critical thinking skills to what was being presented to me as a student. As an educator, I love when students question what is presented as fact, by me or any other source. This does not mean they just don't believe anything; it means that they fact-check and seek diverse perspectives. Students often learn the most in discourse because they are engaged in their own learning, not just trying to memorize material in order to get the "right" answer or pass a test.

Over my years as a student, I read great assigned books, from Nathaniel Hawthorne's *The Scarlet Letter* to *The Diary of Anne Frank.* During high school, I also chose books on my own that deepened my learning, such as autobiographies of Malcolm X, Angela Davis, and Dick Gregory. Reading Mr. Gregory's autobiography was particularly impactful because I had met him a couple of times—his son, Christian, was a friend—making his story even more real to me. Reading became an important part of my learning, and I am still partial to memoirs and autobiographies.

Everyone takes control of their own learning at a different time and pace, but we can all start on this path at any time. At some point, we must all take responsibility for what we know, what we do not know, and what we choose to experience and learn. A grown person who has a lot to say on topics of concern—like income inequality, voting rights, or racial injustice—but cannot reference anything they have learned since high school says to me one of two things: Either they believe what they learned in high school is all they need to know, even if they graduated decades

> *At some point, we must all take responsibility for what we know, what we do not know, and what we choose to experience and learn.*

ago, or they do not want to educate themselves further because it may challenge their current beliefs.

I graduated from high school more than thirty-five years ago. If I was to rely on my high school education to guide my understanding of current challenges to voting rights, for example, my knowledge would be significantly out of date. Put aside the fact that my high school education on civics was severely lacking; even if it had been excellent, it would not have included the changes in law, Supreme Court rulings, and political activity that have occurred over the past three decades. If high school classes were my latest source of information, my perspective would be, at best, out of date.

Nevertheless, many people have strong opinions about topics on which they have little information, or a lot of information that is not based in fact. That brings us back to the need for critical thinking in the face of opinions masquerading as facts that are currently flooding our media and social media "news" outlets. Remember, your social media feed is based on what you "like" and what links you have clicked on in the past. In essence, it's going to tell you what you want to hear, whether it is true or completely made up, because its goal is to keep you engaged, not well informed. If you do not seek out different perspectives, you will be fed what you want to hear—instead of anything even remotely resembling the truth. In other words, if you want to believe that the Earth is flat—for some reason I cannot comprehend—social media will provide you with all the posts it can find to support that delusion just to keep you scrolling and clicking.

As we graduate to self-directed education, we are able to make choices that will inform our understanding of the world. Taking control of your learning regarding racism and antiracism simply requires you to ask yourself, *How do I normally educate myself about something I actually want to learn?* We make choices about what we read, which news sources we consume, and which organizations we belong to, just as we decide where to live, which schools we (or our children) attend, who we socialize with, and so on. All these decisions either expose us to different perspectives and people different from ourselves, or they do not. We either accept racist input at face value, ignore racism, or embrace antiracist perspectives rather than dismissing them because they can be discomforting. And these decisions determine our community, our norms, and our ongoing access to information.

If you choose to limit your exposure to information on any subject, your knowledge on the subject will be limited. Strangely, this often does not stop people who have limited information from holding very strong opinions. Many people who know little to nothing about climate change, for example, have a strong opinion about it. Rather than educating themselves, however, they tend to just go along with whatever the political "leaders" they prefer tell them to believe. This political complacency is both lazy and dangerous.

Developing an antiracist literacy—the ability to identify, comprehend, critically analyze, and communicate a well-informed perspective on issues of race and racism—is the necessary foundation for living an antiracist life. Illiteracy on these issues, considering the vast array of resources available, is a choice.

Antiracist literacy does require effort. For nearly all of us, it requires an effort to learn what was missing from our formal and informal education and to counteract what was inaccurate, made up, and/or biased. What this looks like in real life is taking the time to consider that your education may have been flawed, and purposefully so. From there, it requires thinking critically about areas in which you are familiar with only white historical figures, writers, or originators; finding out that there are (and always have been) important scientists, philosophers, and other luminaries of color around the world; and then learning from and about them through source documents and firsthand accounts.

We can begin with US history. James Loewen, a Smithsonian researcher, wrote his seminal work, *Lies My Teacher Told Me: Everything Your American History Textbook Got Wrong*, to expose the white supremacist US American mythology that passes for history in our schools. Outstanding history texts like Howard Zinn's *A People's History of the United States*, Ronald Takaki's *A Different Mirror: A History of Multicultural America*, Roxanne Dunbar-Ortiz's *An Indigenous Peoples' History of the United States*, and *Black AF*

History: The Un-Whitewashed Story of America by Michael Harriot (to name a few) provide easily accessible information to better educate ourselves. And, from my perspective, the actual history is far more intriguing than the myths and half-truths ever were.

While gaps in available materials still exist in some areas of study, there is far more available than our formal education system introduces to US American students. Maybe you are someone who can contribute to demythologizing your field, providing for the inclusion of diverse perspectives in your area of expertise. If so, write that paper or book, give that lecture, or simply bring it to the attention of your peers so that you can collectively learn more.

To determine the legitimacy of the information that is currently available, we also need to further develop our media literacy to strengthen our ability to discern what is reliable from what is not. There can be a difference between a source that we enjoy because of its political perspective and a source that is accurate. If we want to understand something, we have to be honest with ourselves about whether we recognize a source as reliable or we just find it relatable. While it is not always possible to know for certain the truth behind a story or set of data, we can be honest with ourselves about the source if we know that it is highly partisan and favours one ideology over another, or if we know whether it has been proven to be accurate in the past.

When possible, particularly as educators, we strive to use source documentation. That means original documents, data, records, or media. For example, if your understanding of the US Constitution is based on what you hear from politicians, you could take the time to read it yourself—the actual document. It is not only readily available online and in print form, but it is shorter than any chapter in this book. As you'll see, it also includes sexist and racist statements, and it makes clear that there was an understanding that the "Union" was imperfect from the beginning—and that we have a responsibility to continue working to make it better.

Let's take a major historical event as an example of how crucial taking control of your own self-directed learning can be, and how helpful it can be to use source documents to become more informed. Many people today, for whatever reason, do not want to believe that the US Civil War was fought over slavery. If there are source documents available, wouldn't it make sense to consider what the Confederate leaders had to say on the matter? Well, the Constitution of the Confederate States is available online, as are the declarations of secession written by multiple states that formed the Confederate States of America.[3] Also available are messages from Jefferson Davis, president of the Confederate States, to the Confederate States Congress.[4] All of these documents reveal that the Confederacy was very clear that their right to enslave African people was the primary reason they were seceding from the United States.

Reading source documents for yourself will prepare you to communicate facts to counter racist miseducation, like the revisionist propaganda that claims that the Civil War was not fought over states' rights to allow slavery to continue.

It is also important to read, listen to, and view different perspectives on current issues related to race and racism. Whether the topic is reparations or reservations, immigration or wealth disparities, many books, articles, documentaries, podcasts, vlogs, blogs, and other sources present real discussion and debate on critical race issues. To be clear, I am not talking about one-sided partisan programs or those that regularly promote unfounded conspiracy theories. The wide range of issues related to racism and white supremacy is almost always more complex than what is presented in political debate or on mainstream media. Antiracist literacy means seeking multiple perspectives and accuracy, developing a knowledge base, and being able to communicate a well-informed perspective.

Reading about a group of people can be edifying, but developing a well-informed antiracist perspective also requires learning through engagement with real people. Whenever possible, engage in dialogue and seek relationships that provide an important depth of understanding. Where do you choose to live, and where do you spend your time? If you are white, and your days are full of interactions with white people, then you'll have limited exposure to the perspectives of people of color. If your only interactions with people of color are brief and transactional—with the barista at your favorite coffee shop or with colleagues you see only at work—then you are not going to learn much and your opinion based on a single interaction with one person of color will not be well informed.

Antiracist literacy means seeking multiple perspectives and accuracy, developing a knowledge base, and being able to communicate a well-informed perspective.

Relationships with people who have a different background from your own provide ongoing opportunities to learn. Relationships across social divides help us to move beyond stereotypes, explore different perspectives, and provide context for an understanding around racism and other types of oppression we may not have any firsthand experience with. Of course, you will need more than one friend if you hope to truly understand the experience of any group you do not belong to. It should go without saying, but I'll say it anyway: No single person speaks for their entire race or ethnicity. But developing relationships outside the groups you identify with will help to broaden your understanding of different cultures and perspectives. Whether through friendships, becoming part of diverse organizations, or working in diverse groups (at work, school, or in your community), conversation and relationships across divides can provide opportunities to learn. If nothing else, you will more easily recognize that the diversity within groups is far greater than the differences between groups—which is key to dispelling stereotypes.

Humility and Self-Awareness

I think that having a sense of humor is helpful with regard to communicating across differences. This does not mean you should joke about issues related to race and racism, of course—that is rarely a good idea, especially when you are in the early stages of learning or in conversation with someone who does not know you well. Rather, you should learn to laugh at yourself and not take yourself too seriously. Having genuine humility is important for living an antiracist life, and it matters for many reasons.

First, it takes humility to admit that your understanding of something may be flawed, and to seek guidance on things you feel like you should already know. Too often, white folks who lack humility feel overconfident about their knowledge about other groups of people and their understanding of racialized issues. If you are willing to work on your antiracist literacy, you have probably overcome that hurdle at least to some degree. It will be important to hold on to that humility because, as is true in many aspects of life, the more you learn, the more you realize how much more you have yet to learn.

Consider an issue like racial disparities in the medical treatment of pain. If you are a health-care professional who lacks humility and self-awareness, you may feel confident in your opinion that these disparities are just misunderstandings. It takes humility to consider that the issue might be beyond your understanding—that certain complexities and histories might have escaped your experience or awareness. It takes humility to admit that you do not know something—and that you may need help to learn it.

But the most important reason for humility, from my perspective, is to ensure that you maintain a strong sense of self-awareness. Humility leads to self-awareness because it requires taking a step back, being objective about your beliefs and behavior, and accepting constructive feedback. For example, if you are not able to acknowledge your social location with respect to race—where you fit on the spectrum ranging from "oppressed" to "privileged"—your understanding of anyone else's perspective will be skewed.

Lack of self-awareness is very often the cause of the biggest missteps for genuinely well-meaning white folks when it comes to discussions around racialized issues. Imagine that you are a white person who has never had a negative experience with the police. You may believe this is because you are always respectful and do your best to follow the law. If you cannot take a step back and consider that your whiteness may have something to do with how you have been treated by the police, that may affect your response to a Black person who describes having a negative interaction with a police officer. Without proper self-awareness, you may be unable to recognize that your white privilege may have affected how you were treated, and you might find yourself questioning the Black person's perspective and behavior. *They must have done something wrong*, you might think. What else would provoke the police officer to treat them differently from what has always been your experience? We saw this in the reactions of so many white folks after they saw the video of George Floyd being murdered by police—they immediately assumed that Mr. Floyd had done something wrong, which somehow warranted an extrajudicial death penalty.

Exercising humility and uncovering our self-awareness are essential in the process of developing an antiracist mindset. This type of personal development is a necessary part of contributing to change when it comes to systemic oppression—reflected in the cultural humility concept developed by pediatricians and medical educators Dr. Melanie Tervalon and Dr. Jann Murray-García, which is explicit about the need for a commitment to lifelong learning and critical self-reflection.[5]

For those who were not raised in an antiracist tradition, it may take longer to develop an antiracist mindset, but it is absolutely possible. If you are interested in understanding the impact and mechanics of racism, and how to effectively oppose it, you must become aware of who you are, seek learning opportunities, and engage with humility. You will need to refine and use your critical thinking skills to separate fact from fantasy and to define your own approach to continuously strengthening your antiracist perspective.

Another critical aspect of self-awareness is understanding your social location. This matters because who you are within the contexts of intersecting oppressions will impact not only how you understand yourself, but also how you are heard. We all have to understand that when we speak, it is not just our words that communicate to those listening. We often hear that an important factor in communication is knowing your audience, and I have found that to be true. More important, however, when speaking on racism and intersecting oppressions is knowing who you are. But not just that, knowing who you are generally perceived to be in social contexts matters as well.

For me, as a white man speaking on white supremacy, for example, it is important to provide context and consider the fact that my words are coming out of my face. I have to understand that what I say is heard through racialized and gendered filters and may not land the way I intend if I do not take that into consideration. This is not necessarily because of prejudgment on the part of my audience; it is simply awareness of the racism that exists in the world that we live in. If I do not acknowledge my social location within that reality, my credibility will justifiably be questioned.

It has been my experience that being self-reflective and developing an understanding of my social location is critical to my understanding of my own experiences regarding racism and intersecting forms of oppression. It also helps me understand my perspective—to be aware of where I am standing as I view the world around me. Without that understanding, it is more difficult to consider the perspectives of others, which is a critical aspect of building connection and finding solidarity.

5

THE PACKIE
Developing an Antiracist Lens

If you are neutral in situations of injustice, you have chosen the side of the oppressor. If an elephant has its foot on the tail of a mouse and you say that you are neutral, the mouse will not appreciate your neutrality.

—DESMOND TUTU

WHEN I WAS GROWING UP, everyone in town had an opinion about my family. As I mentioned earlier, my parents ran the Carver Package Store—the local "packie," and we lived in the attached apartment behind it. It was a typical small-town family business, something like a bodega crossed with a liquor store. Since so many people were in and out every day, and because we were seen as a different kind of family, it is no wonder folks developed opinions. They saw us kids growing up, playing basketball behind the store, and working together as a family. The hours were long, and it seemed there was always work to do, but being together made it fun.

Situated on Main Street, the packie was a meeting point between the local communities of color and the quickly growing white-flight neighborhoods, as well as a place where folks just passing through town would stop along the way. Mom seemed to know every customer's story and would talk for hours with those regulars who had become friends, laughing and chatting while waiting on other customers, stocking shelves, or doing whatever needed to be done. Dad was more transactional with customers and not as social as Mom, but he valued his friends and always made time for them. If a friend came in, he would step to the side or invite them to our apartment in the back to hang out for a while. Family was everything to my parents, and their close friends were our extended family.

The packie community wasn't perfect, and occasionally fights would break out in the parking lot. Guns were not as common as they are today, although sometimes conflict boiled over and other weapons, like knives, baseball bats, or tire irons, would make an appearance. Regardless of what kind of drama was going on, everything stopped when one of our parents came out into the parking lot. From drug deals gone bad to high school kids fighting to folks just getting rowdy, everyone looked like kids caught with their hands in the cookie jar when Mom or Dad showed up. Every neighborhood seems to have someone like that—usually an elder or someone else you don't want to disappoint.

Mom and Dad never went out to stop a fight together. After all, someone had to mind the store. Usually, conflicts resolved themselves, but on the rare occasion when it dragged on, Mom or Dad would walk straight into the middle of the melee, and we would rush to the window to see what was going to happen. It was always a sight to see, as everyone who had gathered around just grabbed the nearest person and pulled them back. We wondered if Dad was worried about Mom going out to stop a fight alone, but he would just laugh and say "I'm more worried about what might happen if they don't stop before she gets there." Then he would remind us about when he went to pick her up for their first date and how when he got there, he found Mom breaking up a knife fight in an alley between a couple of guys she knew.

One time, when Kacey and I were watching television in the corner behind the counter, trying to contain little B-J, we heard a bottle smash against the pavement. Then someone yelled the n-slur.

Dad headed for the door.

Mom picked up the three-foot pipe we kept behind the counter and told us boys to sit still. Of course, we followed right behind her.

A small crowd had formed. Mom stood in front of us with one hand behind her, signaling us to stay back, and the other holding that long metal pipe. A close family friend named Roger Santos, a Black man Dad had known since high school, was facing an all-white group of bikers we did not recognize. They were probably just stopping to get some beer at the packie on their way through town. Behind Roger was a group of men, mostly men of color.

Roger saw Dad coming and called out, "Mike!"

"Yep," Dad replied, and he took his place next to Roger, facing down the bikers.

Mom turned and yelled to us boys, "Get inside, now!"

This was not the usual drama. For one thing, Dad had taken a side without even asking what was going on. When Mom grabbed all three of us by the collar, we desperately tried to wriggle away and see what was happening. But we were no match for Mom, who carried us like luggage into the safety of our apartment.

It seemed like hours later when Dad and Roger finally came through the apartment door, disheveled and laughing. Mom went and hugged them both at the same time, checking them as though making sure they still had all their limbs. "What happened, what happened?" Kacey and I shouted, bursting with curiosity.

Dad just said, "They learned their lesson. Everything's all right."

Roger busted out laughing again, like Dad had just told the funniest joke he'd ever heard.

Years later, after Dad had passed and I was in my forties, Roger came by the house to check on Mom, as he would do from time to time. As we all sat on the stoop, reminiscing about those years at the packie and listening to Roger's stories about when he and Dad were young, I asked Roger what had happened that day in the parking lot.

He and Mom looked at each other and chuckled. "What did your dad say? Those guys learned a lesson! All you need to know is that your folks were always on the right side."

I never did get a straight answer. Roger passed a couple of years later, and then Mom, so I'll never know exactly what happened that day. What I do know is that when they heard someone yell the n-slur, our parents did not hesitate to move toward the conflict. Dad saw his friend and immediately knew that the right thing to do was stand with him against racist violence. I do not need to know the details of what else happened that day to understand that Dad did not hesitate to follow Roger's lead as they stood shoulder to shoulder against racist hate and that Mom put herself between us and harm. In that moment, and many others, my parents demonstrated what being partners in antiracism is all about, and we learned from their example.

A Diverse Community of Good Folks

The packie was our home, and I cherish the memories we made there. Every morning, my brothers and I walked through the store to go wait for the school bus, and every afternoon when the bus dropped us off, Mom or Dad would be right there to ask how school went. The regulars would jump right into the conversation, commenting on whatever we had to say, asking about their own kids, or giving their opinion on a teacher.

Whole families—the Fernandes, Silva, and Santos families in particular—all felt like cousins, aunts, and uncles. Then there was Adam Osahowsky, whose foot we would step on for some reason before running away while he acted like he was chasing us. Peter, who snuck up on Dad one day and shocked him with a kiss on the cheek. And so many more who Kacey would've been able to name and tell you all about—more than I ever could. Our community of folks was deep, right there in the packie.

Whenever one of us (usually me) would get kicked off the school bus for fighting or some other disruptive behavior, Mom and Dad would make us walk to school—more than two miles away, no matter the weather. This was never a real problem, though, because one of the regulars would always pick us up. We thought it was a secret, but I found out eventually that Mom and Dad not only knew we would get a ride but expected it. Whoever picked us up would ensure we made it to school in one piece and probably divulge whatever we'd said along the way to Mom and Dad later that day. That's part of how our parents sent us out into the world while still keeping tabs on us.

More often than not, Eddie Spaghetti was the one to pick me up. His real name was Eddie Fernandes, but I did not realize that until years later when I took his granddaughter to a school dance. It never dawned on me that he was just having fun with us kids by telling us his last name was Spaghetti. Like a lot of the Black folks in Carver, Eddie's family was originally from Cape Verde—officially the Republic of Cabo Verde, a country made up of ten islands located off the coast of West Africa, closest to Senegal. Eddie would try to teach me Portuguese, talk to me about Cabo Verde, and seem genuinely concerned as I whined about whatever got me kicked off the bus.

What I did not know was that this, among many other things, was also a part of how our parents intentionally exposed us to different kinds of people. By making sure we had real relationships with good people across differences, we would learn what mattered: that we are all just people, and that everyone deserves to be treated with dignity and respect. Mom and Dad surrounded us with a community of good people from diverse backgrounds. They never discussed this with us explicitly; they just did it. They simply wanted us to understand that good people are not color coded.

Mom and Dad were intentional about a lot of our interactions, taking every opportunity to make diversity normal to us. There was always a lesson to be learned, even when we didn't recognize it right away. Of course, our daily exchanges in the store were the most impactful, and my parents were deliberate in choosing what to read to us or watch on television, but they invoked other means as well. One thing they would do was to include us when they went somewhere to conduct business. We accompanied them to their lawyer's office, where we saw all the fancy folks in suits, and to the distributors' warehouses, to see how the workers used big machines to move whole pallets of beer around. Wherever it was, there were always hidden lessons about respecting everyone, no matter what kind of work they did, and helping us recognize racism and discrimination.

Although our family did not discuss things specifically in terms of "racial hierarchy," "hegemony," or "discrimination," Mom and Dad would point out who was working at different levels, which direction money was moving in, and who was profiting off the labor of others. Without using all the fancy language that I tend to use now, they would simply discuss what was right and what was not, never hesitating to point out inequities. They would call out racism, sexism, homophobia, anti-Semitism, and other forms of prejudice and discrimination whenever they saw them, saying something like "See, that has to change."

Our parents wanted us to understand what was wrong, and to realize that we had a responsibility to do better. They always emphasized when someone made a difference—big or small—and reminded us that we could too. This taught me that opposing racism and other forms of oppression is about the decisions and actions that make up our daily lives.

> *Opposing racism and other forms of oppression is about the decisions and actions that make up our daily lives.*

Our parents' efforts to make diversity normal in our little world were obvious to us, even as kids. Later, normalizing diversity became part of what I strove for as an educator. My master's degree thesis was titled "Making Diversity the Norm in Schools." I thought that if we could somehow just make diversity the norm, everyone would learn and grow out of any racial bigotry. Antiracist social psychologist Gordon Allport addressed part of this as "intergroup contact theory," and the hypothesis showed promise.[1] However, it turns out to be only a marginally successful approach because of all the variables that impact interactions between people, such as what they believe, what they learn outside of school, and so on. Making diversity of interactions normal is a good place to start, but it's not enough to counteract systemic racism. I tried in my thesis to discuss other ways in which diversity needed to become normal, such as in policy and curricula, to make more of a difference.

Our parents already understood all that. Mom was a great writer; in fact, she edited my master's thesis and my doctoral dissertation. After I completed my thesis, she actually asked me if I understood that just making diversity normal is not enough, even if it is comprehensive. Years later, after I defended my dissertation, which focused on more actively addressing racism and other forms of oppression, she said, "You're getting there." Eventually I understood: My parents were not just making sure to surround us with an extended family of people from different backgrounds and perspectives. They went further, doing their best to demonstrate and develop inclusion, equitable practices, and active antiracism in how they lived their lives.

Living Our Values Out Loud

While our parents worked hard to provide this environment for my brothers and me and to expose the evils of racism, it was not the center of our upbringing. The true focus was just on being "good people." That meant doing right by folks, working hard, and acting with integrity. They would not have described themselves as "antiracists"—a term I didn't even learn until my college years. Opposing racism was just part of what it meant to be good people.

My parents demonstrated these egalitarian values as small-business owners. In the late 1970s and early 1980s, when the minimum wage was less than four dollars, they paid more than triple that—not because they couldn't find anyone to work for minimum wage but because they knew that four dollars an hour was not enough to live on. Dad said only employers who were unwilling to work themselves—or who cared more about profit than people—would pay so little. His reasoning still rings true to me.

Mom and Dad were capitalists and believed strongly in entrepreneurship, but they also believed our values should be reflected in how we do business. They did not believe that capitalism and social justice were mutually exclusive. They never became wealthy, but not because they lacked great ideas or business savvy. They just refused to exploit others, even in an environment where other business owners lacked the integrity to follow suit.

Dad's pragmatic business creativity led him to invent a mechanism for using cold air from outside to refrigerate beer in the walk-in cooler, saving money while also protecting the environment: the Air Economizer, which he patented and produced for a reasonable price. He never made a profit, because he could not afford to compete with a large refrigeration company that stole the idea and ran Dad and his partner out of business. Obviously, not everyone shared my parents' values.

If we claim to be antiracist only until opposing racism becomes uncomfortable or threatens our financial security, that is not antiracism; it is just virtue signaling.

That truth served as part of the lesson, though: If you are willing to abandon your values for the sake of stacking up more money—no matter the consequence for others—then those are not your true values. The larger problem our society faces is the loophole in our collective values—the idea that it is okay to set aside even our most core values for comfort or financial gain. If we claim to be antiracist only until opposing racism becomes uncomfortable or threatens our financial security, that is not antiracism; it is just virtue signaling.

Living an antiracist life comes with challenges, just like living in line with any other core values. Something is not a core value if it is so flexible that you can just bypass it when it is convenient, or for the right price. Creating a loophole like that provides a way to live what you claim to be your values more comfortably, but what it really does is camouflage your true values, hiding them even from you. The capitalism that most of us have adopted places money above all else and all others. Racism and other wrongs are ignored in the pursuit of financial gain. This is true even among the majority of us who will never be allowed to benefit from the profits that others gain from the work we do every day.

White working-class and poor folks who believe whiteness connects us to white billionaires have been bamboozled. That path to wealth, through hard work, has never actually existed for us. The truth is that poor and working-class white people have far more in common with people of color, who are excluded from that same US American dream by racism. However, too many of us are so enthralled by our white privilege scraps that we are willing to set aside what we claim to be our most core values, and even our critical thinking skills, in order to maintain this imaginary connection to power and privilege.

The town I grew up in became a destination for white-flighters—white people who left Boston in the 1970s to avoid sending their kids to newly desegregated schools. Carver had been a far more diverse town, with large Cape Verdean and Puerto Rican communities, when my Dad was a kid growing up a couple of towns over in Kingston. Part of the reason he brought our family to Carver was because of that diversity. But the town changed quickly, and Carver became divided. Racist white folks moved in and took over, and the people of color who remained were not willing to put up with their bigotry. Among the kids in town,

> *Too many of us are so enthralled by our white privilege scraps that we are willing to set aside what we claim to be our most core values, and even our critical thinking skills, in order to maintain this imaginary connection to power and privilege.*

there were more than a few racially motivated fights. In fact, most of my fights growing up were, in one way or another, about racism.

One fight happened in the cafeteria after a new student, from South Boston, said something racist. Once the dust cleared a couple of days later, the kid from Southie apologized and wanted to understand why we were so upset with what he said. It took time, but he came around. People can come to this realization in different ways. For some of us, it takes getting hit upside the head—whether literally or metaphorically—before we pay attention. Years later, as a football coach, that same guy from Southie would talk to his teams about standing against racism and how brotherhood across differences mattered. That was his way of being an antiracism advocate.

In my family, we were taught that living your values out loud was paramount. Most of the white-flight kids in Carver were taught racism at home by the examples their parents set. Typically, it was not overt racism—it was more subtle—but many learned their racist ways and never changed much. But some of them were willing to learn and have chosen to do better as adults. All these years later, I count some of them as friends, and remarkably, some of them are among the strongest antiracists I know. In true Massachusetts style, they live their antiracist values out loud. In their communities, they speak up without hesitation when they recognize racial injustice. What's more, they teach *their* children better, and they hold their family, friends, and colleagues accountable. They have learned—just as we did while growing up in the packie—to see antiracism as not just a value but a responsibility.

Leadership Lessons

Growing up living in the back of a liquor store and sharing my daily life with customers is not what most people would consider "normal" or ideal. But my family had fun working together as a team, and the store regulars became an important part of my siblings' and my growing-up experience.

Being underage, of course, my brothers and I were not allowed to sell to customers, but the work we did behind the scenes mattered. Whether filling the cooler, bagging ice, splitting wood to sell, or something else, we knew that our work helped the family in tangible ways, and that made us proud. Being a hard worker was valued as much, if not more, than anything else in our family and community.

Working to support the store was not our favorite thing to do, as you might imagine, but Dad taught us how to enjoy working together. Kacey and I made it fun by singing and dancing to the music blasting from our boom box—an eclectic mix of rap, rock, and pop. When Dad was working with us, he would put on Chuck Berry or Jerry Lee Lewis, and we would belt out that old-school rock 'n' roll at the top of our lungs. Dad also used that time to chat with us, ask us questions, and give us advice. As a parent, I now recognize that he was using that "quality time" to connect with us. If our chats slowed down the work too much, Mom would scold us all about getting the job done. Dad would roll his eyes, and us kids would try not to let Mom hear us laughing. It felt good to contribute, and we were proud of how we worked together, like a well-oiled machine.

Working behind the scenes at the packie was the best possible preparation for the antiracist leadership I would strive for in the decades to come. When I began studying leadership as a doctoral student at Florida A&M University (FAMU), one professor asked us to consider how we had learned about leadership and where we had seen it demonstrated. I had been blessed to be around many people I recognized as leaders, thanks to our parents, and they were the primary sources of my understanding. I have had the privilege of meeting some extraordinary leaders over the years, but none were more impressive than those who surrounded us as children.

In our family, leadership was an expectation, but not the type of leadership that makes headlines. For us, leadership was about demonstrating a strong work ethic and moral integrity and doing your part to contribute to the larger enterprise. It meant that saying something did not matter if you failed to back it up with action. If you saw something that was wrong, you put in the work to change it. It was a blue-collar, lead-by-example kind of leadership—one that sought results, not the spotlight.

My parents demonstrated this type of leadership all day every day. They were true partners, who led our family like a team. That was particularly true when it came to the family business. Dad was always coming up with new ideas for the store, looking for an innovative product or a new way to beat the competition. Mom was all about the details; she kept the books and made sure the store ran like clockwork. Our work was mostly physical labor, but our parents included us in what was going on, too—what was on sale, which new products we were bringing in. They would encourage our opinions on business and marketing matters, like what to name a sale or what to write on the signs. We got hyped up whenever they would use one of our ideas.

We knew our work mattered, especially for "big days" at the packie like the Fourth of July, Labor Day, and Super Bowl weekend, when it was all hands on deck. Mom and Dad could not leave the registers, so they depended on us. We were needed to fill bags of ice and keep the cooler stocked. It was up to us kids to make sure we did not run out of inventory, which would be like throwing money away.

Along with teaching us that work can be fun, meaningful, and community building, Mom and Dad demonstrated leadership in other ways as well. Living behind a liquor store, we saw plenty of conflict that lent itself to important lessons; there were many times we saw them step up the way they did that time when someone yelled the n-slur at Roger, and they did their part in opposing racism without hesitation. With our upbringing, this became second nature for us as well.

My brothers and I were expected to always take the side of anyone being treated wrongly, whether they were family or not. Whenever we were learning lessons at school about big events, like the Holocaust, Mom continued the conversation at home. She made sure that in addition to learning about the Nazi atrocities, we also learned about the people who did nothing to protect their Jewish neighbors—how they were guilty as well. She would also talk about the people who did their part to protect Jews and say that they were real heroes. The lesson was clear: Opposition to anti-Semitism was about living out basic values, and those who stood on the sidelines, unwilling to fight to protect Jews from the Nazis, were simply not good people.

Mom's lessons about inaction are why the words of Ibram X. Kendi—a fellow FAMU alum who, in his book *How to Be an Antiracist*, advanced the concept of nonracist as a false neutrality that only supports racism—resonate with me. A nonracist is the guy who is unwilling to stand against a Nazi, or a Confederate flag–waving bigot, or a racist in a suit practicing racism in the workplace. To be nonracist is about a lack of integrity around any egalitarian values, and my parents made it clear that is unacceptable.

Most folks would not expect lessons about community, leadership, and antiracism to be on tap at the local packie. Unless they grew up in a mom-and-pop shop, it might not occur to them that the families and other characters who frequent the shop become a community, or that it would be such an amazing place for kids to learn life lessons. That was the case for Mike and Maxine's three boys, though. The truth is, in many ways, it was the best and most edifying time of our lives.

Choosing Sides

Another lesson about values that I recall was when Mom made a heart-wrenching sacrifice that showed us what true commitment to living an antiracist life looks like.

When I was born, Papa—my maternal grandfather—would jokingly refer to me as the "bastard child." That was his way of identifying me as the product of Mom marrying a non-Jew. Mom adored Papa, but we all knew that he did not approve of her marrying Irish Catholic Mike McManus. I do not remember my maternal grandmother, who died when I was only a couple of years old, but she was the one who refused to allow my parents' marriage to create an estrangement with her and Papa.

After Nana passed, Papa remarried. One of my earliest memories, from about age five, is of Mom taking us to see Papa and his new wife, Bea, at their apartment in Boston. Mom drove us up to their building, and we saw Bea at the outdoor pool in the back. She was hard to miss: an older Jewish woman with a bleached-blond beehive hairdo.

Kacey and I ran to the gate, but Bea gestured to us to go away, shooing us toward the building entrance. We did not think anything of it until we realized we were not going to be allowed in the pool.

Mom was visibly angry. We knew that look but did not understand what was happening.

When we got upstairs, someone gave Kacey and me some ice cream and sat us in the kitchen. Everything seemed good until we heard Mom arguing with Papa. Next thing we knew, Mom came to collect us and hustled us out the door. "Don't you ever even think about coming near my family again!" she shouted back at our grandfather.

We were done with Papa.

Mom gave me the rest of the story when I was much older: Bea did not want her neighbors to see Kacey. That's why she had motioned us away from the pool gate and why Mom got so angry. When she told Papa what had happened, he responded that Mom was being overly sensitive and asked her to understand Bea's perspective.

Papa's racism was showing, and Mom was simply not having it.

Mom always knew that Papa was racially intolerant. He had tried to explain away his racism and xenophobia by saying that in Germany, Jews were sold out to the Nazis by non-Jews who they considered friends, even family. There is certainly truth to that, but Mom recognized that there was more to his views than that particular fear.

Before Dad came along, Mom had dated outside of the Jewish community on occasion. Anyone she went out with who was not Jewish, she hid from her father. She hid Dad from him for quite a while. She had him meet her for their first date down the street from her apartment so her parents would not see him. That's where she broke up that knife fight in the alley.

Mom loved her father, but she was not going to let his or Bea's racism hurt her children. It took a lot of courage, but as far as Mom was concerned, when we left their apartment that day, Papa was dead to her. She had been trying for many years to persuade him to change, and that day she realized it was simply not going to happen. Papa chose his toxic bigotry over his own daughter and grandkids, and Mom chose to move us on without him.

The strength it took for Mom to end her relationship with her own father was exceptional—another example of how we were taught about leadership. Mom was always willing to do what was right, even if it was difficult. While cutting ties with Papa may have been the most difficult example, she and Dad had to cut some other folks out of our lives for similar reasons.

Mom and Dad led by example, and they said that they never regretted those decisions for one second. More often than not, they were well respected and appreciated for such integrity. After I was grown and moved away, whenever I would visit and be out with either of my parents, people were always stopping us to share a story about how Mom or Dad helped them to be a better person, taught them a lesson of some sort, or somehow saved their life. My parents would always try to downplay the whole thing, interrupting the person with something about the work I was doing as an antiracist educator, but that tended to backfire.

Whoever it was would scoff and say, "Your parents did more to fight racism than you could ever imagine, even with all your fancy degrees."

Just Living

I am sure there is still a lot that I will never know about what my parents did. But what I witnessed myself was more than enough to teach me about leadership—particularly with respect to standing against racism and other injustices. Their leadership was usually quiet, behind the scenes, and unplanned. What stands out to me is the humility that was at the core of how they chose to lead.

As I've noted before, I think we all need to show up with some humility, especially those of us who are white, as we continue in the struggle to end racism. While we definitely need those leaders who make powerful speeches and lead from the front, the rest of us need to lead, too, from wherever we are.

Humility came later for me, but Kacey had that core of humility from birth, I think, and it naturally drew others in because he was more outgoing and accepting. His willingness to meet every individual without prejudgment, and to treat everyone with respect and kindness, was genuinely welcoming. He demonstrated that he cared about you as naturally as taking a breath, and it was obvious that your place in the social hierarchy was simply not of interest to him.

What I learned from the way that Kacey brought people together was that it does not just happen on its own. If you expect people with experiences different from yours to engage beyond cordiality, you have to actually practice equity and inclusion. You have to demonstrate that you are trustworthy and open to different perspectives. Kacey made these values and expectations clear in everything he did, seemingly without effort. He just lived a just life.

What I learned about leadership from my parents and Kacey is that living our own version of an antiracist life is how we can all contribute to real and sustainable change. Despite never giving a big speech in their lives or achieving fame beyond the neighborhoods we lived in, they all had a deep impact on the lives, beliefs, and behaviors of the people who knew them, and occasionally on others who merely witnessed them practicing their own versions of antiracist leadership.

Living our own version of an antiracist life is how we can all contribute to real and sustainable change.

While great speeches inspire and media pundits might persuade, leadership beyond the spotlight is what's needed most. Anyone can just say they agree with public intellectuals who articulate antiracist ideals; it is far more difficult to take on the daily challenges of living an antiracist life, leading by example, and standing up when the opportunity arises to make concrete changes within our spheres of influence.

Even in diverse groups or organizations, the most profound impact occurs when at least three other elements are cultivated:

- regular experiences that actively promote a welcoming and inclusive culture

- the adoption of policies and practices that ensure equity by holding everyone accountable

- the consistent modeling of leadership in opposition to racism and other oppressions

Making these things happen requires a lot of work behind the scenes.

Our parents made sure that growing up at the packie we had the benefit of all three, which allowed us to develop egalitarian values and an antiracist perspective at our very core. Committing to these types of practices, whether within an extended family, a community group, or an organization, helps us to realize the possibilities and benefits of coming together across differences.

Living an antiracist life is similar to a commitment to living a healthy life: While it's easy to agree with everyone who promotes healthy living, it is far more difficult, for me at least, to put it into practice by eating more greens and limiting my intake of coffee ice cream on a daily basis while also putting my laptop aside and getting more exercise. In other words, it is easier to *say* I believe in healthy living than to actually live a healthy life. The same is true about antiracism.

When you live an antiracist life, it will be evident to those around you. It may cause you to end some relationships, and some people might exit on their own. Based on my experience, that will be for the best, and far more positive relationships will begin with people you may never have known otherwise. When you live an antiracist life, nobody who knows you should ever have to ask which side you are on. You should never feel the need to proclaim that you are not racist, because your actions will make that clear.

Perhaps most important, living your antiracist values out loud sets an example for those who look up to you and look to you for guidance, giving them the courage to raise their own voices as my parents did for us.

6

IT'S ME! IT'S MAKKIE!
The Critical Importance of Your Voice

*When the whole world is silent,
even one voice becomes powerful.*

—MALALA YOUSAFZAI

LITTLE MAKKIE AND HER mother, Kecia, finished organizing their lunch and play items on the park bench. Mak was two years old and excited to meet new friends after our recent move to a new town. Once she had decided it was time to meet the other children, she needed no coaxing. Without hesitation, Makkie walked to the middle of the play area, tilted her head slightly, and raised her hands like a celebrity greeting adoring fans.

"Hi!" she said, beaming. "It's me! It's Makkie!" Then she dropped her hands by her side and waited quietly for the other children to flock.

At first there were just a few. But within moments, every single child had come up and introduced themselves. After their mini formalities, they scampered off to play together as if they had all known each other for years.

This was definitely a proud moment for Makaila's mother, and for me when I heard the story, but it was not surprising. The beauty was in how

Makkie embodied a natural confidence, feeling safe to be her full self. To her, everyone was a potential friend. It never occurred to her that anyone would be uninterested in knowing that she had arrived and was ready to play. Young Makkie certainly would never have imagined that anyone would take issue with her skin color. And for that moment in time, she was right.

As Makkie has grown, raising her voice has become more challenging. Her identity has evolved, however, and she finds it necessary to speak up when she feels excluded. She has raised her voice when she has recognized the exclusion or distortion of the histories of Black and Indigenous people, like her, in the school curriculum. She has also spoken up around LGBTQIA+ and immigration issues. Most of these challenges have come in school, with teachers, administrators, and peers (a scenario I know from experience). In school, Mak rarely sees herself—her family, her background, her perspective—in the curriculum. Far too few teachers seem to consider or care about people who look or think like her, or her mother, or her friends. But the problem goes far beyond a racially biased curriculum.

Along with miseducating our children about history, and training them to tolerate or even practice racism, our schools also police the voices of children. Educators focus too much on the type of classroom management that values control and discipline. We need to focus more on classroom approaches that engage diverse groups of students in the curriculum, dialogue, and skills building, so everyone *knows* their voice is welcomed and supported. Without that support, Makkie's love of school and learning— once as strong as her young voice—has diminished over time. She has lost interest because she no longer feels seen.

Kecia and I are both educators who actively oppose racism and other oppressions, but more importantly, we are attentive parents. We know what is happening in school because Makkie has told us, and we listen. We are very much engaged in our child's education, but like all parents, we cannot always be there.

We are not there with our daughter for every class, with every teacher, to address every racial microaggression—those small but harmful racialized assaults, invalidations, and insults. The use of racially offensive language, denying that racism still exists, or questioning how a person of color got into a particular university are examples of each type of microaggression, respectively. The power of those microaggressions is that they are cumulative, compounding with gender microaggressions and piling onto those based on gender identity, sexual orientation, socioeconomic status, and so on. These painful, daily injustices can add up to a devastating impact, especially in an environment of overt, increasingly normalized bigotry.

No parent can protect their child at all times, so each child must learn to raise their voice in order to protect themself. But our children should not have to be alone in this. We need teachers, school administrators, and other parents and community members to step out of their nonracist safe space and step into their antiracist responsibilities. If we are going to protect our children, and ultimately overcome racism and all these other intersecting oppressions, we all need to learn how to use our unique voices to make a difference where we can. We cannot be bystanders at work or in public spaces, in our schools and universities, or in health care and government. We must stop watching racism and other oppressions happen all around us and lend our voices to the cause of progress.

Makkie's exhausting experience at school reminds me of what Kacey endured, and I find that discouraging—and infuriating. With so many people fighting to root out racism, my daughter's experience should not be so reminiscent of my brother's experience forty-plus years ago. Kacey deserved better then, and Makkie and her friends deserve better now.

And by "friends," of course, I mean *everyone*.

Finding Your Voice

Too often, schools serve to restrict the voices of students, focusing more on discipline than on discourse, and teaching our children to behave in the manner that will not disrupt the status quo. For children of color, LGBTQIA+ students, neurodivergent children, and others deemed different, however, the status quo often does not value them or work in their favor. Teaching children to keep their mouths shut translates, later in life, into adults who value not rocking the boat and fear speaking up, even when they know something is wrong. With respect to racism, this promotes the nonracist stance, which only enables racism to persist.

As Makaila's parents, we continue to advocate for our child while trying to help her to heal through the hurt and teaching her to speak up for herself and others. More often than not, we are working against what is being taught, and how Makkie is being treated, in school. We are always looking for teachers who can truly *see* our Black, biracial, Indigenous, interreligious, multicultural child for all she is. The lack of representation matters as well: While more than half of the US population under age eighteen are people of color,[1] teachers of color make up fewer than 20 percent of all educators in US schools.[2] I'm not saying that white teachers cannot effectively teach students of color, but having teachers who look like you and who share key cultural experiences matters. And, unfortunately, too few white teachers have been prepared to recognize and nurture the academic potential, leadership ability, and joyful voices of students who are not white or don't otherwise fit the so-called norm. We can do better at both developing more diverse teachers and ensuring all teachers are better prepared to nurture and educate all children.

The quashing of our voices is part of a system intended to quiet, pacify, and marginalize. An outspoken, confident child of color like our Makaila Imani is even less acceptable than a white child, like I was, speaking up in class when the teacher is glorifying racists or otherwise distorting history. Educators who claim not to hold racist values must actively ensure that all children's voices are nurtured and that none are diminished in order to maintain order in a classroom that includes kids who too many educators do not understand or value. Being a nonracist teacher is not enough. This is akin to someone who "doesn't see color"—someone who may not actively practice racism but is unwilling to oppose racist curricula, policies, and practices in the classroom and the school—and that is unacceptable.

I have worked for many years with preservice and in-service teachers. I have seen many of them become extraordinary educators with well-tuned antiracist lenses. While few have found a school with an administration that fully supports their antiracist teaching and strives to assemble a critical mass of colleagues who share their opposition to racism and other oppressions, I remain hopeful knowing that as they rise through the ranks they will continue to work to create meaningful change.

Of course, cultivating and encouraging strong, confident voices in our children is not a task for teachers alone, but for all of us. Modeling how we raise our voices for our children is important. Whether your primary goal is to advocate for your child, yourself, or your community, or to oppose racism and oppression in general, finding your voice is key. This is true even if your voice has been suppressed in the past by teachers or others wanting to conserve the status quo. We don't all have to raise our voices in the same way; in fact, we are more powerful when we each raise our voices in our own unique ways.

We all have different strengths that we can engage in order to amplify our opposition to racism and other oppressions, and to promote equity, inclusion, and freedom. Some are great orators, whose inspirational words have moved millions, and we certainly need them to inspire the choir to action. But not all of us are ready to speak in front of the United Nations General Assembly, like Malala Yousafzai, or recite original poetry at a presidential inauguration, like Amanda Gorman. And the truth is, speeches alone will not protect our kids from systemic racism.

Most of us will never have the opportunity to speak to a massive audience or have a global platform. Our names may not be known, but together our voices are powerful. Which of your strengths can you use to raise your own voice or amplify the voices of other advocates for racial equity, inclusion, and justice? Are you able to address a school board meeting or facilitate a session at a professional conference? Could you contribute to developing a new hiring or promotion policy? How about writing a blog post or a letter to the editor? Every voice matters, whether you are singing solo or as part of a choir, but you only make a difference if you have the courage to find your voice—and raise it.

While some excel at public speaking or writing, others may shine when organizing events or creating visual arts. Maybe you found your voice on social media, gaining followers because of your ability to creatively edit or make funny videos or share your wisdom through memes. Maybe your voice is most powerful at your book club or in mentoring relationships. Sharing your thoughts, your wisdom, and your own experience can increase awareness of racism, drive interest in antiracist advocacy, and help encourage others to raise their voices. There are endless ways we can raise our voices. The secret is figuring out how to best raise yours. That doesn't mean it will always be easy or comfortable, just that it is a way that works for you.

Which of your strengths can you use to raise your own voice or amplify the voices of other advocates for racial equity, inclusion, and justice?

Because racism is both social and systemic, there are many challenges to take on. That makes it important to develop different strategies that can be engaged depending on the situation. In different settings, communities, and circumstances, there may be ways to raise your voice that are contextually more appropriate or effective. For example, Dr. Ruha Benjamin explores the misguided idea that technology race-neutral, describing how white supremacy and racial and other social inequities are encoded in design—what she terms the "New Jim Code."[3] If technology is in your wheelhouse, that may be where your expert voice is most valuable in terms of antiracist leadership. How do we counteract human biases in coding and the development of new tech?

I remain hopeful that Makkie will keep developing and using her voice and regain her love of education. I am doing my best to help her get there, but it may take time. It took many years for me to develop my voice, and I am always looking for ways to improve my efforts and expand my sphere of influence. It took even longer for me to regain a love for education. Thanks to the challenge Makaila gave me, I am trying to expand my voice by writing this book to advance the idea that if enough of us strive to live our best antiracist lives, we will create real and sustainable change together.

Circles and Spheres

We are always influencing others by what we say and do and when we choose to say or do nothing. We all have different circles of family, friends, colleagues, and followers—different spheres of influence. The degree of our influence varies, as does the reach of our voices. But we all have opportunities to speak up, model, advise, educate, and lead.

It is easy to think that no one is paying attention, but this is rarely true. I am reminded of this every time I do something embarrassing—whether botching a traditional dance at a wedding or inevitably spilling sauce on my shirt at a luncheon—and someone is quick to let me know they saw it all. The folks around you may seem less inclined to point out every time they notice you doing something well, but they are taking it all in.

Once I decided to be more intentional about my antiracist voice, I started taking an inventory of who seemed to be paying attention to me. Which circles and spheres could I influence? I figured that my family and friends were paying at least some attention to me. Then there were students in classes I was teaching, a few of my colleagues, and some folks at conferences that I attended regularly who valued my perspective. I soon began to realize that some people were paying attention to what I posted online, and that when I spoke up in public, the people around me took enough notice to provide feedback.

A turning point came soon after I received my PhD. Friends and family members began expecting me to have answers to questions about racism and other forms of oppression, knowing that had been a focus of my studies. I suppose this is a bit like when newly minted MDs start getting asked to identify the medical ailments of family and friends. I would be at a family function or spending time with friends, and if a current event related to race came up, everyone would look at me. People in my circles expected me to speak up around these issues, but now I was being seen as someone who could provide educated input and valuable insight. Whenever I knew nothing more than what we had all seen on the news or heard in other circles, I was still expected to have a critical take on the matter. They were already looking to me as a resource and expecting me to cite new research, synthesize events, and offer a deeper understanding.

I was clear about wanting to advance an antiracist perspective, so I tried to pay attention to when and where I had opportunities to contribute. But I soon realized that I had no way to predict the impact I could potentially have—that my influence was not something I could turn on and off when needed or just when I felt like it. That's when it occurred to me: What mattered most, more than any particular event or discussion, was living with integrity around my antiracist values. It was more about the fact that my voice was consistent, that it could be relied upon.

Although most folks would think that my brother Kacey and my parents lived pretty ordinary lives, somehow they had an extraordinary influence on the people around them. Their lives had an incalculable ripple effect on their circles of family, friends, and others in the community. The reason behind their remarkable impact was their integrity. They did not live their values out loud only when they knew someone was watching, just to impress. They lived with integrity day in and day out, always guided by their values. It was as simple as that.

Finding your voice begins by looking around to see who is in your life, who you socialize with in real life or online, and who you interact with at work. You may just find your sphere of influence is larger than you thought.

When Makkie was around four years old, her instinct to make friends wherever she went remained strong. Dropping her off at preschool one day, I asked if she was ready to join the class.

"Yes," Makkie responded in a very matter-of-fact way. "I'm ready to go see my friends."

There were a lot of kids around. "Are *all* of these kids your friends?" I asked, smiling.

Makkie nodded. "Some of them don't know it yet, but they are all my friends."

That is why when I say Makkie's friends, I mean everyone. We are all connected, even if we don't know it yet. Each of us influences more people than we think we do, and a lot of that happens when we are just living our daily lives, not thinking about what message we are sending. For our antiracist values to have the greatest impact, I believe they have to be part of *how we live each day*. If we focus on how we live rather than who is watching, maybe one day folks will tell stories about us as well—and not just the embarrassing ones.

> *Finding your voice begins by looking around to see who is in your life, who you socialize with in real life or online, and who you interact with at work. You may just find your sphere of influence is larger than you thought.*

Professional Antiracism

Engaging in social justice dialogue while traveling around the former Soviet Union changed my perspective and trajectory. While I loved collaborating with scientists, the time spent in heated conversations with student groups and in building relationships with other advocates for equity and social justice felt more important to me. I made the decision to switch my major during my third year as an undergraduate at Florida Tech, and I did not look back. I chose to focus on becoming a professional antiracist, although I had no idea what that meant at the time.

During my senior year, I was required to do an internship. My faculty advisor told me about a unique opportunity with the Defense Equal Opportunity Management Institute (DEOMI), a Department of Defense (DOD) organization located on Patrick Air Force Base, only about thirty minutes from the Florida Tech campus. I did a little research and found out that DEOMI had originally been named the Defense Race Relations Institute (DRRI) and that it was launched the same year Kacey was born, in 1971. That felt like a sign that this was the right place for me.

On the heels of the Civil Rights Movement, and with racial conflicts happening on and off base between military personnel, the DOD mandated race relations education for all members of the armed forces. That was the original mission of DRRI, which became DEOMI in 1979 to reflect its growing mission to address additional readiness issues, including sexism and sexual harassment, religious accommodations, and anti-Semitism. My internship started in the Research Directorate under Dr. Mickey Dansby. I was assigned to assist with their DOD-wide climate surveys, which collected data on the cultural climate within military units with respect to equity and inclusion.

The first time I drove up to the gate at Patrick AFB was a nerve-racking experience. My father had served in the army, but I had no experience with the military. My prior experience with police had not been positive, and the soldiers at the gate looked like cops with gym memberships. Inside the base were officers and enlisted service members from every branch of the military—so many different uniforms, insignia, and ranks to learn, my head was spinning.

I had just started getting comfortable driving onto base each day—going to my little corner of the Research Directorate and trying not to refer to a sergeant as a captain, when I was told to report to the commandant: Colonel Ronald M. Joe. As a newcomer, it felt like being called to the principal's office, only this principal was surrounded by soldiers who spoke a secret, acronym-based language and looked ready for a war to break out at any moment.

Colonel Joe had a commanding presence and better posture than anyone I'd ever met. His office was pristine and well organized, and the walls were completely covered with ornate awards and appreciations that all looked very important to me. Having read his biography, I knew that, among his many accomplishments, he was an army colonel and a former tank battalion commander.

Colonel Joe was kind and seemed genuinely interested when he asked why I chose to do my internship at DEOMI. I was nervous and told him half of my life's story. He listened patiently and then returned the favor (more concisely) by telling me about growing up as a young Black man in Florida and why he was excited to lead DEOMI. He made sure that I understood my role, which would adjust based on my performance and aptitude. As it turned out, Colonel Joe felt I needed more work to do.

After a couple of months, I was told to report to the commandant again, this time to shadow him for the day. I had to wake up way earlier than usual, and the day was packed. Remarkably, in between meetings, Colonel Joe took time to make sure I understood what was going on. It was a walking lesson in leadership.

At lunchtime, he took me off base to a favorite spot, offered some professional advice, and asked about my experience so far and my plans for after graduation. We ended the day with a debrief in his office, where Colonel Joe told me that I had leadership potential. He then told me, very matter-of-factly, that I needed to continue my education at Florida A&M University, his alma mater. He followed that up by connecting me with the legendary Professor James Eaton, the founder of the Black Archives at FAMU (now known as the Southeastern Regional Black Archives Research Center and Museum). I took his direction, corresponded with Professor Eaton, and met with him when he visited DEOMI soon after.

During my time at DEOMI, I learned more about professional antiracism, equity, and inclusion work than in all of my college courses combined. The work happening there was dynamic and transformative: Chief Master Sergeant (Ret.) Eugene Johnson, the "Godfather of

DEOMI," taught me the history of the institution and provided guidance for my time there; Lieutenant Colonel (Ret.) Dr. Mickey Dansby introduced me to equity-related research; Navy Lieutenant Lance Harris taught me what service and education truly mean; and Army Staff Sergeant (Ret.) Dorothy J. Maney-Kellum helped me understand how racism is adapted to maintain power.

Another big lesson came six months after completing my internship and graduating from college, when I was asked to return to present on diversity and youth at the DEOMI Worldwide Conference. It was my first major conference presentation, and my sessions were packed with uniformed military—lots of stars and bars that I still could not connect with appropriate ranks if my life had depended on it. They went well, and I was feeling myself a bit, until I went to the plenary session and saw Colonel Joe command the room.

Then Jane Elliott took the stage. I recalled her from that 1970 documentary about introducing third graders to issues of discrimination. Hundreds of attendees packed the room, including Colonel Joe and a group of generals seated behind her. Like a force of nature, she schooled us on the myth of race, discussed how religion is misused to justify racism, and offered her perspective on how racism weakens organizations. Afterward, Colonel Joe brought me over and introduced me to Ms. Elliott.

"It's nice to meet you," she said. "Did you learn anything useful here today?"

When I said yes, she proceeded to make me prove it. Then she gave me a reading list—the first of many that she would assign me over the years to come, and then for Makkie too.

Colonel Joe helped me imagine myself as a leader. By guiding my experience at DEOMI and introducing me to Professor Eaton and Jane Elliott, he helped me understand there are professional paths to follow that focus on antiracism, equity, and inclusion. Kacey had encouraged me to teach others; now, these leaders were helping me find my voice as an educator.

After Colonel Joe retired from the army, he went on to take a position at FAMU. In addition to Col. Joe and Prof. Eaton, I knew a few other folks there as well, including my longtime friend DeReef Jamison and his future wife, Tashala, who were at the university working on graduate degrees. I decided to visit the campus, curious that Colonel Joe and DeReef, who were so different from one another, both spoke so highly of FAMU. Tashala encouraged me to consider applying for a new doctoral program in educational leadership, and I took her advice. That was one of the best decisions I have ever made.

FAMU taught me what higher education should be and how to be an educator. More importantly, my experience at FAMU taught me that education can be a true manifestation of love. It took a long time, from that day in fourth grade, when my teacher tried to tell me that enslavers were great, until graduate school, but I began to see the beauty in education again.

Leading with Love

The philosopher and activist Cornel West challenged us to understand an idea that connects racial, social, economic, environmental, and all other forms of justice by stating that "Justice is what love looks like in public."[4] Few authors have made a greater impact on my thinking around race, revolution, and love, particularly on issues that others have avoided, such as affirmative action and relations between African American and Jewish people. Love is what connects me, as a racial justice seeker, to other justice seekers. I can relate to, and join in struggle with, someone whose passion drives them to focus on equity and inclusion—for transgender people, for example—because love is at the core of why we fight for justice. Love is a shared place to begin, an opening for learning, engaging with empathy, raising our voices, and practicing solidarity.

I had the opportunity and challenge to teach undergraduate courses while working on my doctorate. During my second year, I heard that Cornel

West was going to be speaking across the tracks at Florida State University (FSU) by invitation of their Black Student Union. I had only been on the FSU campus twice, first to protest their use of a Native American mascot and then to protest their defense of a racist psychology professor. I was not going to miss the chance to hear Professor West speak in person, though. In fact, I brought the students from the class that I was scheduled to teach that evening—whatever I was planning to teach could wait.

After Professor West spoke, a number of folks stayed to get an autograph or picture. I waited until the end and introduced myself and some of the students who were waiting for me to give them a ride back to campus. We got to chatting about FAMU, until he became distracted. He noticed his son talking to a young woman off to the side, one of the students from my class. He then started talking about his son, who was attending FAMU at the time, like any dad would, and told me how proud he was of him, and how excited he was to be able to visit.

At one point he asked what I thought was going on with his son and the student from my class. I joked that he was probably finding a way to slip into the conversation that his dad was Cornel West. He said that might be true, and asked if I thought it would work. I hesitantly said no, mentioning that she had two kids and was not easily impressed. He laughed one of those big hearty laughs. He then invited the students who stuck around to join, and he led an amazing conversation that felt like we were all at a jazz club after hours jamming with the band. That is until the student his son had been talking with reminded me that she and a few others had to go.

Before we left, Professor West asked me for my program from the event. He wrote a kind note on it and included his phone number. He said to call him if I was ever in the Boston area. He was a professor at Harvard at the time, across the river in Cambridge. I told him that I would definitely find myself there. I called the number, made an appointment, and had the opportunity to meet with Cornel West in his office. It looked exactly like I had imagined, by the way—as if I had walked into a giant stack of books.

I do not remember a lot about the conversation except that we talked about the book he wrote with Michael Lerner, *Jews and Blacks*. I wanted to know why he chose Lerner as a coauthor. I liked Rabbi Lerner, but he did not seem to know much about Black culture, while Professor West seemed far more well versed on Jewish culture. His answer was simply that Lerner had asked. That answer stuck with me. Sometimes, you just have to ask.

I had the opportunity to meet Professor West a couple more times. Once was when I walked into a hotel in Washington, DC, and saw him sitting at a table in the lobby with Michael Lerner and Deepak Chopra. I know it sounds like the beginning of a joke, but it really happened. I paused, no doubt looking like a deer in headlights, and Professor West actually remembered me and introduced me to his friends.

Seeing Cornel West in that context actually mattered, too. As I have gotten older, I have thought about that moment whenever a student or young professional comes up to a table I am sitting at with some of my amazing friends and colleagues during a conference or event. They are excited to speak with folks who they regard as leaders, not unlike my experience with Prof. West. It made me realize that we are all luminaries to someone. Whether you are an elder sitting in the backyard at the barbecue, a popular student sitting at the cool table, or a professional with a fancy title, imagine the impact you have in those moments when you are seen as a leader, especially if you lead with love.

Imagine the impact you have in those moments when you are seen as a leader, especially if you choose to lead with love.

Permission to Speak

In school, our teachers required us to ask permission before speaking. Life after school is not like that. In general, we have the responsibility to determine whether or not to speak in any given situation. Some of us have a lot to say, but we are shy. Others cannot help themselves and talk so much that they become background noise. Living out our antiracist values in our daily lives sometimes leads us to circumstances where it is necessary to speak up. Whether we personally experience or witness racism, or an incident creates an opportunity for us to promote equity and inclusion, it is important that we know how—and when—to turn up the volume. This is particularly true for those of us who are white.

Sometimes, we are not the ones who need to speak up. Our role may be to support others or encourage them to raise their voices. Sometimes, lending our voice to a choir of voices makes sense. And sometimes, our voice is the one that needs to be amplified.

Too often, those who are targeted by oppressive systems are the ones expected to call it out. Not only that, but they're also supposed to educate everyone else about it while it is happening. The voices of those facing oppression are too often marginalized by definition. As a result, many, if not most, white people tend to have an ear only for white voices. That's when those who benefit from oppression or white privilege need to raise the volume of *our* voices in the fight against racism. Every antiracist voice raised in solidarity extends our reach.

Further, living an antiracist life means more than building a strong antiracist literacy and learning how to raise your voice. It also requires being able to control your volume and use your voice strategically.

Of course, there is no one correct way to raise your voice. Each voice is unique, and the context matters. If you know your strengths, understand your social location, and are aware that voices need to be raised to address an issue, then it is your responsibility to do so in the best way you know how.

I know that I am shy, but I am also passionate. Being quiet is my default, but if a line is crossed, I actually struggle to contain myself. Learning which strategies to use under different circumstances takes time. In some scenarios, a soft touch is the most effective way to get a point across, whereas others require a bullhorn. Many times, I have pulled out my bullhorn and only made the situation worse, but I have learned from those experiences and continue to work on my volume control.

In the best-case scenario, we find mentors and partners who can help us develop our voice and learn how best to use it. That kind of support might come from someone near and dear to you, or from someone you only know online. Either way, their guidance matters if they believe in you and are willing to invest their time in understanding and fine-tuning your voice.

Since my natural inclination is to be quiet until I am so upset that I only have bullhorn mode, it has been important for me to learn how to gain more control and choose my battles. That idea does not sit well with me: How do I have the right to decide how much racism is okay? My mentors have helped me to understand that it is not about some racism being okay but about deciding when and how my voice will be most effective.

Adjusting my voice so I can be more useful, more often, is a process that I continue today. As Gene Johnson asked me back at DEOMI: "Is that a hill that you're ready to die on?" Coming from a veteran, the question had a particular weight to it.

At times, you have to retreat, regroup, and live to fight another day. This is a tough lesson that I have not mastered yet, because I tend to go all in and have a hard time reversing course. Even after all my years trying to learn how to have the best possible impact and influence, I still run up against my own limits.

None of us are perfect at living an antiracist life, any more than we are perfect at living out other core values, like kindness or environmentalism. That being said, I have certainly let "perfect" get in the way of progress at times. This book is a good example: I have rewritten it so many times trying to make it perfect, but all I've really done is delay its publication. I just have to remind myself that perfection is not the goal; progress is. And nothing can prevent all mistakes or erase those we've made in the past. I say be intentional about when and how you raise your voice, but also expect to make mistakes—sometimes big ones. And give yourself permission to be the best version of your antiracist self, imperfections and all, right now.

Even imperfect antiracist effort is better than standing aside and allowing racism to pass unchallenged.

I have used my voice again and again—from trying to protect my brother to becoming a student activist, from giving speeches around the world to transforming systems from within. I have stumbled at times and fallen hard at others. What matters is getting back up and returning to the fight, hopefully stronger, having learned from the experience.

There is no secret recipe here—just encouragement to make all the mistakes, own them, make amends, and keep on fighting. If fear prevents you from speaking up, we all miss out on your wisdom and experience. Every effort matters, and you do not need permission from anyone to speak. I encourage you to raise your voice, lead, be a role model, and make a difference in your circles and within your unique sphere of influence—in that unique way that only you can.

7

SOMEONE FALLS IN A HOLE

The Power of Relationships, Community, and Solidarity

*The most important measure of how good a game
I played was how much better I'd made my teammates play.*

—BILL RUSSELL

My grandfather was a blue-collar guy who dropped out of school in eighth grade to get a job and help take care of his family. He was the kind of no-nonsense guy who saw work that needed to be done and just did it, no complaints—usually no words at all. When he did have something to say, though, it was worth listening to.

When we lost Kacey, our family and friends did their best to console us. All that love mattered and, frankly, kept me from taking my own life—which was all I could think of for a long time. Mom held me as I cried, and Dad encouraged me to honor Kacey by living a good life. But a chat with my Grampa Joe may have made the biggest difference for me.

I was close to Dad's parents. Grandma was the talkative one, and usually the one to give advice. But when we all gathered at their home after

Kacey passed, she just hugged me and told me to go see Grampa. He took me for a ride in his big gray Oldsmobile Delta 88 and told me about his brother, my Great-Uncle Deed, who I knew had suffered with cancer. What I didn't know was that he was a victim of suicide. Grampa understood what happens to those of us who are left behind.

"It hurts, and it's not going to get much better," Grampa told me. "Especially the guilt." That may sound harsh, but I heard it as honest. That was the truth that he understood from experience.

My grandfather explained that Kacey wasn't trying to hurt anyone, and that he would want me to keep going, even if I didn't want to. I would learn how to deal with it, he said, because I would have to be there for the people I love. Someday, I would have to make sure my kids knew about their Uncle Kacey. But for now, I just had to get up each day, get out there, and get to work.

That was what eighteen-year-old me needed to hear.

Years later, one of my favorite TV shows, *The West Wing*, reminded me of that moment with Grampa Joe. As one of the show's characters was struggling with post-traumatic stress disorder (PTSD), another character shares a parable to express his support:

> *This guy's walking down the street when he falls in a hole. The walls are so steep, he can't get out.*
>
> *A doctor passes by, and the guy shouts up, "Hey you, can you help me out?"*
>
> *The doctor writes a prescription, throws it down in the hole, and moves on.*
>
> *Then a priest comes along, and the guy shouts up, "Father, I'm down in this hole, can you help me out?"*
>
> *The priest writes out a prayer, throws it down in the hole, and moves on.*

Then a friend walks by.

"Hey, Joe, it's me, can you help me out?"

And the friend jumps in the hole.

Our guy says, "Are ya stupid? Now we're both down here."

The friend says, "Yeah, but I've been down here before, and I know the way out."[1]

I had become familiar with the flashbacks, nightmares, and other symptoms of PTSD ever since finding Kacey's body, on that cold day in March 1989. When I really could not see a path to a life worth living, Grampa jumped down in the hole with me. And because I knew that he understood, and that he loved Kacey and me, I trusted his guidance and eventually found a way out of that hole.

It took loving pushes from family and friends to help me realize there were reasons to get up in the morning, and I am deeply grateful for that. Over time, I have been blessed to build a community of loved ones who have provided the love and support to get me through each day with purpose, and to even allow myself joy.

Stepping into Discomfort

White people rarely place themselves in situations where they are the only white person. Because of indoctrination, most intentionally avoid those types of situations, especially if the majority are Black. It is uncomfortable for most white people, possibly stemming from the misconception that they would be treated as poorly in that situation as Black people are treated by white folks on a regular basis. It has been my experience that these concerns are unfounded, however, and actually cause white people to frequently miss out on extraordinary experiences and opportunities.

I often encourage white people to consider what they could learn by joining a community or institution where they are not in the majority—and where white folks are not in charge. If that is not part of your regular experience, I submit that it should be. Find an organization with membership that does not look like you but addresses issues you care about or focuses on an interest that you share. Join with the intention of building relationships, learning, and potentially growing your community.

I have had the pleasure of being part of multiple communities led by people of color and where I am in the racial minority. Some are professional associations, and others are social. I also attended FAMU, an HBCU, for my doctoral studies, where I found an academic and professional community that embraced me and taught me far more than I had expected to learn. Because of that experience and what I learned, I do my best to represent FAMU well in all that I do. FAMU alumni are known, for good reason, for our fierce loyalty and pride in our alma mater. Simply put, FAMU shaped me as an educator and made me a better person.

In large part because of my time at FAMU, I am able to bring a different wealth of knowledge, not centered on whiteness, that uplifts Blackness and a commitment to equity and inclusion. In the FAMU College of Education, I learned a different approach to teaching, and gained an understanding of what is possible through an education focused on the motto championed by the president of FAMU during my time on campus, Dr. Frederick S. Humphries Sr.: "Excellence with Caring." FAMU alumni and those that I have met from other HBCUs, and Tribal Colleges and Universities (TCUs) as well, are able to bring critical perspectives because of academic experiences that embrace knowledge and history that historically white colleges and universities tend to ignore, intentionally distort, or exclude.

By building a community of extended family and circles of friends and colleagues who are genuinely diverse, you show others the possibilities that are unlocked by interracial and otherwise diverse relationships. This leading by example is powerful, and as your community becomes more diverse, everyone benefits from the variety of ideas and perspectives that arise, including yourself.

As a basic example, most of us regularly eat foods that did not originate within our own cultural background(s). I am an Irish Jew, and I have a deep love for foods that come out of both traditions. But I also love sushi and pizza and *nsima* and many other foods that come from cultures other than my own. Could I live on Jewish and Irish dishes alone? Of course. But given the opportunity, I find it interesting, stimulating, and plain ol' delicious to enjoy a mixed menu of culinary options.

Your own experience of cultivating a diverse friend group holds even more benefits than diversifying your palate. Beyond just food, cultures have developed traditions to address everything from climate and shelter to building relationships and coping with the loss of loved ones. We can learn a lot from one another if we are willing to engage, with open minds, in relationships that go beyond the superficial.

At the same time, some professional or friend groups may comprise people who look different but are actually made up of white folks and highly assimilated people of color. These types of groups, with people who have chosen not to break the unwritten rules prohibiting different cultural norms, perspectives on race, or challenges to white expectations, do not actually benefit from diversity, because their interactions remain superficial at best. I have seen this in nonprofit agencies, corporate board rooms, and political organizations. It sets a problematic example because it devalues the differences that people of color and other marginalized voices could bring to the table, modeling only assimilation.

My experience as Kacey's brother opened my eyes to racism, but it did not fill in all the blanks. Relationships across the spectrum of racial and ethnic identities have furthered my understanding over time. No one can learn everything from one family member or friend. The more relationships you have that cross social constructs the more you understand, and the more you realize how much more there is to learn. This can help keep your mind open, strengthen your humility, and deepen your appreciation for diverse perspectives.

If you are a white person who is striving to diversify your circle or professional community of practice, you may need to be intentional about leaving behind preconceptions as well as fears you may have learned about racialized others. You may need to allow yourself to feel uncomfortable. You may even need to recognize and accept that what you have been taught before had been distorted, incomplete, or simply untrue.

Engaging across racial and other social divides may require overcoming some discomfort. If you can do it genuinely and with humility, however, the knowledge you will gain, the cultural competencies you will develop, and the new relationships you will begin will be worth any discomfort at the start.

Building Your Squad

For the first several years of our lives, decisions are made on our behalf by parents or guardians. The state makes other decisions that affect us, from school zones, voting districts, and taxes through sorts of regulations, and sometimes even who gets custody of us. Teachers and administrators decide what we will learn and who our classmates will be. The government and corporations make decisions that will determine whether we have access to nutritious food, health care, and clean drinking water. A lot is decided for us.

As we get older, however, some important decisions become our own. The choices we make are still informed to some degree by what we learned and experienced during our childhood, but over time, we begin to make our own way in the world. Among the most important decisions are those regarding relationships, as we've discussed, because they are the building blocks of the communities that we create for ourselves. Developing a community of support—the people who would jump down in the hole with us—is critical for living a purposeful life. When you are committed to creating change, particularly regarding something as grievous and challenging as racism, the support of friends, family, colleagues, and mentors will be incredibly valuable, especially as you encounter difficult times.

I have found great benefits in maintaining a close-knit antiracist circle of colleagues. They have been there for me when I've had to deal with the consequences of my antiracism work: all sorts of threats, being sued for speaking well-documented truths, and even being fired for doing my job well. These colleagues have become friends. Knowing that they have walked, or are currently walking, a similar path is reassuring. They have jumped down into holes that I have found myself in professionally and shown me the way out. And I have been glad to do the same for them.

For anyone willing to lead by example by living an antiracist life, you can benefit greatly from building this type of intentional community of support, in real life or even online. The organizational board structure can provide a framework to describe a few key types of support: your own personal board of advisors (your peers), board of directors (your mentors), and board of trustees (your confidants). I'm not suggesting that you set up multiple boards, just that you include trusted professional peers, mentors, and confidants as you develop an intentional circle of collegial support.

Finding Your Peers and Mentors

My advisors include my closest peer colleagues. We challenge one another, have each other's backs, and provide the encouragement that we all need from time to time. When I need to talk about an emerging issue or get another informed perspective, these are the first people I call. They are my favorite people to work with, and we make the effort to partner as often as possible.

I look to the squad of young progressive members in the US House of Representatives as a public example of how a group of colleagues can work together to promote change. Like these Representatives, the members of my squad live and work in different geographical places, but we support each other's work and come together in partnership whenever possible. We present together at conferences, we consult together, and we develop everything from policies to curricula together.

Your antiracist advisors (or squad) may be a group of professional peers, neighbors who share your values, or fellow parents whose children attend the same schools as yours. What matters is that you seek out those who align with your goals and are doing similar work or advocacy, and that you can support one another. It might start out with making one connection with someone who is willing to support you in your commitment to living an antiracist life. Believe me, there will be days when you need a shoulder to cry on, a compassionate ear to listen, or a partner to work with. From there, your squad will grow.

Finding antiracism mentors—your board of directors—can be a challenge. My first antiracist mentors, aside from my parents, were in my head. I would imagine seeking advice from people I was too shy to approach or who had written books I loved. I would read what they wrote, attend their lectures, or watch their work on television and then ask myself: *Based on what I've learned from their work, how might they guide me?*

Elizabeth Salett was the founding president of the National MultiCultural Institute (NMCI), now the International MultiCultural Institute (IMCI). I met Liz the first time I volunteered for the NMCI Annual Conference. I was a broke graduate student, so I volunteered to help with conference preparations, registration, and assisting presenters, which came with a registration discount that I needed to be able to attend the conference. I was impressed by her patience and poise during difficult conversations—skills I did not have but wanted to learn. She would take everything in and find just the right moment to make a thought-provoking comment or pose a question that would transform a conflict into dialogue. From my perspective, she was a big deal, and although she seemed very approachable, I did not have it in me to ask her about mentoring me. So, she became a mentor in my head.

I am a very direct person, but at times, employing a different, more considered approach can yield better results. Whenever I took a moment to step back and think in the midst of a heated discussion, I would ask myself: *How might Liz handle this situation?* That was my reminder to find a constructive question or comment rather than taking the confrontational approach that came more naturally to me. I learned a great deal from Liz in person, but I also learned from these imaginary conversations in my head.

Some of my most powerful mentors were not the ones writing books or giving lectures or providing their perspective on television, but extraordinary leaders who have simply done antiracist work within their communities and professional fields, living antiracist lives in their own ways. I have met them through my own work, at conferences, and through colleagues. Some guided me for a short time, and others have been willing to provide advice over decades. Some have been formal mentoring relationships, others more informal. I listen to their advice and seek lessons from their involvement in movements, initiatives, and organizations. And when I need specific guidance, I call on them to share their wisdom.

People who are living purpose-driven lives and working in the antiracist tradition, in my experience, tend to be open to giving advice, offering professional guidance, and providing a larger historical context. Over the years, I have overcome some of my anxiety about asking for advice and mentorship and been blessed to learn from people who have advanced equity and inclusion in schools, community centers, and nonprofit organizations. Whether they have made a difference on a large scale, nationally and even internationally, or have made deep change possible locally, all of them have shared valuable stories and perspectives.

Be patient with yourself: You don't need to find a bunch of mentors overnight. Not everyone who is open to mentorship actually knows what they are talking about, and those who do know may want to get better acquainted with you before investing their time. They are not always activists or educators either, and most do not have "antiracism" in their professional title. Be open to meeting people who are experienced in whatever they do and who are also committed to racial justice, and you will end up with mentors from different fields, professions, and communities. There is always something to learn from how others have approached the advancement of equity and inclusion, regardless of how they contribute or which field or sector they may work in.

Guidance from Your Ride-or-Die

People in your life who are committed to antiracism, and who have been invested in you for a long time, are your trustees. They are often like your extended family: people who can remind you where you came from and keep you from becoming overly judgmental of those who are still at earlier stages of learning, just like you were at some point. Your trustees are also the ones who will be there for you if and when life feels too heavy to bear. They are the folks best situated to provide you with much-needed perspective—your ride-or-die folks.

My trustees are folks who have never thought of me as Dr. McManus, because I will always be just Joe-Joe to them. They love me, and I will never have to doubt that. Their motives are clear: They are Team Joe-Joe all the way, and nothing will ever change that. They give me the courage to keep going because I know they will always be in my corner.

They are also the people who can check me—they are unafraid to call me out on my mistakes and challenge my assumptions. Sometimes we become so focused on our purpose that we get tunnel vision. No matter how woke you think you are, or how experienced you are in your work, everyone makes mistakes. We are all human, and while some are far more aware than others, our collective awakening is still in progress. Sometimes we need our closest loved ones—those ride-or-die friends and family—to give us a smack on the back of the head that brings us back to our senses.

Just as important, these are also the people who pick up the pieces when we fall. Living an antiracist life requires taking risks, and sometimes those risks do not work out in our favor. I have failed big and small. And though I have done my best to learn from my mistakes, sometimes it is easy to get stuck. It is not just the big flops that hurt. The smallest mistake can hurt big too, and sometimes we feel defeated when those small failures accumulate. Keeping a few people close who know your heart, and how to put it back together, can help you get up on even the toughest mornings.

Recognizing who your trustees are is not enough, though. You must also be willing to rely on them—to put aside your ego and share when you are feeling broken or like a failure in your antiracist work or advocacy. It is not always easy to ask for help when you need it. I know that for many people, including myself, it's a lot easier to offer help than to ask for it. It may help to consider that people who care about you actually want to be there when you need them, just like you want to be there when your loved ones need you. No matter how strong you are, there are always times when your strength is depleted—when you must check your ego at the door and accept support.

As you look around at your closest confidants, you may find you are blessed with support from surprising corners. My child is a key member of Team Joe-Joe because she inspires me, keeps me centered, and reminds me of my purpose in a way that is singular among all of my relationships. Makkie is suitably unimpressed with my accomplishments and helps me focus in the moment. Watching Makkie and her friends also inspires me in a distinct way. Don't be fooled into thinking the younger generation of US Americans is naturally solving racism just by being a more diverse population. Despite being less encumbered by the weight of the years, they face all the same systems of racism, plus a few new online ones thrown in for good measure.

What I gain from my daughter's insights, and from watching her generation interact, is a sense of hope stemming from how they are understanding identity in more complex ways and recognizing connections between movements. I have also benefited greatly from the support of my former students: those who took classes taught by me or participated in programs that I ran and who have continued to keep in touch. Watching them grow as people, as professionals, and as leaders has been powerful for me. I continue to learn from their experiences, their new ways of looking at the

> *It may help to consider that people who care about you actually want to be there when you need them, just like you want to be there when your loved ones need you.*

world and the work, and their unique perspectives on current events and social issues.

Some former students have become educators, of course, but others have ventured into other fields, such as health care, finance, government, the military, social services, and law. I do my best to remain a resource and even a mentor for them but, just as often, I receive guidance from them as well. The beauty of wisdom is that it can be shared in both directions.

Online Community

At its best, social media connects us with each other, supplies us with interesting and credible information, and provides extraordinary learning opportunities. Technology can help us build relationships in many ways, allowing those with access to interact with loved ones, hold important meetings, and maintain a sense of community even at a physical distance, as we learned during the COVID-19 pandemic. Social media has not lived up to its potential as a connecting force, however, and in many ways traces a downward spiral with respect to the quality of impact. In becoming more about propaganda and bullying in the pursuit of profit, these platforms too often serve to further divide us. But even with all these problems, most of us choose to have an online presence, living part of our lives virtually.

When using online tools to connect, educate, and organize, it is important to build our capacity to recognize untruths, propaganda, and hate on our screens. Just believing whatever we see or hear through the media has never been wise, and today—given the lack of integrity among social media profiteers and political opportunists—it is particularly ill-advised. There is a learning curve for this type of online media literacy, and we are way behind that curve. Collectively, it is of vital importance that we quickly develop a far more critical eye.

The onslaught of extremist content online has people believing the Earth is flat, Trump won the 2020 election, and the pandemic was a hoax. All these statements are absurd, but many people accept what is fed to them as long as it feeds their beliefs or biases. Spreading with ease throughout the population, disinformation not only miseducates and deepens social divisions among us but also distracts from legitimate, well-documented problems that we need to address: health care, education, housing, police violence, predatory capitalism, and so many other social issues plaguing our nation. Meanwhile, solutions are becoming increasingly difficult to find and implement, because they are obscured by misinformation and confounding lies.

The challenges we face in fighting racism are not new; they have just adapted to new platforms. Technology has given us new opportunities to connect and communicate, but that same technology is available to spread racist ideas, forged histories, sham science, xenophobic fantasies, and fake facts. At the same time, social media provides a means to out those who demonstrate their racism publicly.

In addition to building our social media literacy, we must assess how we choose to engage online. Is getting caught up in online arguments about racism and politics with people you'll never meet an effective use of your time and energy? I used to spend hours trying to make a point to people who were clearly uninterested in considering a new perspective or facts that contradicted their racist fantasies. At some point, we learn to see this as a pointless waste of time and refuse to fall into that trap, just as we refuse to expend time and energy in real life with a person who is unequipped to listen.

We are all still learning about the challenges and benefits of online relationships. I enjoy staying in touch with friends and family that I do not see often. Seeing pictures of what they and their families are up to and sharing funny memes and political stories helps me feel connected to them. Granted, some of my social media friends are people I might not recognize if I walked past them on the street. However, many are genuine friends who I might not have otherwise been able to keep up with when I have moved, or folks I've met during my travels that I'm glad to be able to stay connected to. Still others are colleagues and professional connections that deepen my network.

The online world has potential as a place where meaningful and productive dialogue can occur, if you can (and want to) make it work for you. I encourage using social media to engage with antiracist organizations, find antiracist community, and signal-boost antiracism creators, initiatives, and movements. Powerful connections and learning opportunities can be found in the cyberverse. While I remain concerned about how racist organizations and trolls use the internet, I have to acknowledge that online tools and apps have enabled me to maintain much closer relationships—especially internationally—growing my community of support and expanding my learning opportunities and access to resources many times over.

Activists, advocates, and educators are using the internet in thousands of exciting ways. Just think of how hashtags, shared videos, and online platforms have been employed to shed light on racist "Karens" and "Kens," the murders of unarmed Black people by police, missing Native American girls and women, and in amplifying the online voices of creators of color. The internet is paradoxical, an innovative tool that is being used to spread white supremacy and all sorts of other hateful and oppressive ideologies while also providing opportunities to overcome, resources to dismantle, and connections to advance racial and social justice. I don't think of it as an answer, just another space that requires our attention as we continue in the antiracist tradition.

Professional Community

For those seeking to learn from and contribute to the abolitionist/antiracist tradition, professional organizations and conferences are another space where positive community exists. More organizations than ever are focused on equity and inclusion, engaging across sectors in the fight against oppression. They offer opportunities to learn, share experience, collaborate, and develop relationships.

Multiple conferences and professional membership associations provide meaningful PD around antiracism and DEI. The DEOMI and NMCI conferences were the first professional conferences I ever attended. Others include the National Association for Multicultural Education (NAME) conference, where I met the authors and editors of books that I had been studying, including James Banks, Geneva Gay, Carl Grant, Sonia Nieto, and Christine Sleeter. To graduate students focused on multicultural education, they were rock stars—"the big five"—having authored critical texts that were foundational for our studies at the time. I soon learned that these pioneers, who were approachable at the conference and provided advice and guidance to many of us, were just the tip of the iceberg.

The National Conference on Race and Ethnicity (NCORE) continues to be the most focused on antiracism and intersecting oppressions in higher education. Going to NCORE sometimes feels like a family reunion. Opportunities are not always available on our home campuses to gather with large numbers of colleagues who are committed to the work of antiracism, but at NCORE, many of us are able to come together.

My favorite conference of all, the White Privilege Conference (WPC), led by my friend and colleague Dr. Eddie Moore Jr., is laser-focused on antiracism, bringing antiracist activists, advocates, and professionals together across sectors, fields, and communities. Dr. Moore has done extraordinary work as an educator, author, and advocate, and the conference that he and his team have developed over the past twenty-plus years brings it all together. Open to everyone, WPC is a critical forum for building relationships and often offers sessions that challenge even the most experienced antiracists.

Some conferences feel more like a retreat or an intentional community, like Diversity 2000 (D2K). Using open space technology to frame the experience each year allows discussions and sessions to develop more organically than at a traditional conference. With no agenda, no preplanned workshops, and no list of sessions to browse, D2K is an opportunity to address issues deeply, challenge one another, and create the conference that you want to attend while you are attending it. Because it is small by design—usually around forty people—this type of intentional community also provides chances for deeper relationship-building over the years.

My professional community has helped me learn and grow in my work while providing many opportunities to partner with colleagues and develop lifelong friendships. Finding conferences like these, within your own field or community of practice, you will begin to develop your own network of professionals who can provide support, guidance, and information about new thinking, as well as feedback on your work and opportunities to partner. And you may find, as I have, that collaboration can be the foundation for some of your best work.

The Power of Solidarity Across Communities

On a humid morning, in August 2000, I walked across the stage, shook President Humphries's hand, and received my PhD from Florida A&M University. My parents smiled and cheered as I was hooded by my dissertation chair, Dr. Janet Guyden. It was one of those surreal moments that I will never forget. But my feelings of accomplishment and joy did not last long.

By the end of the year, I was depressed, unable to stop thinking about Kacey. Sometimes, I have experienced what I think of as "relapses in coping" with the loss of my brother to suicide. The joy I had experienced brought on guilt, and the loss just felt heavier. As I tried to work through my depression, I wondered if Kacey would have been proud of my accomplishment. Reaching my goals felt hollow without a big bear hug from my brother, and selfish, considering that he never had the opportunities I was enjoying. Escaping into movies or television series sometimes helped, sometimes it helped to play basketball or work out, other times I would just walk on the beach at night and get lost in the sound of the waves.

Sometimes life feels like a bad country song: just a long list of bad things happening to us. None of us get to choose the body, family, community, or culture we are born into. We do not choose where in the world we are born, what language we will learn first, what we look like, or our family's socioeconomic circumstances or educational attainment. Each of these things will have a very real impact on our lives, yet we have no say in the matter. Add to that the fact that life can just be hard. Building and depending on communities of support, both personal and professional, can provide the love, encouragement, and assistance to get us through difficult times. Ultimately, it took my parents and closest friends to pull me out of the depression that followed my graduation from FAMU.

The more privilege we have, the more choices we have. The privileges that I am afforded made it possible for me to make decisions about my life's direction, including my educational path; my inherited privilege also allowed me to miss and even screw up some opportunities on my way to eventually getting some of it right. Racism and other forms of oppression create disparities of opportunity, and it frustrates me when privileged people squander their numerous opportunities while criticizing the choices of people with far fewer options.

Whatever opportunities we may have, building robust and supportive communities helps boost our chances for success. I have held faculty positions, founded a leadership academy, and served as a university diversity officer. I have traveled, lived, worked, and grown my community locally, nationally, and in other countries. I have also experienced the blessings of being an educator, not the least of which has been when former students reach out to let me know that I somehow made a difference in their lives—and that in turn, they have impacted others as teachers, parents, and leaders of all sorts.

My path has been both frustrating and rewarding, but it has always been guided by my core values—and most particularly, by my efforts to oppose racism, in solidarity, across social divides and oppressions. Looking in the mirror each day, as my hairs continue to gray and my athletic body softens into a "dad bod," I take comfort in knowing that I'm doing my best to improve the world that my amazing child and all her young friends will inherit.

Kacey never knew how many people found hope in his spirit, were touched by his kindness, and were taught by his actions. Likewise, you and I will never fully know how much of a difference we make. Yet I remain confident that together we can make very real progress in fighting oppression and injustice. Racism does more harm than most people can imagine or want to believe. Choosing to advance equity and inclusion in how we live our lives matters because it brings us together in unity, favoring and promoting love over hate.

When you speak up or take action to oppose racism, there will almost always be resistance. Sometimes there will be harsh consequences for doing the right thing, and there is no magic shield to protect you. But the community you build—those who will not hesitate to jump down into the hole with you—will lift you up and bring you a type of joy that feels just. In return, you will be fortunate to have opportunities to do the same for them. For me, these experiences of solidarity are among my most cherished memories, because I believe that solidarity is what love looks like in community.

Solidarity is what love looks like in community.

8

CHECK, PLEASE!
Racism as a Deal-Breaker

> *What we need now more than ever is a human rights movement that challenges systemic racism in every single context.*
>
> —OPAL TOMETI

I WAS EXCITED: AN ACQUAINTANCE in Tallahassee had set me up with a friend of theirs, a graduate student at another local university. I had arrived a bit early at the restaurant to say hello to a few FAMU students who worked there. I had no idea what my date looked like, but she told me not to worry, because she had seen me speak at an event.

When my date arrived, she came right over and introduced herself. She had a beautiful smile and bright eyes, and she was white—that became relevant a bit later. Once we were seated, one of the waitstaff came with a menu and told us about the specials. He was a student in one of my classes—a couple more students were peeking over and not so subtly ear-hustling, from behind some potted plants—and assured us that everyone would make sure we had a great meal.

Looking over the menu, we chatted about the restaurant, how awkward first dates can be, and how nice it was that her friend had set us up. She seemed smart, told a couple of funny stories, and was a good conversationalist. Plus, she had a great laugh. I was mostly just trying not to slouch or spill anything on my shirt. So far, it seemed to be going well.

After we ordered our meals, she told me about her experience as a graduate student—her department, her colleagues and classmates, what she was studying—and it seemed like she was enjoying our conversation.

Then she asked why I was doing my doctoral studies at FAMU.

I had a feeling where she was going with this, but I wanted to give her the benefit of the doubt.

Unfortunately, she followed that up with a comment that left no room for mistake. "Aren't you uncomfortable, always being around so many of them?"

I asked her to clarify, and sadly she did, expanding on how she could not imagine being "surrounded" by Black people all day and explaining that she would not feel safe. To top it off, she went on to question FAMU's academic rigor.

When she finally paused to take a breath, I pointed out the racism in what she had said, schooled her on why I was a proud FAMU Rattler, and told her it was time for me to go. She protested, but I was done.

On my way out the door, I could hardly miss the students reacting to the implosion of my date. They had heard pretty much everything and were ready to accidentally spill some food in her lap. We laughed at the idea but agreed it was best to just let her sit there and deal with why the date had ended so abruptly. I learned later that she told them I had left because of an emergency.

When does racist or otherwise hateful behavior become a deal-breaker?

The next day, before class started, the students from the restaurant brought me a to-go container with the exact meal I had missed out on the night before. I chose not to explain the details to the rest of the class, but my lesson plan for the day changed. We proceeded to discuss an important topic: At what point is it okay to say "Check, please!" and give yourself permission to cut off a relationship—old or new—with a bigot?

When does racist or otherwise hateful behavior become a deal-breaker?

Deal-Breakers

Some of the most frequent questions I am asked about living an antiracist life involve relationships. Our relationships with romantic partners, family, friends, and work colleagues are complicated even without the additional complexities brought on by racism. Relationships present some of the most profound challenges to our racial and social justice goals because they tend to be where our commitment is most tested.

There are many facets to our lives. We have roles in our families, friend groups, workplaces, and communities. We are neighbors, members, and consumers. We may be students, parents, or alumni. As adults, we likely have the opportunity to vote and get involved in politics some other way. These and other aspects of how we engage in the world provide daily opportunities to live our antiracist values out loud. In order to contribute to racial justice, we have to be conscious of our vulnerabilities, influence, and impact in all these roles, and thoughtful about our decisions.

In thinking about the different ways that you engage with people and how you can have an antiracist impact, it is important to set clear expectations and establish what constitutes a deal-breaker in any type of relationship. In dating or seeking a partner, for example, there could be any number of deal-breakers: Is the other person rude or self-centered? Do they want (or not want) children as you do? Upon confirming that there are no deal-breakers, you would likely continue exploring a potential relationship. Ultimately, it is about what is important to you. If you are antiracist, then, naturally, racism is not something you would tolerate in your relationships—racism is a deal-breaker.

On more than a few occasions, while working with students and families to provide independent educational opportunities focused on antiracism and racial justice, I have encountered a parent who claims they were unaware of their spouse's racist views and behaviors until after they were married and had children. Some say they have tried to help their partner learn and change. Others acted as though it was just some quirky aspect of their partner's personality that they learned to live with. These types of disclosures are difficult for me to digest. Even for those who are far removed, by choice and privilege, from the impact of racial oppression, it hardly seems possible that racist beliefs and behavior would not be evident prior to the wedding day. More than a red flag, if you claim to be antiracist (or even nonracist, I would think) it should have been a clear deal-breaker.

Anytime I am just getting to know someone, bigotry has always caused me to lose interest in any relationship with that person, unless my role was to educate. The choice to stand against racism and oppression is available, in one way or another, to us all. You simply have to decide what type of behavior, in your perspective, constitutes an impossible barrier to overcome.

But what about once a relationship becomes more serious, or when bias exists in a lifelong relationship you cannot avoid? The answer here may not be so simple.

Perhaps the bottom line is that your opinion should matter to the person on the other end of the relationship, so you should expect willingness from them to address your concerns directly. Once you've pointed out their racist conduct and made your position clear, see how they respond. If they are able to see their bias and commit to working to release it, that could be a sign of potential growth, and perhaps a healthy relationship could continue.

The same is true in reverse. Be clear with people that if you demonstrate a bias, you hope they will help you see the error of your ways as well. If a partner in any type of relationship is not willing or able to address their bias, that may be an insurmountable problem and could, and possibly should, end the relationship.

Antiracist Dating

Most of us have some set of characteristics we tend to be attracted to in a potential partner, whether they make good sense or not. Personally, I have a weakness for a nerdy woman with a good sense of humor, someone who makes me think and has some street smarts—and if she has a raspy voice, all the better—I have no idea why. The red flag would be when racism masquerades as a preference, becoming just another way of saying "whites only."

Employing a white supremacist hierarchy in dating, or in anything else, is obviously racist. For the sake of clarity, I am not saying that it is racist for a white person to be attracted to another white person, but if your "preference" for dating white people is rooted in stereotypes or racial value judgments, that is racist. On the flip side, for example, a non-Asian man's "preference" for dating Asian women can actually be racial fetishization, which is rooted in racist stereotyping. People of color have been sexually fetishized and objectified as a means to minimize their humanity—an example of where intersectional oppressions collide, as racial biases intersect with stereotypes about gender, gender identity, culture, sexual orientation, and other identities.

But antiracism in dating and romantic relationships goes beyond the race of the person you choose to date. It also includes questioning a potential partner's beliefs and behaviors: If you are striving to live an antiracist life, at what point is a person too racist for you to continue to date them, to say no to a proposal, or to call it quits?

Once I saw the disgust in the eyes of my date when she spoke about Black people, I was done. Now, I realize that we are all works in progress, and if she had been a student in one of my classes, I would have been willing to work hard to help her learn and develop an antiracist lens. If she had been a friend or family member—someone who I believed I could get through to—I might have been more tolerant. But I have always been the kind of guy who looks toward the end game, even on a first date. And I certainly cannot see myself thinking about marriage and children with someone whose bigotry is so blatant that it becomes obvious on a first date. I am grateful that it came out quickly, though, before I caught feelings. I just hope that my walking out on her might have caused some reflection.

It tracks that my tolerance level for racism is low, and I admit that I have been quick to unfriend folks both online and in real life. In the past, I have been challenged by friends to realize that my propensity to quickly sever relationships with people who express racist thoughts or beliefs is an example of white privilege: My privilege permits me to ignore the problem at no likely cost to me. By not doing whatever I can to help someone see the racism in their words or deeds, and to encourage change, I am allowing racist behavior to persist without doing my part to address it. This has continued to be one of the most difficult challenges for me—to stay engaged with folks I have no interest in knowing.

To effectively counter racism, it is our responsibility (particularly white folks) to actively oppose racism whenever possible, especially when there exists a relationship or other reason that offers you even a slightly better chance of changing someone's heart and mind. This does not mean you have to dedicate your life to trying to change the mind of every single obstinate racist you meet. But it is our responsibility to make a genuine effort, not to walk away just because they are annoying or frustrating. Once you've done all you can, if success seems unlikely, it may be wise to move on and use your time more productively. Still, you never know when your engagement with someone might help you make an impact.

When it is possible for me to educate or otherwise break through a person's racist perspective, I have learned to accept that responsibility. Friendship and kinship bonds can produce opportunities to be heard in meaningful ways. If I have honestly made my best effort and someone still refuses to examine their racist perspective, I will delete them from my life, but only as a last resort.

I had no hesitation or remorse about exiting that date at the restaurant all those years ago. I would do the same again today. I had no other connection with her, and when it comes to seeking a life partner, bigotry is a deal-breaker for me. When considering a relationship that could lead to sharing my life with someone, the bar has to be higher, especially now that this person could have a role in my child's life. Continuing to build a relationship while hoping that a partner will eventually become antiracist is a risk I'm not willing to take.

Family Ties

As is true for most folks, family is deeply important to me. In some families, as in mine, the history and the web of relationships are complicated. Given our strong ties and deep connections, addressing racism within the ranks without putting our familiar relationships at risk can be tricky. Years ago, in my family, Papa's unwillingness to let go of his racism cost him his relationship with his daughter and his grandkids. There are consequences for opposing racism, which we'll discuss later, but there can also be serious consequences for holding on to your racism. Papa learned that the hard way.

Our families play critical roles in our lives. From the time we are born, they protect, support, teach, and challenge us. For some, *family* means their closest relatives, like parents and siblings. For others, it includes every branch of the family tree, including all the cousins many times removed. *Family* can also mean a chosen family, or those who fill the void left by relatives who are unable or unwilling to be present. Regardless of how we define them, our familial bonds provide us with an unrivaled feeling of security, a sense of home, and a foundation for who we are in the world.

When my brothers and I were growing up, we had a favorite cousin who was a few years older, so we thought he was cool, plus he was seriously funny. Whenever he visited, he always pitched in when there was work to be done—and there was always work to be done. That earned our respect. As we got older, my cousin and I did not see eye to eye on politics, but that did not change his status as my favorite. I never minded sparring about politics because I felt that I knew his heart. Fond memories of how much fun Kacey and I used to have with him caused me to give him the benefit of the doubt more often than I would for someone who was not my favorite cousin.

When the time came for his wedding, Mom was unable to attend, but Dad, B-J, and I were looking forward to it. The entire event, starting with a rehearsal dinner the night before the ceremony, was at a fancy country club. We figured we would do our best to blend in and pretend we enjoyed the fancy food. But during dinner, a friend of the groom told a story that ended with a punchline that relied on the racist trope that Black men are to be feared.

The groom—the favorite cousin—did nothing. He just moved on with the program.

As we squirmed, Dad, who was sitting between us, put his hands on our knees. "This is not the time," he said, looking at me and then B-J.

Everyone who knew us looked uncomfortable and tried not to make eye contact with us. But it felt like their discomfort was less about the racist story and more about their concern that we might make a scene.

So we sat there quietly, among all those white folks—aside from the waitstaff. We had never expected a lot of diversity at his wedding. After all, he was a Republican, and his friend group looked like the Republican Party. Although he had grown up in a predominantly Black city, his friends that we'd met were almost all white, but we had always made the excuse that he went to a mostly white private school—even though we didn't know if it really was—and that he had moved around a lot. But I realized I could no longer give my cousin a pass, regardless of all the fond memories.

I was so angry at myself. That night was a wake-up call, but the signs had been there all along: My favorite cousin was in the nonracist camp—never overtly racist, but tolerant of racism—and I had given him a pass all these years. Two questions hit me: How could he be Kacey's cousin *and* be okay with racism? And what did giving him a pass say about my commitment to antiracism?

My cousin apologized to us and tried to explain it away. I think he may have even made his friend apologize to us—not to everyone present, of course, because no one else was really bothered. In fact, most of the guests seemed to enjoy the story, especially those who had obviously heard it before. I do not remember the actual wedding day, or if we even attended; it was all overshadowed by how painful that evening had been. I remember Dad saying, "That would have broken Kacey's heart." And it broke our hearts too.

Because of our family bond, the wedding experience was not exactly a deal-breaker, although it came awfully close. While the relationship with my cousin did not end, it changed, at least from my perspective. I appreciated that he understood the story was problematic, and I do believe that he learned something from the experience. We hardly ever talk or see each other, but I do wonder if he is teaching his children to be nonracist, or if he has taken a more antiracist approach. Truth is, I have not done my part to stay engaged—an example of my own imperfect antiracism.

As many challenges as there are with family, there are even more opportunities. I have seen deep divides within families over racism, but I have also seen extraordinary learning occur when someone has taken the risk to plant seeds of antiracism. I saw this recently within the family of a friend. My friend is white, and she has had the same best friend since college—more than twenty-five years—and that friend is African American. My friend's family has always treated her friend well, but initially her parents thought of her as an exception. They would make comments to their daughter that her friend was different from other Black folks, or that they didn't see her as Black. Of course, making her the exception allowed them to hold on to their stereotypes and racial bias.

My friend had a very difficult conversation with her parents after it became evident to her that this was a problem. From then on, not only have her parents changed what they have said, but over the years they have worked to educate themselves and actively discuss this and related issues with their daughter, and eventually with her friend as well. My friend made the effort to engage in a difficult conversation—multiple actually—with her parents about race and let them know that she needed them to change. Their relationship with their daughter mattered enough for them to stay engaged rather than dismissing her concerns, and then to make the effort to learn and change their perspective.

We tend to try harder and make more allowances with family because most of us are taught that family comes first. They are our first teachers, and family members tend to share core values. My parents were intentional about antiracism and racial justice being core values, although they did not use those terms. They were the ones who planted the seeds, and they also had to establish deal-breakers. Knowing that they worked to establish those core values and that they sacrificed relationships when they felt it was necessary made me respect them even more.

Some of the most important decisions that parents make are about who is allowed to spend time with their children, particularly when those children are very young. Exposing kids to people who hold racist beliefs, including beloved family members, can have a dangerous impact on any child's learning, self-image, and socialization. I make the effort to include family and close friends and their children in Mak's life as much as possible, even across great distances. I simply do not include those family members who do not share our antiracist and otherwise inclusive values.

Addressing these concerns in the context of familial relationships is complicated. So much of family life is. Still, establishing antiracism as a norm in our homes and as an expectation of anyone who we allow to spend time with our children is a must.

Friendship

It may be less obvious how antiracism is relevant to your social life, but, without a doubt, it is. Just as antiracist dating is a thing, there are opportunities for antiracism in socializing, choosing our friends, and even as a sports fan.

Like many people, I consider my close friends to be the family members I get to choose. I love and value each of my friends, for many different reasons. They are the walking and talking history of my life choices, holding memories that I cherish and, of course, some that I might like everyone to forget. As I get older, some of my favorite moments are sharing funny stories and good memories with friends, particularly stories that include loved ones who are no longer with us. For me, sharing those beloved memories helps to keep loved ones' spirits alive long after they have passed.

Because we value our friends and our shared histories, we often grant friends some of the same leeway as family when it comes to their behavior. Every friend group has one or two difficult relationships, but we tend to give those people grace because they are part of a group and shared memories that are meaningful to us. But friends are different from family for the very reason that our circles of friends are based on our own choices. You did not get to choose your racist aunt or your homophobic cousin, but you chose your friends. Perhaps some were chosen for you because of family connections when you were a child but remember: You have chosen to keep them around.

Because I am outspoken on issues of racial justice, it is exceedingly rare that a friend would spout off something overtly racist in my presence. But friends have made uninformed and racist comments related to current events—like shortly after 9/11, when I heard a friend make racist comments about Arab Muslims. This friend was someone I would have described as antiracist and part of a circle that included my dear friend from college, Joya, whose hope that her father was still alive in the rubble of the World Trade Center turned to despair, and then mourning. I understood and shared my friend's anger but recognized that it had become misguided to put blame on all Arab Muslims because of rhetoric absorbed from media coverage.

Sometimes our anger needs somewhere to go, and racism is often a tempting route for directing that anger. Consider who that serves, though, and to what end. In this case, I confronted my friend about the comments coming across as racist. My initial attempt was met with indignation and the accusation that I was siding with terrorists. I could see that our conversation was not going in a good direction. I left it by just focusing on the heartbreaking death of Joya's father, making it clear that I understood the gravity of the situation.

My friend and I did not see each other for a while. When I got a call about a month later, I was unsure what to expect. We talked guardedly about other things until my friend steered the conversation to our conflict, saying, "Thanks for checking me. I don't know what I was thinking. It wouldn't be fair to condemn me, as a white Christian, for all the evil that supposedly Christian KKK members do."

We were good after that. My friend now sees my challenge as the act of someone who cares about them.

Of course, it does not always go the way you hope. I have lost friends over issues of racial and social justice. People's perspectives change over time, and not always for the better. Friendships evolve, and some come to an end. Precisely because we value our friendships, however, it is worth making the effort to address potential deal-breakers like racism as they emerge. Because your friends value and trust you, you may be in a good position to help them avoid going down an unjust path. These conversations are always difficult, but it is often only a trusted friend who can get through. I believe it is our responsibility to try.

You have the power to have a positive influence among your friends with respect to racial justice. Likewise, your choice of friends sends a message to those influenced by your example. As a parent, I also think we have a responsibility to note that who our friends are, and what they say and do, can have an impact on our children. Think twice before you expose your children, or anyone else who looks to you as an example, to friends who express racist and other bigoted beliefs. I don't mean hide them; I mean try your best to help them change, and if that doesn't work, say goodbye. These hateful attitudes could influence what your child believes about themself and others—not to mention what they will come to believe about you for harboring friends with such attitudes.

I encourage you to consider how you address challenging issues with friends. As in any relationship, there are lines that cannot be crossed without consequences for the friendship. How have you, or how would you, address racism within your friend groups? Where is the line regarding racial justice that, if crossed, will cause you to end a friendship?

> *Where is the line regarding racial justice that, if crossed, will cause you to end a friendship?*

Choices at School

I encourage us all to show up in support of those living their antiracist lives as educators. As students (or as parents of students or as local community members), once we understand the role our educational institutions play in perpetuating racist views and systems, it becomes critical that we support those antiracist educators in actively promoting accurate and inclusive education, beginning in early childhood. Schools and universities comprise a lot of moving parts, and a variety of different interests are at work. Being aware of those interests and keeping an informed eye on key indicators that may deserve praise or calls for concern is essential.

My website and others list resources that provide more detail on assessing your school or university around racial justice and inclusive excellence. I encourage you to use the latest resources that are available. It is our responsibility as students—and as parents, educators, and members of the larger community—to hold our educational institutions to a higher standard. That standard includes the expectation that our schools both teach and practice antiracism and inclusive excellence.

We must expect—and when necessary, demand—that our school boards or boards of trustees make every effort to be diverse and inclusive.

How much exposure to racism in our education is acceptable before we decide to speak up, vote differently, or choose to study elsewhere?

The same goes for our expectations for a diverse faculty that employs equitable teaching practices and teaches an inclusive and antiracist curriculum. Administrations must be held to account for all aspects of the educational experience, from who is represented on the walls to ensuring the highest possible graduation rates for *all* students.

When racist and oppressive campaigns do threaten our school campuses, we must be willing to counter them with constructive resistance. This resistance could take many forms, from organizing walkouts and protests to running for election to the school board or as a trustee. As we learn and engage more with our schools and institutions of higher learning, we must ask ourselves: How much exposure to racism in our education is acceptable before we decide to speak up, vote differently, or choose to study elsewhere?

Justice at Work

Antiracism is obviously relevant in the workplace, and our interaction with colleagues over time will almost certainly provide opportunities to promote equity and inclusion. As part of your job responsibilities, perhaps you impact who gets hired, promoted, or mentored. If you have a critical ear, you likely have overheard or been part of a conversation at work that exposed racial insensitivity, bias, or discrimination in the workplace. Knowing how to address these concerns is anything but simple, particularly considering the web of power dynamics in the workplace.

Doing anything you can to shut down racist comments may be a start, but when those comments could influence systems—whether hiring and promotions, research and development, or something else—the challenge becomes more complicated. Given these complexities, it may be difficult to know how best to raise your voice to promote change.

Of course, reverting to strategic white ignorance is a much easier path. In fact, often we are rewarded for ignoring racism, pretending not to notice racial injustice, or making excuses for racial disparities. For white people, this is understood as the path to continued white privilege. For those people of color who choose to look the other way, their collusion with systemic racism is often rewarded by recognition as one of the "good ones" and possibly a measure of access to some privilege scraps—though still less than their white counterparts.

We can examine countless possible scenarios to determine when to raise our voices in opposition to racism or to promote racial justice in the workplace. Do you raise your voice when you recognize racial microaggressions at your social club? Do you raise concerns when you see that a candidate pool at your workplace lacks any racial diversity? How about when you recognize disparities in how students are disciplined at your school?

Racial inequities, exclusion, and injustice can be found in any field or sector of work. We may notice disparities in hiring, promotion, salaries, issues related to the impact of the organization on communities, and how products and services either advance or oppose racism. Ultimately, raising the concern is a critical first step. Once racial bias is identified in the workplace, it is our responsibility to consider the potential impact and address both the initial concern and the potential areas of systemic corruption in order to find a path for change.

As in other aspects of our lives, antiracism in our work life is about decision-making. Weighing the risks and the probability of success against our personal and professional integrity, we must decide how much oppression is too much. How much racism are we willing to tolerate in the workplace? For many, this question trips a defense mechanism and opens a tiny escape hatch based on the idea that it will not matter if they speak up—a clear example of nonracist avoidance. The truth is, inaction directly supports systemic racism. More than anything else, in fact, the inaction of nonracists is what enables systemic racism to persist.

Of course, powerful forms of resistance are in place, which protect systems corrupted by racism in the workplace. This is why we need to report concerns over things we see and hear and support colleagues who speak up and work to create change. Reporting an incident of concern with respect to racial equity and inclusion may not produce immediate results, and may cause fear of retribution, but it can be helpful in finding a pattern of systemic bias. This is a critical piece of the proverbial puzzle: By identifying paths for potential bias, we can address interpersonal and systemic opportunities for change.

Ideally, promoting antiracism at work would also include taking more of a macro-view of the changes required in how we expect our businesses to behave. Currently, our society allows (even promotes) predatory capitalism, which measures success by only one metric: profit. This system remains centered on maximizing profits for investors, owners, and executives, whose goal is to keep expenses as low as possible—including what is paid to workers—and to charge consumers as much as possible for goods and services. This is the modern-day manifestation of a plantation approach to business.

The truth is, inaction directly supports systemic racism. More than anything else, in fact, the inaction of nonracists is what enables systemic racism to persist.

Some free enterprise models measure success differently, through a "triple bottom line"—considering shared profit, stewardship of the planet, and socioeconomic justice for all people involved and impacted. With this model, the rising tide of corporate profits could actually serve to lift all boats. Call me idealistic, but I am interested in creating shared wealth, not maintaining a small group of billionaires (soon to be trillionaires) on the backs of billions of us working for as little as they can get away with paying us.

If you are having a reaction to my comparison of predatory capitalism to the plantation model, or the idea that profit should be shared and not hoarded, I will ask you to take a breath. Consider where your discomfort is coming from and who you serve by supporting our current version of capitalism.

We value the idea that capitalism is fair competition and based on skill, intelligence, and hard work—this is drilled into us in school and through the media. We are taught to believe that we live in a meritocracy. However, the starting line is not the same for all of us. Some have a very real head start. Significant advantages are afforded to those with generational wealth and access to education, networks, and opportunities. It is also true that, in addition to the challenges we all face, systemic biases place hurdles and barriers in the paths of people of color and other marginalized groups. This works to maintain power structures for those with generational advantages. In other words, we don't live in anything even remotely resembling a meritocracy.

The insightful author Minda Harts writes what I have heard countless times from friends and colleagues of color: "I was under the assumption that every hard-working employee would have equal opportunity to advance; little did I know that this whole meritocracy thing was a sham. I had to do my job in addition to jumping through so many hoops, kissing a lot of babies, and performing at a level that would make me stand out, but some of my white colleagues could do the bare minimum and reap the benefits."[1]

In the US, and increasingly around the world, we are taught to respect, and even idolize, the rich, but how a person became wealthy is almost always left unexamined. The roots of capitalism, particularly in the US, are in profiting off the hard work of the exploited and enslaved. That wealth did not disappear, by the way, when slavery was outlawed; it was passed on and built upon. The system of profiting from the labor of others also did not go away; it adapted. So, if we genuinely value the idea of a meritocracy, we will need to work toward that becoming a reality, which will take significant change to our current economic system and way of doing business.

Large-scale change in the workplace will require us to raise our voices in unison and vote for those who will change relevant tax, finance, and other business-related laws. It will also require a shift in how we define success for ourselves, our businesses, and our nation. As with any large-scale change, though, it all begins with seemingly small first steps. If a candidate or official up for reelection resists taxing those who benefit most from predatory capitalism—deal-breaker—vote for someone better; if a business you frequent is shown to have racist or exploitative practices—deal-breaker—find a competitor to support; and if you are an entrepreneur or business leader looking for a vendor or partner and you find that a business does not employ equitable and inclusive practices—deal-breaker—find someone else to work with.

Consumer Choice

As consumers, we make decisions every day that have the potential to support or oppose racism in many ways. Consider what happens when we eat out at a restaurant: We are interacting with a business that hires, promotes, and fires people, and our meal is made possible by someone's labor. The practices of whoever supplies the food matter, too, and those suppliers work with other businesses along the product chain that provide all sorts of services to them. Although we may feel as though we're innocently eating our meal, we are supporting the practices of all these businesses, and their respective practices.

How much exploitation would it take for you to stop supporting a business? You could be doing business with a company whose practices support environmental racism, or you could choose their competitor that practices inclusive sustainability. Your decisions matter.

Check, Please!

On one end of the supply-and-demand model is the consumer. We are all consumers to some degree. Most of us do not produce much of what we need to survive, so companies provide goods and services. They also use very sophisticated and targeted marketing to get us to buy whatever they produce. From personalized ads on social media to influencers, celebrities, and athletes who are paid to wear or promote products, companies will do anything to get us to buy their goods and services.

We purchase what we need. The basics for living—food, water, clothing, shelter, health care—all cost money in a capitalist society like ours. We also purchase things we don't really need, all of which presents us with bills, of course, but also with opportunities and power.

> *How much exploitation would it take for you to stop supporting a business?*

The power of the consumer to support, disrupt, or even end a business was made clear to me at an early age, when I learned about boycotts after making the mistake of admiring a particular German-made car. My mother told me in no uncertain terms that she believed that no self-respecting Jew would buy a Mercedes, BMW, Audi, or Volkswagen. She explained the role that many powerful German automotive companies and other businesses (pharmaceutical companies, banks, etc.) played during the Holocaust.[2] I knew if she so much as saw me riding in a car made by one of those companies, she would be disappointed, and for a kid like me, the last thing I wanted to do was disappoint Mom.

I chose my mother's respect, and my own self-respect, of course. Having done my research, I have chosen to follow Mom's lead on this. Once, I even called my mother for permission, and forgiveness, when I was in desperate need of a ride in South Africa and the only option I could find was a Mercedes taxi. We joked about it, but part of me still feels bad about getting in that cab.

Some automotive and other companies have admitted, long after the fact, their involvement with the Nazi government and profiting from the labor of enslaved Jews. A few have provided modest reparations. Others continue to hide how they benefited from their complicity in the murder of millions, all in the name of white supremacy and anti-Semitism. The issue is complicated, because many auto companies have gone international and become part of large conglomerates, and the same is true of other companies who benefited from doing business with the Nazi regime.

As a Jewish person, I am not interested in supporting any people or companies who sympathized with or profited from doing business with the Nazis, no matter how long ago. But in the interest of solidarity, taking this stance is not so easy as just saying I will not buy certain German cars. The same types of collusion were carried out by banks, insurance companies, and other businesses that were built on profits from the triangular slave trade, the attempted genocide and subsequent displacement of Native Americans, and the many colonial and genocidal atrocities that have been perpetrated around the world.

Businesses built on systemic racism are not a thing of the past. Many businesses and business executives have openly supported the overtly racist Donald Trump and his MAGA movement. As a result, many people will no longer support those businesses, including me. Not having the business of a single person may not matter, but I am not alone. Boycotts have had a cumulative impact on business reputations, stock values, and, in some cases, profits.

One example from the Latinx community was a protest of Goya Foods due to their CEO Robert Unanue's support of Donald Trump after he had made offensive statements regarding Latinx people and immigration. One of the boycotters was someone I'm very close to, Francesca Lozada, a proud Puerto Rican woman born and raised in the Bronx. Her pantry used to look like the shelves at her local bodega—stocked full of Goya products—but that changed rapidly. Goya, whose primary customer base is Latinx, tried to distance the company from Unanue's vocal support of then president, Trump. Still, he remained CEO, and for Francesca, that was a deal-breaker. The impact on sales is unclear since Goya is a privately held company, but the board of directors reportedly put a "full stop" to their own CEO speaking with the press about politics or the company. If nothing else, Goya lost a very loyal customer, and she wasn't the only one.[3]

Economic boycotts have had a very real impact on the way corporations do business. Many have realized that their internal practices and impact on communities matter to consumers and have accordingly made changes. The cynical view is that they only make whatever changes they have to in order not to lose money but, regardless of their motives, their responsiveness to consumers can make a difference.

When it comes to wielding our power as consumers concerned with racial and social justice, there are many concerns to be addressed and multiple options available for taking a stand. Those who are able to make a large purchase, like buying a home, can potentially make a significant statement.

How do you make the decision about buying a home with an antiracist lens?

Housing in the US is fraught with racist history, and in many ways, not a lot has changed. Redlining is not formalized anymore but is now accomplished in more informal and subtle ways. The results are evident in the housing segregation that endures and in racially discriminatory practices still used today: real estate companies steering buyers to neighborhoods that reflect their perceived racial identities; the use of racially biased school rating systems; and employing coded language like "good" and "safe" neighborhoods, which translates not to places with less crime, but to places with fewer people of color. These practices still exist and impact home values and continue to contribute to ongoing segregation in many neighborhoods.

As someone who appreciates diversity, I prefer to live in neighborhoods where I see a multitude of cultures—people of different racial and ethnic backgrounds and local businesses run by and catering to all sorts of folks. But the truth is, it's difficult to find a diverse neighborhood in the US because of centuries of racist housing practices, which boil down to the decisions made by each of us about where we want to live and who we want as neighbors. The trend in recent decades has seen white people moving into less expensive areas, bringing financial investments that end up forcing out local residents who cannot afford increases in rent and other living expenses. This gentrification has a racist impact, even where the motivations may be relatively well-meaning.

We can all be more intentional about supporting companies recognized for equitable, inclusive, and sustainable practices.

So, where do you choose to buy a home? Which real estate company do you engage, and where do you send your children to school? These are relevant questions when you are committed to opposing the racially discriminatory practices that surround real estate, school districting, and educational access.

In every financial decision we make, from shopping at certain stores to buying a home, we support the company that provides us with a product or service. When organizations engage in racially discriminatory practices or support racist politicians, your decision to strengthen those companies with your dollars is essentially making a financial contribution to white supremacy. That is a heavy statement, but a true one: The world still runs on financial transactions, large and small.

The good news is, plenty of online resources provide information about the social, economic, and environmental impact of most large companies, so you can do your research and feel good about your choices. When we do our best to be well-informed consumers, we can make a collective impact on how business is done. We can all be more intentional about supporting companies recognized for equitable, inclusive, and sustainable practices.

Voting Your Values

Every time we donate to a candidate or political party, volunteer for a campaign, or vote (or choose not to vote), we make a statement about racial justice. Racist, nonracist, or antiracist positions, taken on a variety of issues by candidates or political office holders, have real-world implications. Government policies on housing, taxes, health care, immigration, the justice system, education, campaign finance reform, policing, military spending and actions, and many other issues have direct racial and social justice impacts. Holding our political representatives responsible is among our most important duties—and opportunities—in the fight against racism.

One important lesson from the Trump presidency is that approximately half of the US American electorate was, at least, willing to overlook racist positions and policies advanced by his administration. The ongoing attacks on DEI continue through what has become Trump's Republican Party. His hateful comments and actions, both as a candidate and during his presidency, were so overt and such an integral part of his campaign that no one could say they were unaware. People who either consciously embraced his bigotry or were willing to overlook it—and those who simply did not care enough to vote against him—elected an openly racist and otherwise bigoted person to the US presidency, and now he is looking to return to power.

The scope of the problem is not news to those of us who have been doing antiracism work. Racism did not disappear when Lincoln signed the Emancipation Proclamation, or on Juneteenth, or when the Jim Crow system was dismantled, or even when President Obama was elected. While legal action has caused some positive change over the decades, it has not changed the minds of at least half of us about race—and now millions of our fellow citizens are so invested in their privilege scraps that they refuse to believe all the evidence that Trump lost the 2020 election to President Joe Biden, fair and square. We remain a nation divided over white supremacy and racism, the same as we have been since any of us were born, and even before the colonizers inked the US Constitution.

Biden, too, has a problematic history with respect to racism, but that wasn't a deal-breaker for the Democratic Party, despite alternatives that included more progressive candidates, including candidates of color. To be fair, President Biden has progressed in his views and has worked to become more antiracist. For me, it is important to not only promote change but to appreciate it when it happens. Racism today is not owned by Republicans alone, but they have certainly embraced it, and they currently count white supremacists as a core constituency of their base.

Too many US Americans convince themselves that voting for the same political party preferred by the Ku Klux Klan, skinheads, and the Proud Boys does not mean anything. They act as if a preference for a political party is no different from their preference for an ice-cream flavor. This could not be further from the truth.

Membership in a political party or voting for a candidate for office from that party connects us to the organization's beliefs and behaviors. No political candidate is perfect, and often we dislike at least one thing about every candidate in the race. But we choose to vote for one of them anyway—perhaps as "the lesser of two evils." Instead of voting for a mediocre candidate who promises to mildly oppose racist policy, we are actually voting against a worse candidate who promises to reverse progress on racial justice, put racist judges on the Bench, or advance regressive policies designed to deepen racial inequities and limit established freedoms.

Many people who vote for racist candidates claim they will be better for the economy. What I hear is the belief that the economy is racist, so a racist candidate will be good for business. If we look at Trump, who lowered taxes on the wealthy to the detriment of the rest of us, many of those who voted for him—poor and working-class white folks—voted against their own financial interest and that of their loved ones. Trump did not work in the best interest of the majority of white people who put him in office. Yet record numbers voted for him in 2020 because they did not like the positions of the Democratic candidates on social issues. In other words, they voted against their own pocketbook to avoid supporting the idea that

Black lives matter and that white supremacy should be evicted from the White House. Trump voters, in huge numbers, made a statement that they were willing to hurt themselves financially in order to oppose racial justice and hold tight to their privilege scraps.

Then there are the voters who understand and agree that racism is not a good thing but still vote for racist candidates because of their stances against abortion, gun control, or taxes. So, in addition to overtly racist voters, there are also a significant number of nonracist voters for whom a racist candidate is just not a deal-breaker.

So, ask yourself: How overtly racist does a candidate have to be to lose my vote?

Our votes are political power, which impacts decisions made on local, national, and international levels. Its implications range from what is taught (or excluded) in our local schools, how we address racism in policing, how we make decisions about military engagements against racially minoritized peoples, and hundreds of other important issues. Given the implications, we must consider how much of a priority we place on racial and social justice as voters.

Becoming Global Citizens

As travel, international business, and social media continue to expand our access to one another, our world has become more intricately connected. Our interconnectedness comes with a wide variety of socioeconomic consequences, both positive and negative. The global COVID-19 pandemic demonstrated how a virus can spread across the entire planet faster than ever. The same can be said of business practices, innovations, and ideas.

As global citizens, we make choices about who we connect with, where we go, and how we get there. Whether virtually (for those of us who have access to social media) or in person (for those of us who can afford international travel), we have increasing opportunities to journey within and between nations and to develop relationships across distances, cultures, and borders. All these opportunities also allow for sharing information and misinformation.

Social media adds a new layer to existing friendships, and also provides opportunities to connect with people who we might not have the chance to meet off-line. Through social media, our decisions can be amplified and influence the choices others make as well. This is particularly true for influencers with large online followings, but when a friend or family member makes a recommendation, it tends to hold even more weight.

For those of us with the privilege of expanding our experiences and friend circles through travel, there are multiple opportunities to make antiracist choices. For example, we are consumers when we travel. We purchase airline, train, or bus tickets or, if we drive, fuel and car services. We typically have to pay for a place to stay. We might partake in some tourist activities, eat out, or do some shopping. Having grown up in a family business, I always advocate shopping with locally owned mom-and-pop shops both close to home and when I travel. As travel consumers, we can educate ourselves, particularly about the larger-ticket items, and make choices to do business with more equity-minded companies and businesses that benefit local communities. Conversely, we can also decide not to do business with airlines, hotels, restaurants, and other businesses that have demonstrated white supremacist ideologies through racist practices.

Checking someone for a racist comment or racially offensive behavior while on vacation is another way to exercise your commitment to antiracism. When some people travel—and US Americans certainly are no exception—their privilege and biases often show. Perhaps they expect no consequences for their behavior because they are away from home—like online trolls, but in real life. And sometimes there are none: Bad behavior from tourists is often tolerated because of their financial impact on local communities or in the name of hospitality. People in the travel, tourism, and hospitality industries bend over backward to ensure that guests are happy, and often that means that they put up with racist and otherwise offensive behavior.

Unfortunately, white supremacy is one of our most potent exports, spread all over the world by tourists, corporations, and our government's actions, as well as "expats." The term "expats" is what white folks call themselves when they live outside their home country instead of "immigrants," kind of like how they used to call themselves "settlers" instead of "colonizers." In all of these capacities, those who carry white supremacist ideologies and racist practices tend to spread them like a virus.

When I feel obliged to check white US Americans for their racist behavior while traveling abroad, they are usually quite surprised, as though I'm breaking some sort of white travelers' code; I guess they expect me to show solidarity with fellow white folks traveling abroad. When white people make racist remarks or inside jokes while traveling that belittle the people of color around us, there is pressure not to interrupt anyone's good time, because everyone is just trying to enjoy their time abroad. But that does not change the impact of racist statements or behaviors—or our responsibility to speak up.

What happens outside our borders matters as much as what happens back home. Being on a trip does not come with a free pass to spread bigotry, or to take a break from living your values. Don't forget to pack your antiracist, anti-oppression lens when you travel, and make decisions based on what you know to be right, not what you can get away with. Deal-breakers shouldn't take a vacation just because you do.

> *Don't forget to pack your antiracist, anti-oppression lens when you travel.*

Reclaiming Philanthropy

Most of us are never referred to as "philanthropists," but I think more of us should be. That term is usually reserved for obscenely wealthy people, many of whom donate in order to see their names engraved on plaques and buildings, or to appear to care about something that they got caught not caring about, or to just dodge more taxes. To be fair, I'm sure that some of the giving by wealthy folks is for respectable reasons. However, I don't believe that their giving should be valued more, particularly because those of us with far more modest bank accounts give at least as much, relative to our income, than those praised so publicly for their generosity. Why shouldn't generous people at all income levels be recognized for their philanthropy? Given that there *are* generous people at all income levels, we should be intentional about our philanthropic endeavors, no matter how modest. Many charities, nonprofit organizations, schools, and museums rely heavily on the accumulation of small gifts. Collectively, small donations made online are becoming a major stream of donations for political campaigns and social movements as well. Every donation matters, so we should recognize the potential for our giving to promote racial justice and be clear about deal-breakers for our philanthropic giving.

When you donate money that is not earmarked for a particular purpose, it is called an "unrestricted donation," which means there are no limits on how the money can be spent. Unrestricted donations are valuable to their recipients, but you have no say in how they are used.

If you would like to ensure that your donation is used to support racial equity, inclusion, and justice, let the organization know that you would like to restrict your donation accordingly.

Big-money donors often dictate where and how they want their money spent. This is called a "restricted donation." If you donate to a university, for example, you can earmark your donation for a particular scholarship fund or to be put toward the purchase of more books by authors of color for the library. You can also choose specific books and send them as what is called an "in-kind" donation. If you would like to ensure that your donation is used to support racial equity, inclusion, and justice, let the organization know that you would like to restrict your donation accordingly.

As antiracist philanthropists, we can seek out options for giving with intention. As a donor, you have the right to earmark funds for a specific purpose or to restrict your donation to certain types of initiatives. Deal-breakers are avoided by determining what your donation must be used for prior to making your contribution. Whether you are an alumnus giving back to a school or university, a donor to an international nonprofit, or contributing to a local museum, make it clear that your money comes with strings attached, the same way that big donors do.

Breaking Our Silence

Antiracism is rooted in a fundamental opposition to oppression in all its manifestations. It would be hypocritical to oppose racism while supporting sexism, or while claiming neutrality in the struggle against heterosexism. If you want to fight oppression, then oppression of any sort becomes a deal-breaker.

Solidarity in opposition to all forms of oppression deepens our credibility and is the most important key to making sustainable progress. Intersectionality illuminates how oppressions are connected and how each is fortified by the next. This is why no singular anti-oppression movement can fully succeed without solidarity in opposition to other oppressions. This is how we counter the divide-and-conquer strategy for maintaining power through oppression.

Our progress toward social justice is about the math. We get closer to justice for us all as our deal-breakers merge, as we break our silences, and as our support across social divides grows

If you want to fight oppression, then oppression of any sort becomes a deal-breaker.

in numbers. For example, as a Jew, I cannot expect our society to eradicate anti-Semitism unless we also join in opposition to racism, sexism, and other oppressions. This brings to mind the well-known confession of German pastor Martin Niemöller, lamenting his own complicity and the cowardice shown by his fellow Germans who chose not to stand against the Nazis:

> *First they came for the socialists, and I did not speak out—*
> *Because I was not a socialist.*
>
> *Then they came for the trade unionists, and I did not speak out—*
> *Because I was not a trade unionist.*
>
> *Then they came for the Jews, and I did not speak out—*
> *Because I was not a Jew.*
>
> *Then they came for me—and there was no one left to speak for me.*[4]

In this, and far too many other cases, a critical mass chose a neutral stance, claiming not to support the oppressors but also choosing to do nothing about their rise to power. By choosing to be bystanders, they enabled atrocities.

The nonracist stance too many of us take today reflects that fatal neutrality. I do not make this comparison lightly. Neo-Nazis and other white supremacists are increasing their representation and power in Washington, DC, in state and local school boards and government, and in police and military forces. They have strategically cultivated power in these same ways in other parts of the world as well. Many of us oppose them, and our numbers are increasing, but there are still far too many who have chosen not to take Niemöller's cautionary reflections to heart.

Niemöller listed what he knew were wrongs, but notes that they were not deal-breakers until it was too late. While he was not targeted, he remained silent. What if we were to replace the groups named by Niemöller with examples from our current circumstances in the US?

When they beat Matthew Shepard to death, was that a deal-breaker,
or did you remain silent because you are not gay?

When they came for Trayvon Martin and Tamir Rice, did you speak up,
or make excuses because your children were safe?

When they came for Mike Brown and Sandra Bland and George Floyd and Breonna Taylor, did you take up the cause,
or did you blame the victims because you are not Black?

When they took out Heather Heyer, in Charlottesville, did you step up,
or remain silent because you were not an antiracist?

When people of Asian heritage were attacked as COVID-19 scapegoats, did you act,
or did you look the other way because you are not Asian?

When police officers were killed during the insurrection at the Capitol, did you disavow the failed coup,
or did you minimize it to suit your politics?

When they enacted laws restricting voting rights, did you call for securing the vote for all,
or did you stay quiet because your right to vote is secure?

A truly comprehensive list of the deal-breakers we should have heeded begins with the colonization of the Americas, continues through attempted genocide, and includes deaths from the middle passage and slavery, the Civil War, lynching, and so on. What if the list were global? Humanity has a lot to atone for. But we can choose to be honest with ourselves about our past, address our current challenges head-on, and ensure a better future for generations to come.

Being firm in our deal-breakers and standing in solidarity against wrongs even when they do not impact us directly could become the norm. Regardless of our social standing or level of privilege, there are choices each of us can make to contribute in our own way, in service to equity, inclusion, and justice.

This is not a naive proposition. It is based in history, reflecting how every global shift, good or bad, has happened. It has to begin somewhere, and the truth is that the struggle against oppression began long ago. We have the choice to join the struggle, decide where to make our stand, bring increased solidarity to bear, and use our voices to advance change. When we finally reach critical mass, our effort to do better will shift the world away from systems of privilege and oppression. We could reach the tipping point that changes our collective direction toward equity, inclusion, and justice for all of us sooner if more of us are willing to raise our voices.

From my perspective, solidarity is most possible when we can see one another as family. When you see a video of another Black child murdered by police, imagine your own child in their place, and I believe you will find motivation.

The next time you hear about another Indigenous woman being sexually assaulted and found murdered, imagine that was your sister or your mother, and I hope you will feel the need to act.

And when people taking peacefully to the streets ask us to see that they are being violently oppressed because of the color of their skin, imagine that you or a loved one could be next, and I expect you will be ready to stand up.

If your empathy is based on whether you think you are immediately vulnerable to the same fate as someone else being excluded, oppressed, or killed, then I implore you to heed Pastor Niemöller's words. None of us are exempt from one day being caught in the crosshairs of intersecting oppressions. From my perspective, it seems prudent to act now.

9

KILLED, FIRED, CANCELED
Being Prepared for Backlash

If you don't stick to your values when they are being tested, they're not values; they're hobbies.

—JON STEWART

I HAVE BEEN FIRED FOR doing my job well, hated on for speaking up against blatant racism, and called "race traitor," "reverse racist," and all sorts of things outside my given name. I have been assaulted verbally and physically, lost opportunities, and been sued. I have been accused of hating myself, hating all white people, and being a self-hating Jew. I feel like I've heard it all, but some inventive bigot is always out there working on a brand-new way to insult me or anyone else who opposes their precious white supremacy or threatens their privilege scraps.

I have also been assaulted by police at protests, and my home was even shot up once. Luckily, none of us were home at the time. You never become comfortable with the potential for negative responses or threats of violence, but I have become somewhat accustomed to it. Even when speaking loudly, though, I am at less risk than a lot of my friends of color when they are simply driving home after work. So, I try to keep it all in perspective.

I was recently honored to serve on a panel at the National Association of Diversity Officers in Higher Education (NADOHE) conference titled "When Free Speech Isn't Free: Navigating Risk and Harm in Institutional Response to Palestine-Israel." As my distinguished colleagues and I prepared for our session over the preceding months, I received numerous warnings of the potential backlash. University presidents have come under fire over their handling of protests and statements they have made on the situation. Knowing that I advise college and university presidents and diversity officers, well-wishers were concerned about my livelihood and even my safety.

None of this was new to me. Although our panel raised concerns that some may see as controversial regarding settler colonialism, oppression, and genocide, it was very well received and brought critical insights to the ongoing discourse. So, from my perspective, it turned out to be worth the risk.

At other times, I have experienced far more negative reactions. When I have publicly shared stories about Kacey, recalling fond memories, good times and bad, what I learned growing up as his brother, and how we lost him, I have received some intense responses. I believe that most of the feedback, even some that is difficult to hear, comes from a place of love and a desire to push us all to do better. But not all of it.

Sometimes people who are stuck in their racism threaten and insult me at a distance or from behind a keyboard. Others have criticized my parents for adopting Kacey, declared that Kacey's soul is burning because he committed a sin by taking his own life, accused me of using the tragedy of his death to push a political agenda, or directly blamed me for my brother's death.

I have thought a lot about whether Kacey would have been better off if he had been adopted by a family that shared his racial background, or if his biological parents had been able to keep him. All I know, without any doubt, is that Kacey was loved, and that his memory lives on in all of us who knew and loved him.

Of course, considering what happened in the end, if another outcome had been possible, I wish more than anyone that Kacey's path had been different. And it is also difficult to hear negativity cast toward my parents, who were beautiful people. But the criticism and blame levied toward me does not tend to land the way it is intended. I am more critical of myself than anyone who has ever thrown shade my way. I have already lived through the tragic loss of my brother, so I am well able to put taunts and accusations in appropriate perspective. From my perspective, sharing stories about my life experiences and the important lessons I have learned, in hopes that I can contribute to change, outweighs all the hate, threats, and hurtful statements that come my way.

I am aware of the risks, and I've decided to use my voice anyway.

A Cost-Benefit Analysis

Though what I propose is simple—making racial justice a core value that we live out loud—doing so may require sacrifice. Saying otherwise would be dishonest. Like many others, I have endured a wide range of consequences for living my life in the antiracist tradition. There are risks and potential consequences of living an antiracist life, and you have to be prepared to take them in your stride.

This is where we lose a lot of white people.

Writer Ijeoma Oluo puts it this way: "Plenty of people of color have met the white antiracist who is all for Dr. King's dream until people of color start asking white people to make actual sacrifices for racial justice."[1] What we do not need are more mediocre white nonracists who know the language, like to post antiracist memes, and call others out but are not willing to sacrifice any of their own comfort or privileges for racial justice.

Life, in general, can be difficult. This is true even if your skin color is not systematically used to make it more difficult. But my challenges, though significant and even painful at times, pale in comparison to what many people of color face on a daily basis. I offer my experience in stark contrast to the consequences that Kacey and so many others have suffered.

The sacrifices of white antiracists are rarely on par with the losses endured by people of color as a result of racism and oppression, but they are significant and can take a very real toll as well.

In life, as in business, we compare the possible cost of an action with the potential benefits. This holds true when determining whether to oppose racism in a particular situation or to participate in actions designed to advance racial justice. I am sure that reading about people being killed, fired, and canceled in the name of antiracism is unsettling and could make someone nervous about those potential grave costs. So, we should address those very real, persistent threats directly.

> *As part of our cost-benefit analysis, we must remember that it is more dangerous for a person of color to simply live in the United States than it is to be the loudest, most public white advocate for antiracism.*

I cannot stress this enough: As part of our cost-benefit analysis, we must remember that it is more dangerous for a person of color to simply live in the United States than it is to be the loudest, most public white advocate for antiracism. If we sincerely care about our siblings of color, this has to be a major factor in our cost-benefit analysis. We must consider not only the *possible* costs to ourselves if we act, but also the *certain* costs to ourselves, loved ones, and others if we choose not to act.

We will ultimately move our nation and our world toward a state of intersectional racial justice. People will look back (as we always do) on past injustices and wonder why it took so long to recognize wrongdoing and demand change. I often hear students say that if they had been there during the time of slavery, the Holocaust, and other extreme wrongs, they would have fought for what was right. Unfortunately, history tells a different story. Over and over, most people have chosen to do nothing in the face of even the most hateful and obvious injustices. Change tends to happen only after small groups of people take big risks until a critical mass is persuaded to join the fight.

One way that we avoid the risks is by pretending that we do not see the wrongs that are done to others, even when it happens right in front of us. This form of deliberate ignorance does not ultimately protect us. As we were reminded by Niemöller, they eventually come for us all. That's why we must do all we can to protect each other's well-being and have each other's backs. Our solidarity is both the act of a true ally and an act of self-preservation.

Still, from my perspective, choosing racial justice as a core value is a question of conscience. I will not allow cowardly bigots to intimidate me, and neither should you.

Confronting Resistance

To prepare for potential risks or consequences of our antiracist efforts, it is important to understand the resistance that we are facing currently in the multiple forms of racist backlash. We are still dealing with the racist reaction to the Obama presidency in the form of the ongoing MAGA movement. We are seeing attacks against DEI programs designed to move institutions to become more equitable and inclusive. And books that address issues of race and racism are being banned from schools and libraries across the country. This is causing deep concern and real fear, both in communities impacted directly and in those advocating for progress, but we must be willing to stand against racist backlash.

There are times when efforts to address racism are welcomed, and change comes readily to an organization, school, or community that is ready. Those experiences give us hope and energy to continue the work. But even though most declare their distaste for racism, real change in the direction of racial equity, inclusion, and justice is still rarely welcomed with open arms. Resistance takes many forms, and we need to recognize it when the time comes.

The US collectively experienced one sneaky form of resistance following the 2020 election: a large-scale "comfort trap" playing out as people were advised to come together in unity following the narrowly won election of President Biden and Vice President Harris and the subsequent insurrection of January 6, 2021. As you probably know from your own introspective work, addressing racism tends to be an uncomfortable endeavor. This, and the desire not to make others uncomfortable, often results in such comfort traps: when our desire to be comfortable, and to ensure the comfort of others—especially white folks—is used to slow or even stop progress in dismantling racist systems.

Asking those of us who care about racial justice to unite with those who supported the MAGA-fueled insurrection is unrealistic and counterproductive. If we were to "just move on" with this type of false unity, we would be choosing to support white supremacy by failing to hold our fellow US Americans accountable.

For some, the priority would be to ease the conflict by appealing to national unity. However, if we don't address the racism behind the movement that culminated in the January 6 insurrection, that so-called call for unity is actually about making racists and those who colluded with them comfortable. The divide between racist and antiracist will continue to deepen until we address the white supremacist elephant in the room. Until then, any attempt to call for unity is disingenuous and premature.

To reach any real solution, we first need to recognize that the divide is not between races. The actual divide is between those who want freedom for some and oppression for others and those who favor freedom for everyone. Those who want to maintain oppressive systems because they benefit directly from them, or to hold on to some privilege scraps, will claim they are fighting for conservative values. This divide is not about conservative values either—that is, unless one of those values is white supremacy. If that is the case, we have to be honest with ourselves about it. True unity will require atoning for our nation's original sins of slavery, attempted genocide, and all the manifestations of systemic oppression that have followed. If we want to heal our national divides, we must stop hiding behind political euphemisms and patriotic mythologies about ourselves, reconcile our actual (not imagined) differences, and work in solidarity to make the idea of "liberty and justice for all" our reality.

This may sound like a massive undertaking, but we are a nation that, at a time before email, video games, or GPS, sent the first humans on a half-million-mile journey to the moon and back. We did that during a time of social unrest, only a year after ending legal lynching and the assassinations of the Reverend Dr. Martin Luther King Jr. and Robert Kennedy. As with so many things, the question is not whether we are capable; it is whether we are willing.

At the level of organizations, institutions, or companies, we see systemic resistance up close. Let's consider a common comfort-trap scenario: A proposal is made to a leadership team to reform a system that has produced racial disparities. A white member of the team says that they are not comfortable with the change, that it seems to go too far. Rather than interrogate the concern, everyone goes into compromise mode. The white team member who raised a concern did not even need to give any details or reasons—only to say that they were uncomfortable.

> *If we want to heal our national divides, we must stop hiding behind political euphemisms and patriotic mythologies about ourselves, reconcile our actual (not imagined) differences, and work in solidarity to make the idea of "liberty and justice for all" our reality.*

This is an example of resistance that happens all the time. When compromise is made automatically, simply to make white folks feel comfortable, it inevitably weakens the antiracist initiative. Sometimes that white person isn't even real, they are hypothetical—someone in the group just has to say "What if this makes white folks uncomfortable?," and the system kicks in.

Since dismantling racism requires challenging well-entrenched beliefs and practices, discomfort should be an *expectation*, not a roadblock or a reason to change direction. Providing feedback that could potentially improve an antiracist initiative must be welcomed, but discomfort alone is neither feedback nor a reason to change a constructive initiative. I encourage us all to lean into this particular discomfort; the benefit far outweighs the cost.

Some other common forms of resistance are intended to look like support. A classic is the unfunded mandate for DEI initiatives: Leadership declares that the organization is committed to examining and improving all systems with respect to DEI. Leaders throughout the organization are encouraged to present strategic plans for improving the policies and practices in their divisions and departments. They all comply, and a brand-new strategic plan is born. All good, so far. The problem arises when no resources are provided to accomplish any of the stated goals, and no one is held accountable for anything aside from saying that DEI is important to the organization. The result: successful resistance. The plan spends the rest of its life as binders on office shelves, collecting dust, or in easily accessible computer files that go unopened—which is by design, because leadership never wanted any change to happen in the first place.

Another common example happens when an organization hires its first executive diversity officer. Suddenly, the organization, once eager to prove its commitment to change, discovers it is not only unprepared for change but actually adverse to the initiative. When the diversity officer demonstrates what is needed to advance DEI goals, the organization pushes back, undermining efforts at every turn. This often manifests as withdrawing support from the person they hired, setting them up for failure, letting them go and hiring someone else—rinse and repeat.

Recently, in Southern California, a large multinational technology company with thousands of employees worldwide concluded, after repeated challenges about the company's lack of diversity and inclusion, that it should create a vice president of diversity. However, no international search was performed for a highly qualified and experienced professional. Instead, the tech company shifted a longtime organizational leader who had zero related experience, training, or preparation of any sort into the newly minted role.

Would this or any other tech company fill a vacancy for an engineer, even at the lowest level, by hiring someone with no training or experience as an engineer? Of course not. The company invests in the success of its engineering division by recognizing the correlation between education and experience in engineering and the ability to successfully perform a job in engineering. So, why hire a vice president to lead diversity and inclusion initiatives for a multibillion-dollar company who has no education or experience in the field?

At best, the company is only interested in superficial change that will unfold very slowly, guided by a familiar company officer—and here again, we have circled back to comfort as the priority over real, substantive change. At worst (and this is the case far more often), the company has no interest in making any substantive change. This can be recognized because the leadership of these massive organizations are not stupid; they are strategic.

In addition to hiring someone who is not prepared to successfully lead antiracism and DEI initiatives, institutional resistance can also be accomplished by underfunding, understaffing, or the allocation of little to no authority. Another strategy is to donate money to a social justice cause and accept praise for supporting an antiracist mission while doing nothing to address racial inequities in the organization. All sorts of strategic maneuvers like these can be employed to uphold a pro-diversity or nonracist image while actively maintaining systems that have demonstrably racist impact.

Genuine change is coming, however. Demographics, expectations, and power are shifting with each new generation, in the US and in other parts of the world. Companies, institutions, and organizations that are able to overcome resistance, and embrace racial justice and inclusive excellence, will be the most successful over time. In the meantime, as they make choices about which path to take today, the world is watching.

The desperate opposition to all things antiracism and DEI that we see playing out in our local, state, and national politics, as well as on the global stage, is particularly absurd because we know what is behind it: They see change coming. Demographic shifts alone cannot create the change we seek. But as we continue building solidarity against intersecting oppressions, global change is taking root and causing panic among those wedded to bigotry, racism, and white supremacy as means to gain wealth and maintain power.

So, if you were sure, as a child in history class, that you would have been on the side that fought against slavery and other atrocities, this is your opportunity to prove yourself right. History is being written, right now.

Protecting Your Physical Well-Being

Many lives have been taken in the global struggle for racial justice. These losses continue today, part of a wide range of violent acts against those who dare to resist colonization, enslavement, and racial oppression. The constant threat of death is intended to maintain a white supremacist order, and this has worked for hundreds of years.

Millions have died fighting colonizers and slavers: in the hulls of slave ships, in battles for freedom, or in efforts to escape oppression. Indigenous resistance efforts like the battles led by Chief Tecumseh in the US, revolts on slave ships like the *Amistad*, and rebellions like Nat Turner's were met with murderous vengeance. White abolitionists like Elijah Parish Lovejoy, John Brown, and others were killed for their part in opposing slavery and white supremacy. These are names you have likely heard, but millions of people you've never heard of have fought for the same cause, and their stories of sacrifice have been suppressed.

These losses are not limited to the past, or to the United States. For example, the global thirst for technology has produced laptops, cell phones, and electric vehicles all powered by batteries. The lithium-ion batteries they use require cobalt, 75 percent of which is mined in the Democratic Republic of the Congo. The conditions in the cobalt mines are disgraceful.

The mines themselves are extremely dangerous, with severe health risks, high rates of sexual assaults, and all for two dollars or less per day. I do not believe that the global community would find this acceptable if the miners were white. But this is a part of the world that has been colonized and looted for centuries, all justified by white supremacy. This is also an example of extreme oppression, with which nearly all of us are complicit—including me, as I sit here typing on my laptop and listening to music on my mobile phone.[2]

White supremacy has been a blight on the entire world. From colonization to the Maafa (African Holocaust) through the Shoah (Jewish Holocaust) and the array of modern oppressions, there is no way to know the exact number of precious lives lost. And make no mistake: Every one of those lives was *precious*, although we are taught to devalue the life of anyone who is minoritized, marginalized, or simply not considered white. Part of becoming antiracist requires recognition that every life is precious, that the murder of a dark-skinned father is no less tragic than the murder of a blond-haired, fair-skinned daughter—that every life is as precious as your own.

There can be little doubt that if George Floyd had been a young white man, he would have almost certainly lived through that encounter with convicted murderer Officer Chauvin and his accomplices in blue. We have seen videos of countless armed white men—some who had just finished an actual killing spree—somehow taken into custody without injury. Meanwhile, video after video surfaces where people of color are killed on the spot who were unarmed and had not killed anyone. The term "modern-day lynching" is not too strong to describe this tragic reality.

> *Part of becoming antiracist requires recognition that every life is precious, that the murder of a dark-skinned father is no less tragic than the murder of a blond-haired, fair-skinned daughter—that every life is as precious as your own.*

Yet as scholar and educator Toni Battle has explained to me, the barbaric practice of lynching never really disappeared; the extrajudicial murders of people of color by police today are a continuation—examples of what lynching looks like in our current context. The motive behind the lynchings prior to 1968, when it became illegal in the United States, is the same as the extrajudicial murders we see today: to serve and protect white supremacy.

Think about that year: 1968. How many people living today supported lynchings or perhaps even participated in the practice? How many posed for, sent, or received the postcards printed to commemorate lynchings? How many knew what was happening in their own town and chose to do nothing?

Many of us do not want to face the reality that lynchings—like colonial conquest, attempts at genocide, various forms of slavery, human zoos, forced medical experimentation, and other things we recognize as abominations—are part of our recent history. We want to see them as part of a distant past or erase them altogether. No wonder so many folks don't want us teaching accurate history in schools. Being on the wrong side of history does have consequences—and sometimes there are pictures, videos, and other documentation of the folks standing knee deep in the muck on the wrong side. I imagine that may have some folks concerned about what their grandchildren may learn in school.

The murders that sparked the Black Lives Matter movement—and that continue today—would simply not be tolerated by the majority of white people without the persistent belief that people of color are less human than people who are deemed white. As Dr. Rheeda Walker explains, "At the root of racism and racial disparities is the belief that Black people are not fully human and do not deserve access to the same rights as others."[3] To me, that is the only explanation that makes sense—only this persistent belief could make lynching and the ongoing murders of people of color by the police acceptable to so many.

Whether or not you term these murders by police and white supremacists as "lynchings," they are a very real threat to people of color, which far too often goes unpunished. Too many of those with power in the US and other parts of the world continue to simply value the lives of white people more than people of color. It is evident in domestic and global policy, in how our government responds (or doesn't) to violence at home and abroad, and in the decisions made about when to intervene militarily and on whose behalf.

Anyone living an antiracist life puts their well-being at risk, simply for declaring that the lives of people of color matter—that they are as valued and precious as the lives of white people. The fact that there is any danger at all in making that statement is shameful. Yet the death threats received by activists and advocates for racial justice are real, as are the assaults on protesters and others who speak out against oppression.

The violent insurrectionists (many of whom were avowed white supremacists) who attacked the US Capitol on January 6, 2021, had no more respect for the lives of those in their way than their racist counterparts of the past. Those who died at the hands of the insurrectionists were casualties in the ongoing struggle against white supremacy and oppression. If we fail to take seriously the intentional and violent actions of the white supremacist organizations that were part of the insurrection and have such influence on our political leaders, the threat will continue to grow. As demographic changes enrage violent bigots and their supporters in police forces, in the military, on school boards, and in government, the risks increase exponentially.

> *Too many of those with power in the US and other parts of the world continue to simply value the lives of white people more than people of color.*

The more committed we are to ensuring that the most vulnerable among us (due to global systems of oppression) are safe and valued as human beings, the safer we all are from suffering similar fates moving forward. Working in solidarity to advance freedom from oppression, we can champion measures that will protect everyone and provide us all with the full spectrum of opportunities to live our best lives.

Concerns About Financial Well-Being

Of all the reasons for hesitancy I hear from people who want to oppose racism more actively, fear of financial consequences is the most common—far more common than fear of any type of physical violence. Many have concerns about speaking up at work, the primary source of income for most of us. Our income matters to those who rely on our financial support, so the threat of losing your job, having your reputation damaged, or being excluded from opportunities to advance is a real and understandable concern.

Again, this threat of financial consequences must be considered in context. Disparities in employment and salaries, for example, have always existed between white people and people of color in the context of the United States. On the global stage, similar disparities of opportunity and compensation exist as well. Our economic system in the US, built upon the foundation of colonization, was designed to maintain these disparities, and they persist to this day. Again, global colonization primarily by European nations has led to similar results in other parts of the world that also suffer the ongoing impacts of colonization.

So, as we discuss the financial consequences for engaging in antiracism, those of us who are white need to keep in mind that the risks we take, while certainly meaningful to us and our families, must be considered in the context of the financial disadvantages built into the system for people of color in the US and globally. Again, this does not mean the risks are small or do not matter for white antiracists; I just think it is wise to recognize our privilege and the context of this particular risk.

With respect to our economic systems, the US American brand of capitalism was built on stolen land, slavery, and economic oppression based on a racialized caste system. Reparations have not been made for these colossal wrongs—which created the massive gap in wealth between the generationally wealthy and those starting from scratch and earning lower and middle incomes. And while our systems have adapted, they have not transformed into an equitable and inclusive model. The "need" to maximize profits for owners, investors, and executives promotes ongoing oppression of those who do the labor. The less that is paid to workers, the more profit for those at the top. This is why predatory capitalists and those privileged by generational wealth still fight to keep the minimum wage as low as possible. It is not because there would be no profit if workers were paid a living wage—or more appropriately, if workers received their true share of the wealth generated by their labor. It is because the goal is to maximize profit to further enrich those already at the top, far beyond their needs or worth.

We know that systems resist change, and racist systems are no different. Educator and civil rights advocate Septima Clark felt the resistance to change when she was famously fired from a position with the Charleston, South Carolina, Board of Education in 1957 because she was a member of the NAACP.[4] She was not the first nor the last person fired for their racial justice activism. More recently, I have known multiple executive diversity officers who have been fired for simply attempting to do the work outlined explicitly in their job descriptions; unfortunately, I have had that same experience myself.

Transforming racist and otherwise oppressive systems into those that value equity, inclusion, and justice is no easy task. In fact, sometimes it is not possible, and those systems will need to be fully dismantled and replaced. This sort of change, even when an institution is fully committed to the task, is uncomfortable at best, and too often costs the people doing the heavy lifting opportunities, and sometimes their livelihood.

A few months ago, a friend and colleague of mine at an elite university, who does excellent antiracism and inclusive excellence work, was let go from her position directing an extraordinary teacher education program centered on social justice. The programs she was hired to implement received public praise and recognition and had begun to change the practices and demographics of the institution and have an impact in the city's schools. That ultimately caused resistance from the university—initially decreasing funding and eventually forcing a reorganization, which changed the direction of the programs and pushed out the leader who had driven their success.

This description will sound all too familiar to anyone who works professionally in opposition to racism and intersecting oppressions. Diversity professionals and other leaders working to promote inclusive excellence put their jobs in jeopardy practically every day. Changing biased and oppressive systems is at the core of their job description, and that change is resisted vehemently. Far too often, when progress becomes evident, those driving the change are targeted. When those leaders are fired for a job well done, too few colleagues, partners, and outside constituents are willing to stand up to oppose the injustice—more of the unhelpful nonengagement of nonracist bystanders.

This is not a risk limited to professionals in DEI. When Super Bowl champion Colin Kaepernick and his San Francisco 49ers teammate Eric Reid chose to kneel during the national anthem, seeking to call attention to issues of racial inequality and police brutality, there were serious consequences. Kaepernick lost his job and was never accepted to play in the NFL again.[5] Similarly, Emmy Award–winning journalist and former ESPN commentator Jemele Hill, as she discusses in her memoir, *Uphill*, suffered extreme backlash and a major threat to her career for stating the obvious about racist comments made by Donald Trump.[6]

Librarians have lost jobs for not removing banned books from libraries.[7] Employees of tech giants have lost their jobs after speaking out against racism, as have doctors who have taken up the challenge. People from all walks of life have spoken out against racism at work, and many suffer consequences when their colleagues choose not to have their backs because they fear similar retaliatory consequences that could threaten their own financial well-being.

I have faced financial consequences on several occasions for doing the job I was hired to do. As with the colleagues I mentioned, and so many others, the more significant the impact of my work, the more serious the backlash has been—including not having my contract renewed. My career in antiracism and inclusive excellence is something that I am proud of, but to be honest, it has brought with it a great deal of financial instability.

Even my decision not to include many of the names of racist individuals and institutions described in this book is, in part, about protecting myself from litigious bigots. I share the experiences because they provide you with relevant examples and reveal that such experiences are far from abnormal. The truth is that none of my stories are out of the ordinary. The bigots and racist organizations that I have challenged are not special. They are no different from the ones you know and deal with every day.

I am far from alone in my constant concern about my financial situation and how racist reactions to my work impact those who rely on my income, most importantly my daughter. My choice to prioritize antiracism has limited my future income potential and, even more concerning, my present financial stability. This has caused problems in my personal life and challenges for my family and has been infuriating for me personally and professionally. Still, despite sometimes having to check my bank account balance before I "splurge" on groceries, in no way do I regret the work I do, and I have no plans to stop.

Ultimately, we all have to make financial decisions, and sometimes this requires working for organizations and individuals for whom we harbor no love. But remember, there is a difference between maintaining employment so you can sustain yourself—an admirable path—and choosing to collude in order to ensure financial gains to enrich yourself. Using privilege to chase wealth at the expense of others has never been an option I have considered, and I hope it is not an option you will choose either.

By describing these risks, I hope to ensure that you are more informed than I was, and that you will be better able to plan accordingly as you move forward with your antiracist commitment. Some of my colleagues have been more savvy with their money over the years, which has protected them a bit more when they have lost a job or had difficulty moving up in an organization. You may never have to face financial retribution for your antiracist actions, and I sincerely hope you do not. However, it is best to understand what is possible so you can plan for any challenges that could arise.

In my field of work, many have realized that we need side hustles to fall back on. I know people who invest in small businesses that are not part of the diversity and inclusion field. Others, like me, maintain a consulting business that we try to ramp up when necessary. Some folks have formed collectives, contributing money to help any members who need assistance during a difficult time. Still others choose to do their primary antiracist work outside of their profession, through membership organizations and volunteer efforts. Perhaps one of those alternatives would work best for you.

Tending to Your Social Well-Being

Of the many risks to my social well-being that I've encountered in telling my story, the greatest comes in response to talking about losing Kacey to suicide. Only people who have lost a loved one this way can fully understand that specific type of pain or what it feels like to hear the harsh judgment imposed by others who see it as an opportunity to place blame. On this particular subject, I have been heckled by both opportunistic racists and those who would claim to be antiracist. Since I began speaking in public more than thirty years ago, however, many things have changed. In the past, I have been shouted at, challenged in newspapers, and threatened on quite a few occasions. Now, we must also deal with online trolling, doxing, and other increasingly sophisticated online attacks.

Thanks to social media and our connected world of advanced travel and communications, most of us live more publicly than ever before. This has made it more difficult for people to hide their biases, bigotries, and other problematic beliefs and behaviors, except, of course, when they are hiding behind a keyboard, making anonymous comments online. For those who prefer to share their racism freely, getting signal-boosted online makes it easier than ever to spread hate, misinformation, and smear campaigns about anyone. The social threat that has been increased by online platforms is the threat of being "canceled."

Being canceled can include public shaming or discrediting, and can lead to loss of support, credibility, and opportunities. Sometimes it is a legitimate consequence for repeated egregious behavior. At other times, it can happen to someone who just made an honest mistake. Solidarity has always been difficult, but canceling one another for showing our humanity certainly does not help advance our cause. The question is: Where do we draw the line between behaviors that should come with major consequences and those that should elicit guidance?

> *Where do we draw the line between behaviors that should come with major consequences and those that should elicit guidance?*

Beyond that, now we are facing the use of artificial intelligence (AI) to produce deep fakes, including videos that are becoming more and more difficult to discern from the real thing. The use of these deep fakes already includes attempts to get people canceled.

Another strategy of racist trolls is to hijack social justice language. I was told, for example, that my problem with the blind date that went racist real fast back in Tallahassee was about toxic masculinity, not racism. The person claimed that my male ego was bruised because my date had a different viewpoint, so I canceled her to prove that I was woke.

First, it is important to understand that racism is not a legitimate viewpoint. The racist beliefs expressed by my date did not threaten my masculinity; they demonstrated her bigotry, and that caused me to lose interest. The person trying to discredit me knew all of that and was attempting to legitimize racism as a conservative viewpoint and use social justice language to pit *feminist* against *antiracist*. This is part of why antiracism requires opposition to all forms of oppression. Solidarity is the only way to effectively oppose those interested in preserving their illegitimate power by pitting us against one another.

As an antiracist, you may find yourself at risk of having your words and actions twisted to fit a divisive narrative. You may even be challenged by other antiracists who, at times, forget that we are all imperfect. It is expected that racists will lash out at antiracists. Being canceled by those we value as colleagues and partners in the work is far more concerning than the predictable hate that we receive from entrenched bigots. As horrible as the consequences coming from racists can be, the threat of being canceled by those you tend to be aligned with on sociopolitical matters can be even more daunting.

We must find it within ourselves to practice empathy, compassion, and patience if we hope to receive the same courtesies in return.

Whether you are concerned about being canceled because of a bigot's twisting of your words or by an unforgiving comrade, you are your own best protection. When you demonstrate your commitment to racial justice, and your opposition to intersecting oppressions, over time you develop the credibility necessary to receive the benefit of the doubt. This is similar to the credibility that you might earn by consistently being a good friend or a team player. As the work and language of diversity, equity, inclusion, and justice evolve, we must continue to learn, and learning is often accompanied by mistakes. It is easier to forgive mistakes when they are owned up to, not repeated, and when you have already developed relevant credibility over time.

It can be difficult to reserve judgment of one another as we struggle to end racism and other oppressions. The work can be frustrating, exhausting, and demoralizing at times, which sometimes causes us to lose patience, even with each other. Too often, when pushed into fight mode, even for good reason, we end up being critical of one another rather than the systems we are committed to changing. I have been guilty of this more than I would like to admit. I have learned that we need more voices, though, not fewer. When we are able to locate our own humility, it helps create a greater appreciation of one another's best efforts, even in difficult times.

Tending to our social well-being is more than maintaining a social life. It includes being thoughtful about what we put out in the world through social media, being patient with how others grow into their antiracism, and refusing to be overly judgmental when people make mistakes. We must find it within ourselves to practice empathy, compassion, and patience if we hope to receive the same courtesies in return.

Threats to Your Psychological Well-Being

Very real threats to our psychological well-being come with addressing racism in ourselves and others. Additionally, the American Psychological Association has stated clearly that there are significant psychological impacts of racism and discrimination on people of color.[8] In fact, racism-related stress has been shown to be more harmful than many stressful life events, in part because it is an ongoing stressor, not something that comes and goes. According to Dr. Rheeda Walker, "There is sufficient research that shows that racism is not just another stressor that people deal with. For Black people, racism is linked to poorer mental outcomes and emotional stability even when more general life stressors like work stress, relationship stress, and financial stress are taken into consideration."[9]

Racism certainly took a toll on my brother Kacey's psychological fortitude. I cannot know for sure, but I believe that he would be with us today if it was not for the additional strain, beyond the usual stresses of adolescence, that racism put on his heart. Sometimes people ask me why I feel the need to say that Kacey was a victim of suicide. Sure, it would be easier to just say that he passed, but it would leave an important part of my brother's story untold. For me, the way I say it matters as well. Saying that someone "committed" suicide comes across to me as placing blame on the victim; I choose not to do that.

Another psychological challenge is regret. It is like a heavy bag we must bear on our backs—one of life's most difficult consequences to endure. It takes a toll on our psyche and impacts our well-being in quantifiable ways. My most profound regret is that I did not go back to Kacey's room that fateful night to listen more and encourage hope. That night haunts me, for what I said and what I did not say. It did not occur to me that we would not have another day.

There is great pain where regret meets loss, but also a great lesson that I take seriously, out of respect for my brother. I have learned to cherish time with loved ones and not postpone showing love, because we cannot assume we will have another moment together. I have lived this truth. I spent many years afraid of the impact I could have on others, particularly loved ones. It has been difficult to share my real emotions with anyone, worrying that if I say something hurtful, something difficult to hear, or something that brings up painful memories, there may not be another chance to bring comfort or joy.

I do not know how much of a difference I have made, but I have no regrets about trying.

A testament to the power of regret is that it provides the opportunity to reflect on those precious moments when it was absent. I am able, by contrast and necessity, to look back at the great times Kacey and I had together: singing along to Helen Reddy or Little Richard in the back of our parents' Pontiac GTO Judge, pretending to be superheroes in our black-and-green capes, racing in Grandma and Grampa's swimming pool. There are far more moments that I do not regret than the few that I do.

No matter how you choose to live your life, you will encounter highs and lows, love and loss, opportunities and brick walls. No matter our level or type of privilege, none of us can avoid all the consequences of our choices. For me, among the hardest to cope with are the outcomes of a failure to take a stand or act when I knew better. I do not regret the times when I was able to summon the courage to stand against hate that was meant to hurt, belittle, or marginalize my brother and other loved ones, even if they were not always effective. That I did not hesitate in those moments—whether I was by Kacey's side or on my own—never causes me a single moment of regret. I do not know how much of a difference I have made, but I have no regrets about trying.

To embrace racial justice as a core value means choosing to take those opportunities to correct a wrong or change a mind instead of shying away just because you can. It means stepping forward to make your voice known instead of staying awake at night wishing you had. You may have already encountered some regret around moments when your voice might have made a difference but instead you chose silence. Living a life in line with your antiracist values will make you more conscious of these decisions. I encourage you to let regret be a deterrent and peace of mind be your reward.

For people of color, systemic and interpersonal racism already poses extreme risks to their mental health. Actively opposing racism adds another layer of risk. For white antiracists, our risk does not include the same daily threats or psychological impacts, but that does not diminish the stresses we do face. For all antiracists, our efforts to oppose powerful, and often dangerous, systems of oppression add significant stress to our lives, and we must protect our mental health as much as possible.

There is no getting around the fact that additional stress, regardless of the cause, can put our mental and physical health at risk. But there are ways to protect ourselves and others from the damage caused by the stress we take on, at least to some degree. Exercise is a primary example. I used to take my stress out on the opposing team on the basketball court. Now I talk to myself while shooting baskets at the local court. When the stress gets really bad, I beat on my heavy bag. Another go-to for me is watching a good movie or a television show—perhaps even one that I have already seen; it can be like visiting with an old friend. Comedies can be especially therapeutic because they make you laugh, or science fiction because it helps us escape.

Talking about what weighs on us can relieve stress, too, whether with family, friends, or a professional—someone who understands what you're going through and can handle the weight of your story. Some people find therapy to be helpful, particularly regarding issues that it might be hard to trust others with. Counseling is becoming much more accessible financially these days, so more of us can benefit from it. The bigger challenge for some of us is getting over our preconceived notions, but the stigma within some communities around therapy and caring for our mental health is (happily) beginning to fade. For me, getting past my own resistance to therapy has proven fruitful.

Perhaps you deal with stress by leaning on your faith, seeking guidance from sacred texts and religious leaders. Some people practice yoga or meditate; others like to swim or hike or play pool or cards. Ultimately, we all need to do our best to tend to our health—although most of us are better at giving this advice than taking it. Whatever works to relieve your stress, do more of that.

Living an antiracist life comes with mental health challenges, but at some point, we realize that the psychological consequences of living in collusion with racism can be far worse.

The Risks of Ignorance

I arrived in Malawi, known as "the warm heart of Africa," on September 6, 2001. In deciding to take the yearlong visiting professor position at the University of Malawi's Chancellor College, my intent was not necessarily to do antiracism work. As I had learned during my time in the former Soviet Union, when I was an undergrad, my education about the world was not strong. I had continued to travel when I could, and worked on my global literacy, but I hoped that my time in Malawi would provide me with another intensive learning experience outside of the context of the United States.

I was proud to have gotten the teaching position through Leon Sullivan's organization, the International Foundation for Education and Self-Help (IFESH). Because Sullivan was the founder, I trusted that it was not just another paternalistic nongovernmental organization (NGO) that does little more than further colonial propaganda. As expected, IFESH was different, and my experience was more educational than I could have imagined.

Unfortunately, my understanding of the colonial history and the neocolonial realities in Africa—and particularly in Malawi, a nation I had barely heard of—was much like my understanding of US history: full of gaps and misconceptions. As it turned out, my miseducation was truly global. While I was well versed in culturally responsive education within the US context and had no delusions of being some sort of great white savior, I did routinely get checked on my lack of knowledge. I was pretty well versed on colonialism, though I had less of an understanding of neocolonialism and the part the United States currently plays in the ongoing suppression of nations and oppression of peoples around the world.

One conversation with a group of students meandered into a conversation about John Nkologo Chilembwe, the US-trained Malawian minister and revolutionary who led an unsuccessful uprising against British colonial rule in 1915. Chilembwe was tracked down and killed without a trial, but the uprising continued to inspire his people, up through Malawi's regained independence in 1964. The students had thoughts about his time in the United States and how he studied Booker T. Washington and Frederick Douglass; they compared him to John Brown and Nat Turner, using US American references to help me understand.

When I attempted to draw parallels between the American Revolutionary War and the Malawian fight for independence, one student spoke up. "But while the US colonizers won independence from the British, the Indigenous Native Americans remained colonized, and Africans in America remained displaced and enslaved," she pointed out. That should have been obvious to me, but it clearly was not. She and the other students proceeded to school me on the United States' use of corporations, NGOs, and political power to suppress and exert control in African nations and globally.

That conversation, and others with students and colleagues, opened my eyes about everything from the Berlin Conference and the ruthless carving up of the African continent to the role of religion in colonization to the use of predatory capitalism in neocolonialism. My experience in Malawi helped me further understand global forces, challenges, and opportunities for change. I learned more about the impact of colonialism, the capitalistic white supremacy that drove it, and the impact of ongoing racism today. I learned not only from my colleagues at the university and my students but also from friends that I made in the course of living in the town of Zomba.

And I learned another lesson in the risks of ignorance.

When we remain ignorant of the world around us, we put ourselves at risk of being deceived and misguided by our political and social leaders. How many African authors did you read in school? How about authors from Asia, Latin America, or really anywhere outside the US and Europe? What do you know of history told from the perspective of Indigenous peoples? How much do you know about any nation that does not come from the perspective of white authors? Our ethnocentrism puts us at risk of remaining stalled at the dangerous intersection of overly confident and obliviously ignorant.

Our ethnocentrism puts us at risk of remaining stalled at the dangerous intersection of overly confident and obliviously ignorant.

While this book has focused primarily on living an antiracist life within the US, it is necessary for us to lift our heads to see the impact and opportunities for change globally. Here in the US, unfortunately, we do not spend a lot of time learning about the rest of the world, and our world news is rarely more than updates on wherever we are waging war. As a result, US Americans are generally seen as only concerned with ourselves and uneducated (or miseducated) about the rest of the world.

Less than a week after my arrival in Malawi, while in the capital city of Lilongwe to complete my training, I happened to be visiting the US embassy when I learned of the attacks taking place at home. It was September 11, 2001. I was worried about friends, and relieved when I got good news from those who worked at the Pentagon. When I finally reached my close friend Joya on the phone, she was still holding out hope for her father, Winston Grant, who never made it home from the thirtieth floor of the North Tower at the World Trade Center. While I struggled to communicate with friends and loved ones at home, and grieved for Joya and her family, I was struck by the empathy shown to myself and my colleagues from the States. Many of the Malawian people around us were Muslim and had felt unseen and stereotyped by US Americans, many had had bad experiences with NGOs from the US, and most had felt disrespected by US American tourists, businesspeople, and government officials in country. In spite of all of that, the "warm heart of Africa" did not disappoint.

Our nation, led by the politicians we elect and by wealthy US-based multinational corporations, has an enormous impact on the entire planet. America is not the best in the world at everything, although we are taught that we are, and tend to believe it. Nor are we always a force for good in the world. In fact, when it comes to freedom, justice, and equity, we are far too often among the villains. I'm not trying to bash us; I believe that we US Americans, in all our diversity, have awesome potential, and I love a great deal about our cultures. It is our political and economic systems that I recognize as problematic, domestically and internationally.

We will not make progress if we limit our scope of understanding and only practice antiracism when it is safe and without consequence.

Living an antiracist life requires us to consider more than the diverse perspectives within our own nation or the diversity of immigrants who arrive at our borders. We must also be much more aware of global diversity and the equity, inclusion, and justice issues that exist worldwide. That includes the roles we play as individuals and as a nation on the global stage. Our political engagement, military actions, and economic impacts are far-reaching. We will not make progress if we limit our scope of understanding and only practice antiracism when it is safe and without consequence. The consequences of our white supremacy and systemic racism are not limited to our own experiences in the United States either, and neither should our attention as antiracists be.

10

WANT THE BALL
Making Your Unique Contribution to Ending Racism

*If you think you are too small to make a difference,
try sleeping with a mosquito.*

—THE DALAI LAMA

My youngest brother, B-J, is a big, blond-haired, blue-eyed, pickup truck–driving guy. As an "essential worker" during the pandemic, managing a corporate pharmacy in a small military town in North Carolina, he was required to wear a mask to work every day. He saw that as an opportunity to wear a mask with the Black Lives Matter (BLM) logo, to show his support for the movement.

When Kacey died, B-J struggled too, and it was years before I was able to be a decent big brother to him again. Now, B-J and I live significantly different lives, but we share most of our core values, including racial justice. He never finished college and has spent most of his life in construction and retail, yet sometimes he can more effectively challenge racism simply because of how he is seen. B-J's commitment to antiracism looks different from mine, but he is no less serious, and his contribution matters.

B-J has a different type of credibility than I do, with all my formal education and professional experience, and sometimes his efforts are significantly more effective than mine. Within his sphere of influence, I am often seen as an out-of-touch academic—to put it nicely. Most impressive to me is how my, and Kacey's, little brother never hesitates to act when someone makes the mistake of saying or doing something racist anywhere near him. I have never seen him show any fear, whether the situation became physical, his job was on the line, or there was some other potential consequence.

When he wore his Black Lives Matter mask while waiting on customers, some did not appreciate his advocacy for racial justice, and he was encouraged by his supervisor to wear a different mask. He responded by pointing out that the company was not providing masks, and there was no policy against wearing any specific types of masks. His supervisor backed off.

Customers continued to express their disapproval of B-J's support for the Black Lives Matter movement. He was confronted several times a day, and each time he responded with his brand of charm and quick wit, questioning why anyone would oppose the idea that the police should not murder and terrorize Black people. The complaining customers would sometimes get angry about being challenged for making a racist comment. Some were confused as to why B-J, based on how they saw him, would care about fighting racism. Some confronted him, some asked questions, and a few actually left rethinking their position.

After some time, the national chain that employed B-J wrote a policy banning masks with any political statements. B-J argued that he was not making a political statement; it was a social justice statement. Even so, he was told not to wear the BLM mask anymore.

B-J complained about the racist policy. But while they were busy ignoring his complaints, he decided to avoid getting fired and wear a different mask—his Inclusive Pride flag mask. When confronted, again, by his supervisor, B-J said, "It's not a political statement. I just really like rainbows." Meanwhile, the new mask brought even more opportunities for B-J to discuss both racism and homophobia with customers, along with more than a few complaints.

When racial justice becomes a core value, it serves to guide your actions in every aspect of your life, and using your own authentic voice will help you make your best contribution as an individual. B-J's antiracism looks different from mine, and that is a good thing. The ways that our antiracism manifests can be different even though we share the same core value of racial justice. The fact that our approaches are different, and that we are perceived differently, makes it possible for us to reach more people with the same racial and social justice message.

Too often, people just want to perform opposition to racism or other forms of oppression. They want a list or a description of how to be antiracist. But living an antiracist life is not about performance or matching the correct canned responses to similar circumstances. It is about shepherding your own transformation through introspection and making your own unique contributions to change. Guidance on what antiracism looks like and examples of successful actions are helpful, but at the end of the day, your way of actively opposing racism and intersecting oppressions will be uniquely yours and distinctly effective within your sphere of influence. While we can learn a great deal about different approaches, there is no list or singular answer to how we should all be antiracist.

> *The ways that our antiracism manifests can be different even though we share the same core value of racial justice.*

B-J and I do most things differently, but I will always appreciate the unique impact he has by living a fiercely antiracist life in his own way. His voice matters not just because he speaks truth to customers and challenges unjust policy at work but because antiracism is one of his core values that he lives out loud every day.

Of course, this is not surprising. After all, B-J is Kacey's brother too.

Unlearning Racism

When folks initially decide to embrace antiracism, they often want to jump into action immediately. Without knowing how best to do so, however, they find that this can (and often does) backfire. Imagine if we took that approach to rock climbing or skydiving, where making a mistake because you lack critical knowledge or a necessary skill could be deadly. Similarly, without taking the time to develop your antiracist literacy, you will likely set yourself up for failure. The point is not to aim for perfection but to ensure that we are well informed. Failures will come as you learn, and that's okay, but preparation can help us avoid some predictable mistakes that might otherwise be discouraging.

Of course, how well you prepare impacts how well you perform. Preparation is critical for success in most endeavors, and actively opposing racism is no different. If you want to be good at it, spending some time preparing yourself is advisable.

Antiracist engagement begins internally, with unlearning racism and building up an antiracist literacy.

As we have discussed, antiracist engagement begins internally, with unlearning racism and building up an antiracist literacy. We do this by determining which lies our teachers told us, digging into learning diverse perspectives and examples of greatness beyond the accomplishments of white men, letting go of bad habits like strategic white ignorance, and figuring out how to practice antiracism in our own unique ways.

Despite preparation, we all make mistakes and missteps. That's fine, and to be expected. Just keep learning, make amends, and move forward.

Unlearning racist ideas taught to us by family members is a common challenge for those who have recently begun to acknowledge the racism around them. This relearning process is particularly difficult because it can sometimes feel like you are judging or rejecting someone you love.

Rejecting a loved one's perspective on the proper way to make your bed or manage your finances may not feel like a judgment or rejection of the whole person—just a minor disagreement. But because racism is seen by most people as a fatal flaw, and something that makes you a bad person, we resist seeing racist behavior among loved ones to avoid rejecting them—like the way I gave my favorite cousin a pass for so long, dismissing his behavior instead of confronting it.

It is easy to categorize someone who has espoused racist beliefs as evil and dismiss them, but real life is more complicated than that. People who hold racist beliefs, or who do not share your antiracist perspective, are not all Klansmen. They are family members and other loved ones, friendly colleagues and new acquaintances, all of whom may also have some genuinely beautiful qualities.

The true test of a person's character is in how they respond when confronted about their racist statement or behavior. Do they double down and dig in, or are they willing to open their eyes to reality?

Some people believe that their inability to comprehend something is a legitimate argument against it. Infants think this way before they are capable of understanding object permanence—that's why peekaboo is so fun for babies. Until we have the mental capacity, we cannot comprehend that something is still there when we cannot see it. The problem arises when millions of adults still believe that when they cover their eyes Grandma ceases to exist, or that racism is magically gone.

Too often, people will attach themselves to easily disproven narratives for the sole reason that those narratives fit their perspective. This is true for flat-earthers, those who deny that systemic racism exists, and those who think Trump is still secretly president. Even given overwhelming evidence to the contrary, they cannot see anything that does not match their viewpoint. But just like Grandma was right there when you uncovered your eyes, racism still exists even if you refuse to see it.

Opening our eyes may force us to face situations that are difficult to accept. It is not easy to overcome our own resistance when we want to protect our image of loved ones, or of our beloved nation for that matter, but it is a necessary step on the path to unlearning the racist ideas our loved ones may have taught us. Not only that—it is our responsibility to do our part in countering racist beliefs in those same loved ones. Over time, some will come to share our antiracist values; some will remain works in progress; and some may remain stuck in their own racist muck, and we may choose to leave them there and move on. Either way, once we have committed to learning, whether on our own or with family, friends, or colleagues, we are free to focus on developing our antiracist literacy.

It is not as simple as just turning on a switch. Learning and embracing who we are as individuals, as members of families, communities, and cultures, can be a long process. Unlearning racism and growing into antiracism are part of this process. Racism persists until a new, antiracist thinking process replaces the old, racist one. As with any learning, it takes time to get on track. It requires working on how you view the world and respond to situations and then practicing until it's automatic, like muscle memory.

Muscle memory happens when you repeat a movement so many times through practice that your body can automatically reproduce that movement without conscious effort. Typing is a great example: The more you practice, the less you have to think about where a letter is on the keyboard, and the faster you can perform the task. In time, your fingers move to the right place at the right time, with speed and proficiency, and without conscious thought.

As a basketball player, I was taught to practice shooting free throws with the same form and rhythm every time. The intention is to promote shooting a high percentage of successful free throws, and it works. Once you have established the routine, your body just knows what to do, and you become more confident in your shooting ability. Living an antiracist life can require fighting against some old muscle memory. The only way to overcome this is to practice a new way, over and over again, until the old routine is replaced by a new one. It works when you develop a bad habit shooting a basketball, when getting used to a new keyboard, and when it is time to adopt a new way of thinking as well.

As you work to develop your own way of living an antiracist life, it is important to address residual racism in your unconscious mind. Consider how you respond when someone says they are facing racism from a mutual friend or colleague: An automatic nonracist response might be to say something like "I'm sure that's not what they meant." An antiracist response, on the other hand, would be to listen, empathize, and remain open to learning whether racism is at play and then to serve as a partner to help your mutual friend learn and do better.

Over time, responding in an antiracist manner will become automatic. You'll still make some typos or miss a few free throws, but you will become better the more you practice.

Nonracist Is Not Helpful

People often say they want to get involved, but they do not feel prepared. Understanding this sentiment, I encourage entry-level involvement that will provide learning opportunities. Offering your skills, knowledge, assets, and talents to those already doing antiracism work is an excellent way to get involved before you feel prepared to raise your own voice.

When it comes to opposing racism, taking action and getting involved is critical. Most people in the United States claim to oppose racism—even our "forefathers" paid lip service to "freedom from tyranny" and "equality for all," though they failed to live those values even more than most of our neighbors do

Offering your skills, knowledge, assets, and talents to those already doing antiracism work is an excellent way to get involved before you feel prepared to raise your own voice.

today. Therein lies the problem: We know better, but too often we choose not to *do* better.

That's the essence of the nonracist stance: people saying "I'm not racist" while doing absolutely nothing to stand against it. To the nonracist, it is enough to not use the n-slur or to tell their children that racism is wrong without ever doing anything to oppose it. To opt out as nonracist is a choice, and the problem with that choice is that it allows racism to go unchecked. It may sound harsh, but choosing to be nonracist is essentially choosing to support racism.

As the saying goes: "Don't talk about it. Be about it." It is far past time for more of us white folks to locate our integrity, to live our values through action. We need to be about it—to act in harmony with the racial justice values we profess to hold.

What good are values if they only exist in your mouth?

Far too many people say they are all for racial justice but then refuse to stand up against racist gaslighting in our schools and political discourse or refuse to oppose racial discrimination in their own workplace. There is always plenty of work to be done in furthering racial equity and justice goals, from the simple, like volunteering to prepare materials for conferences or leaflets for protests, to the more complex, like grant writing, teaching a course, or rewriting a policy. Find out how you can share your strengths at the same time as you learn.

> *What good are values if they only exist in your mouth?*

Volunteer your services during downtime, not just leading up to an event. Your time is often more valuable when help is sparse, such as during planning phases or for the day-to-day DEI work at a university, corporation, or other organization.

Your ability to organize, manage a project, or find resources can be quite valuable, too. The same can be said of professional skills: If you are an attorney, an accountant, an event planner, or someone with experience in marketing, communications, or any number of professions, offering your services pro bono can make a significant difference, especially to a small operation. Every event, project, initiative, and movement can benefit from the support of those who care and who genuinely want to contribute.

When you have the privilege and opportunity to volunteer, explain that you are hoping to continue learning about the work being done. My colleagues and I always make the effort to provide educational opportunities for volunteers who express interest. In addition to sharing what we have learned, I see it as a way of showing appreciation for the time, effort, and talent people are providing.

Leading by Example

Leadership takes many forms, but first and foremost, we lead by example. Perhaps our most important leadership role is as an example to those around us. People look up to you. They value your example. How you behave matters. What you say in daily conversation or in response to the news matters. Your relationships matter. Your example sends messages to those all around you—maybe most especially when you think nobody is looking.

Leadership is as much about stepping into an opportunity as it is about whatever position you may hold. There are leaders of antiracist organizations; leaders of other institutions and corporations; and community leaders who want to practice and promote antiracism. There are opportunities to lead in our neighborhoods, schools, and workplaces. Leadership in all of these spaces can be very impactful.

Should you take on a leadership role in opposition to racism? The short answer is yes. To be successful, you'll need to work in solidarity, and you will need humility, political savvy, and, above all, a genuine commitment. You will face moments that are more difficult than you expected. Are you ready to enter into dialogue with your racist uncle who runs a business in town, whose decisions matter to his customers, employees, suppliers, and others?

Are you up for challenging your boss, the board of trustees at your university, or the bank that holds your mortgage? How about stepping forward when Karen or Ken is putting a Black man's life at risk by calling the police because he is trying to walk his dog, or jog around the neighborhood, or read a book on a bench, or anything else that upsets their fragile white sensibilities?

It is important that you lead when you are able, that you step up when you have the chance. Your leadership matters. But no matter how tempting the spotlight might be, remember that you do not always need to be up front. Your ability to locate your humility will make all the difference. If you are not Black, you do not need to try and become the new face of the Black Lives Matter movement. If you are not a person directly impacted by the oppression being addressed, then your voice must be secondary—loud, but secondary. This is not about superficiality or identity politics but about who is most informed, most experienced, and most able to represent the people who are being targeted by oppression(s).

You can still lead, and you can still be useful. Your skills, knowledge, understanding, and experience may have prepared you for a leadership role, but perhaps, in this case, your leadership will be most helpful in a supportive or advisory capacity. That's okay. It is important to develop the political savvy to know when the cause is better served by you stuffing envelopes or making signs, drawing up a new policy draft, or otherwise working behind the scenes.

And if that sounds like too much right now, then start with one of the best ways to lead by example: in your family. Love is a powerful thing, and who you show love to sends a message to those around you. That does not mean just loving your partner or spouse, or your kids, but also friends and extended family, the folks who are like family, and the people you speak highly of—they are an extension of you. Who you choose to be "family" sends a very real message. If you allow the people you love to make racist statements or behave in a racist manner, that sends the message that you cosign with their bigotry. If you exhibit love only for white people, that message is louder than anything you say.

As the Black Lives Matter movement took hold and white people began asking friends, colleagues, and acquaintances how to help, their lack of close relationships across racial lines was sometimes exposed. They might have talked a good game about diversity and inclusion, but their circle of friends told a different story. There is no short-term solution to developing such relationships. Many white folks ended up seeking guidance from people they barely knew.

Real relationships across differences matter not only for genuine learning but also for the example you set. People who look up to you will take notice of who makes up your circles. They will notice when your claimed values are not reflected in those people you hold dear. As community builder Bellamy Shoffner of Revolutionary Humans puts it:

> *It is insufficient to only tell your children that racism and racists are bad. It is insufficient to simply explain "we love people of all colors."' It is lazy and near damaging to proclaim a love for all people but never make the leap of actually reaching out to people of color or adding tangible diversity to your life. In a world filled with empty rhetoric, our children don't need to hear words from us without action. They need to see us embody the beliefs we claim to hold dear.*[1]

Her words hold true regarding not only what our children need to see but our example for everyone around us.

The people who were important to my parents were always around, especially when we lived behind the packie. As kids, we knew who the important ones were, the people our parents cared about most. Their close relationships were an extension of their values, including racial equity and inclusion. That doesn't mean they didn't have white friends—they did, and they were held to an antiracist standard. What it did mean was that our parents also had close friends of color. They became friends with who they liked, and those relationships became close over time. They never had to tell anyone that they had a Black friend or that they were not racist. They lived their values, and we valued their example.

So many of those important people attended the memorial services for Kacey and were there for our family, and many were there later when we lost Mom and Dad. They influenced countless people during their lives. We all influence more people than we know, and maybe more than we want to believe, because that comes with a lot of responsibility. On the other hand, it also presents a lot of opportunity and hope as well.

Making Activism Your Own

I cannot tell you exactly when and where you should stand up and demand change. Only you know if you are not raising your hand when the opportunity arises. But living an antiracist life requires more than stepping up only when it is comfortable, when it poses no risk, or when it is popular. Too many people do the superficial and safe, "like" the antiracist memes, and show up at all the cultural events, but are nowhere to be found when their voice could make a real difference.

I cannot tell you exactly when and where you should stand up and demand change. Only you know if you are not raising your hand when the opportunity arises.

My introduction to public antiracism efforts was through activism. I had seen protests on television and read about them in books, but the first protest I ever attended was in 1986, my tenth-grade year. I went to protest the Ku Klux Klan at a rally in Washington, DC, to demonstrate that their racism and anti-Semitism were not welcome.

News of the protest caused the Klan to move their event. When we learned of their change of plans, we marched toward their new site. What was most disturbing—and I have seen this many times since—was that the police were poised to "protect" the Klan from our demonstration. We marched until we reached the point where the police decided that we needed to stop. I was near the front, along with many other young people, and as we tried to stop, the momentum of those behind us pushed us into the police line.

Things became tense. The police worked to serve and protect the Klan, one of the most terroristic and murderous hate groups in US history, against those of us who were peacefully protesting their hate. Perhaps that is no revelation, considering what we have seen at Black Lives Matter marches in more recent years. Indeed, systemic racism within our police forces has been the norm since the inception of slave patrols. The only thing that has changed is the technology: Being able to record a video of their behavior means we can expose it to the world. Not as much of a game changer as I would hope, since so many people are still able to access their bigotry easier than their critical thinking skills, but still, these videos are beginning to make a real difference.

Activism can take many forms. Some people are not comfortable marching in the streets. They may be legitimately concerned about police violence, for example, or retaliation at their place of employment. I have learned from many exceptional activists who have engaged by providing educational materials, participating in civil disobedience, holding teach-ins, and promoting hashtag campaigns that draw attention to social justice issues and initiatives. Recently, I have seen many activists provide young people with access to banned books, start banned-book clubs, and provide funding for the purchase of banned books. My local Barnes and Noble even has a banned-book section—I loved to see that and took Makkie straight to it! I have also seen online examples of activism on websites, blogs, and even social media accounts that center diverse perspectives and provide access to critical resources. How you can become involved in antiracist activism is only limited by your creativity and willingness to participate.

Your activism may also be situational. When I was nine years old, Larry Bird and Magic Johnson were drafted into the National Basketball

Association (NBA). Magic went to the Los Angeles Lakers and Bird went to the Boston Celtics. My favorite player at the time was Julius "Dr. J" Erving, but it was impossible not to get caught up in the Celtics–Lakers rivalry; it was epic, and they were both phenomenal players. I particularly loved how they played team ball—they each had an uncanny ability to find the open man and make the perfect pass.

Unfortunately, the rivalry had already been tainted by racism among fans and in the media. It was not by accident that, for the most part, white folks favored Bird, and Black folks rooted for Magic. While the Celtics had actually been the first team in the NBA to draft a Black player, first with an all-Black starting five, and the first with a Black head coach, Boston fans were another story. And when Larry Bird came to town, their racism went into overdrive.

Of course I was a Celtics fan: Kacey and I were both named after Celtic greats (K. C. Jones and JoJo White) after all. I had always rooted for the Celtics, but during the Magic and Bird era (basically the 1980s), I made a point to only wear Lakers gear. Even as a kid, I could see what was going on, and that was my way of saying that I was not going to align myself with the racist white folks who made Bird their great white hope and who demonized Magic and the Lakers. They took the rivalry between teams, which had existed for decades, and turned it into a racial litmus test.

Wearing my Lakers shirt was my way of saying "I'm not with the racists." It was my way of protesting, and believe me, it got plenty of attention. I was called everything from a traitor to an n-slur lover—mostly by white adults. They weren't mad at me for being a fan of the awesome "Laker break"; they were mad because as a white kid, I was supposed to cosign with their bigotry.

Activism can be a great outlet for creativity. A number of individuals have volunteered to assist me and my colleagues with everything from graphic design to proposal writing. I have seen artwork that stirred critical questions, heard spoken word that uplifted, and encountered creative memes that genuinely made people think. These are activist efforts as well, and I'm all for it.

Find the type of activism that best fits your personality, skill set, and circumstances. Activism is what you make it; as long as it serves to promote racial equity and justice, it is all good. If you find yourself deeply concerned about racism, I implore you to engage in some way as an activist, or to do your best to support others in their activism and efforts to create change.

Finding Your Voice as an Advocate

While activism focuses on taking disruptive action to bring attention to a cause, advocacy is simply about expressing support for a particular initiative, position, group, or opportunity for change.

Advocacy, like activism, takes many forms. You can advocate for a particular public reform, a policy change at work, or a change in your school's curriculum. Your advocacy can be personal or professional, focus on specific change in an organization or community, or seek support for major social change.

Engaging in advocacy often requires articulating your perspective to potential supporters, including those who may not initially agree. This requires not only antiracist literacy but also a depth of understanding of the specific change for which you are advocating. As with most forms of engagement, there are behind-the-scenes opportunities as well—for example, doing research to help legal advocates make their case or working to inform and motivate potential supporters to engage with political advocates.

Another way to advocate is through philanthropy. As antiracist philanthropists, we have the opportunity to advocate by centering racial equity and justice in our giving choices. If you are able to organize with other donors, you can amplify your advocacy even further. As writer and social justice leader Vu Le points out: "We need to acknowledge that the things that most donors care about, the things that make them feel good, are often the things that will *least likely* change the systems of oppression and exploitation that make philanthropy necessary."[2] Your advocacy through giving can create a shift *away* from fundraising with ulterior motives and *toward* philanthropy in solidarity with antiracist organizations.

Racial justice advocacy does not always need to occur within an action focused only on racial justice. Within a racially unjust society like ours, a racial justice lens is always valuable. You may choose to engage in environmental justice advocacy, promote gender equity in an organization's leadership, or speak at a city council meeting to address food insecurity. Bringing an antiracist perspective to the table as an advocate for other social and environmental issues is another critical way to advance racial justice. Your antiracist voice, raised within another movement, is valuable because it can help those involved to see the connections between causes and find opportunities to engage in solidarity. So, keep fighting your fight, but also consider whether racially diverse voices are included at all levels and how racial justice applies within other social movements.

I have sought to advocate by bringing my racial justice lens to efforts to recruit more teachers, address suicide on college campuses, and promote shopping with small businesses. I have served as an advocate for changes in hiring policies and practices, and for hiring specific job candidates who, in my opinion, were not being evaluated equitably. I have advocated for changes in everything from curricula to international faculty exchanges. The way I see it, when racial justice is a core value, it simply goes where you go.

Advocacy is not easy. Many people find it difficult to raise their hand in support of racial equity and justice. Race and racism have been made taboo in many spaces. This is a form of resistance; if you make it difficult to even speak about racism, change is less likely. The pressure to maintain the status quo is real, and peer pressure is just as intense in the workplace and in politics as it was in grade school. People who believe change should happen sometimes fail at the time when they could best advocate for change, because they fear being labeled or that they may experience retaliation.

Advocacy is often met with resistance. There is no way around this truth. Speaking up at the right moment requires the courage to set aside the taboo and take some level of risk—which, predictably, is likely higher for people of color and other marginalized folks. If this makes you hesitant, continue to discuss your passion for advocacy in conversations with friends, or at your child's school, and during family dinners to build experience working through that discomfort. That may help you eventually feel more confident speaking up in public, at work, or in larger forums.

When people who believe in racial justice (particularly white people and others in privileged positions or roles) choose not to speak up and advocate for change, this makes the work of DEI professionals even more difficult, and success less likely. My colleagues and I can all recount painful stories about folks we have worked with who understand the issues and claim to be supportive of the work but are nowhere to be seen when their voice could make a difference. I have seen many initiatives fail, and many diversity and inclusion leaders lose their jobs, because people who claimed to support the work chose to remain silent when their voices mattered most.

Member, Alum, Elder: Wielding Your Influence

Our relationships with institutions and organizations provide us with additional opportunities to promote racial equity, inclusion, and justice. Whether you are a member of a religious institution or a club, an alum of a school or university, or an elder within a particular field or community, your status holds weight. Highly privileged families never doubt their influence; they know that their money and power can exert pressure on educational institutions and advance their agenda. As an educator, however, I have seen firsthand how students, parents, and alumni can have a major impact on admissions, curricula, teaching practices, policies, and more.

Our relationship with our schools, colleges, and universities are critical to our success, and also to the continued success of those institutions. Yes, major donors have far more power and influence than they should. But the student community does not realize how much power it could wield. Despite students sometimes choosing not to exercise that power for fear of retribution or simply due to apathy, their voices have a great deal of influence. Schools and universities are concerned with their reputation, and some actually want to do better around DEI. Once we realize our power and become willing to take action to cultivate support and attention, we have the opportunity to promote real and sustainable change.

As a student, I was not fully aware of how to use that collective power. Most of us had no idea about the inner workings of our schools and school systems, or the extent to which external players control decision-making, and we didn't know how to access that information. My efforts would have been much more effective and consequential if I had understood how the power structure worked and who the actual influencers and decision-makers were behind the systems we were trying to change.

Today, many student efforts initially take the form of a hashtag, followed by multiple video posts addressing related issues and concerns. Sometimes, because students do not know what they do not know, they are too easily appeased by temporary, partial, or superficial changes promised by administrators. But during my years as a university administrator, I saw the concern and well-hidden panic that results when student-, parent-, and alumni-led activism and advocacy hit their target. Of late, we have seen this on display with the pro-Palestinian/anti-genocide encampment protests on campuses across the US and internationally. While some of these protests have received major media attention, and some changes in investing practices have been reported at a few universities, we are not seeing a true cross section of these protests and their impact.

More often than not, a great deal is being left on the table. Members of school communities and other organizations can trigger far more change if we refuse to settle for scraps, and if we follow our activism with well-informed negotiations and binding agreements. We are seeing more substantive and potentially sustainable results as activists make it a regular practice to engage experienced advisors who are knowledgeable about the systems and powers at play, as well as attorneys willing to assist in negotiating and drafting agreements. Seeking advice and assistance is proving effective, which is why we hear such external organizers, advisors, and professional collaborators referred to as "outside agitators" in an attempt to vilify those supporting students interested in advancing social justice through their activism and advocacy.

We should not underestimate our influence in spaces where we have invested our time and in organizations that value our membership. Raising your voice to encourage change, and being clear when potential deal-breakers arise that could cause you to withdraw support or sever ties, can provide the jolt necessary to ensure racial justice is considered in decision-making.

Change Agency

When an organization or movement seeks to support social justice within its ranks, a theory of change—a description of why and how a particular change will be accomplished—will develop. As leaders and managers know, in order to best ensure success, this should be followed by developing and implementing a strategic plan, measuring progress to ensure the intended change takes place, and continuing to adjust and work toward progress over time. This is a standard process, which doesn't make change easy but does provide a road map for the work.

When it comes to DEI, many people point to some type of diversity training as the goal of the work. It is actually just a tool for promoting understanding or to advance specific objectives through education, not an end goal.

Let's say a brick-and-mortar retailer wants to change their business to focus primarily on online sales. The retailer would not expect any significant change to come from training employees about the benefits of online sales and then doing nothing else. But that is exactly what we are expected to accept as a genuine effort to address racism and intersecting oppressions in today's organizations: "Here is your two-hour training on diversity, and we're done. Now we are antiracist, right?"

Intentionally impotent efforts to "check the diversity or antiracism box" are the rule, not the exception in far too many organizations. When organizational leaders truly want to address racial equity and justice, they know what is necessary to make systemic changes. Anything less than what they know would work is simply meant to pacify and serve public relations purposes while avoiding meaningful change. And far too often, we accept this as a "step in the right direction," hoping it will lead to an actual commitment to change in the future.

But organizational change around racial equity, inclusion, and justice is complicated, and most often involves addressing deeply entrenched cultural norms. There is truth in the old-school management aphorism "Culture eats strategy for breakfast." No matter how strategic and sustainable your plans are, change will be a hard sell if the culture of your organization (or your nation, for that matter) disagrees with the intended change. In this context, performative mission statements and policies that are never put into practice serve only as superficial public relations efforts. Change agents know that promoting culture shift must be incorporated into any process of change management alongside strategic planning.

What that means for our efforts to promote racial equity, inclusion, and justice is that it is critically important to directly address resistance and challenge problematic norms. This is difficult for organizations to accomplish without the guidance of professionals (internal and/or external) who specialize in this work. Depending on your position with your employer, your change agency may involve advocating for the necessary hiring of consultants, being actively involved with the strategic planning, or participating in plan implementation as a vocal advocate for systemic change.

The first step in becoming a change agent is to understand how change happens in your organization, community, or wherever you are trying to promote progress. Once you understand the process, you will be prepared to advocate for initiatives with real potential for success. Numerous resources (including benchmarks, strategic frameworks, and educational materials) and professionals are available to assist in research, strategic planning, implementation, and measurements of progress.

Hiring and promotion practices are an area where change is often necessary—and effective—in efforts to promote a more diverse organization. Writing an antiracist policy is not particularly difficult. Many organizations have excellent hiring policies on paper but continue to racially discriminate in practice because the organizational culture simply ate their new hiring policy and continued to do what has always been done. Then, when the hiring has not produced any more diversity, the response is to defer blame—"Hey, we tried the new policy, but it just didn't work"—when the truth is that a new policy was written but not actually put into practice.

The first step in becoming a change agent is to understand how change happens in your organization, community, or wherever you are trying to promote progress.

This resistance to progress in hiring works when new equity policies have no "teeth"—meaning that nobody is held accountable for implementation and success. When leaders want a new policy to work, they will not only promote it and provide resources but also build implementation and success directly into evaluations and performance reviews. People are held accountable.

In addition to developing goals, resources, metrics, incentives, and accountability measures, we must also interrogate resistance. There is no magical process that will work for every organization. The process must make sense within the organization's structures and norms and must acknowledge how challenges to organizational values have been successfully addressed in the past.

If an organization is serious about change, then a shared learning process must be established, encouraged, and properly resourced. To effectively embrace racial equity and inclusion at the institutional level, individuals will need to increase their antiracist literacy (from different starting points), and the organization will need to adopt an intentional process for organizational learning. By doing this, an organization will develop the sustainable racial equity and inclusion policies necessary to see progress. But, in order to benefit from all of that work, leadership must follow through with implementation.

Since basketball has been so important in my life, I'll use it here to illustrate another critical point. On a team, it is important that each player continues to learn, practice, and work out in order to contribute their best to the team. If a player works hard to become an excellent shooter, learns technique, and practices hard, it will only matter in the game if they are not afraid to take the shot—in other words, they have to want the ball. The same is true when we talk about organizational change or change within any community. You can learn everything you need to know about antiracism and organizational change, but you have to be ready and willing to use your voice—you have to want the ball!

As individuals learn and develop their antiracist perspectives, and as the organization develops new policy and institutes new practices, including holding one another accountable, a foundation is built to support progress. As time goes by, new approaches may become necessary, but the value placed on antiracism in the organization can be maintained and improved upon because it has become a value, and changes in practice become the norm within the organizational culture.

Antiracist Freestyling: Do *Your* Thing

Not all antiracist efforts are planned out or can be easily categorized as activism, advocacy, or change agency. That's a good thing: There is no need to limit our efforts, regulate how anyone lives their own unique antiracist life, or restrict ourselves to formal, planned, or organized action.

We never know what might make people rethink their perspective. Instead of a teacher, parent, mentor, or prominent leader who challenges someone to think differently, it could be just something that happens in the moment to spur change: the way a friend reacts to a news report, or an impromptu statement by a coach, or a server in a restaurant challenging an overheard comment. Or it might be a big, pickup truck–driving, good-old-boy-looking guy behind the counter at the local pharmacy wearing a Black Lives Matter mask who makes someone consider a different perspective.

I think of those situations as "antiracist freestyling."

To extend the basketball metaphor a bit, you can think of this as playing a pickup game. No coaches, no game plan, and no set plays—just the opportunity to play, to take that shot you've been working on or make that assist that gives a teammate the opportunity to slam it home. These opportunities happen for antiracist action as well, and it is not always about directly opposing racism. Sometimes, the most powerful antiracist actions are actually about providing opportunities for others—the assist.

In higher education, possibly the most critical and powerful antiracist action is focused more generally on the progress of people of color. In spite of the system of racial oppression that threatens to obstruct their success, HBCUs, like Florida A&M University, provide opportunities for students that may otherwise be excluded. Not only that, HBCUs work to counter the white supremacist ideologies and racist practices that are the norm in our schools. FAMU and other higher education institutions provide examples of

> *Sometimes, the most powerful antiracist actions are actually about providing opportunities for others—the assist.*

Black excellence in curricula and among students, faculty, staff, and the administration, and produce alumni who intentionally lift as they climb, which may be the greatest contribution of all.

But you do not need to be a university or some other large organization to advance racial equity and justice, and it is not all about decisions made by CEOs and politicians. Whether it is addressing the underlying racism in how the white instructor of your spin class imitates African American Vernacular English when playing hip-hop music or making the effort to include someone who is being excluded at a social function, these are opportunities that matter. Our daily interactions with one another tend to have a far more immediate and personal impact. These are all opportunities to freestyle.

Perhaps you make the intentional decision to frequent a business that has been targeted by anti-Asian hate, or seek out Latinx employees for leadership roles. Maybe you financially support water protectors and land defenders, or bank with a Black-owned financial institution, or contribute as much as you can to a scholarship fund for students of color. There are many ways that you can actively promote racial equity and justice by showing love and support. You are uniquely qualified, so do your thing—whatever that is—in support of the advancement of racial equity and justice.

When you wanted to deepen a friendship, how did you do that?

When you were upset that your child's school stopped offering music classes, what did you do?

When you felt a policy at your job was unfair to you or a friend, how did you promote change?

Do your thing—whatever that is—in support of the advancement of racial equity and justice.

You know better than anyone how you learn, build relationships, address problems, and work with others to make a difference. This is no different. It simply takes the will to educate yourself and figure out how you can have your best antiracist impact. With some guidance, you will absolutely be able to employ your strengths and experience to contribute to the advancement of racial justice both within organized structures, like schools or workplaces, and as opportunities present themselves in your daily life.

Paraphrasing the abolitionist Theodore Parker, the Reverend Dr. Martin Luther King Jr. said, "The arc of the moral universe is long, but it bends toward justice." I believe this to be true. Over time, we will end white supremacy and all forms of oppression. How long will it take? How many lives will be lost or limited in the process? I can only respond by saying that it will take less time if you join the struggle.

We need people working at every level and in every nook and cranny of every community. There is no one right answer that will end racism or poverty or any other massive sociocultural problem.

We need brilliant authors to write the next *Race Matters*, *Lies My Teacher Told Me*, and *Caste*.

We need policy wonks to dig in and write antiracist policies that will transform practices in all of our institutions.

We need lawmakers to transform our tax laws and the justice system, along with political leaders like Mayor Keisha Lance Bottoms of Atlanta and Mayor Melvin Carter of St. Paul (both FAMU alums), and to make decisions with racial justice front of mind.

We need educators and influencers to teach us all how to do better.

And we need you to want the ball, to cultivate progress within your sphere of influence whenever the opportunity arises, like only you can. It is too late in the game for those who oppose racism to still be sitting on the bench! It is time to get in the game and contribute.

AFTERWORD

FOR ALL THE MARBLES
How We All Benefit from Choosing Solidarity

*You cannot fight racism with racism.
You have to fight it with solidarity.*

—BOBBY SEALE

WE CANNOT FULLY UNDERSTAND anyone else's truth—only our own. In my young life, the person who knew me best was my brother Kacey. Still, I will never know what it was like to walk in the world as Kacey, and he could not completely understand what it was like to be me. Still, we walked together through our young lives, and I have never been closer to anyone since. That experience has been unique in my life, and one that I have difficulty describing to people.

For years, people told me to watch the television show *This Is Us*, about a white couple pregnant with triplets, one of whom dies during childbirth. As fate would have it, another infant, Randall, was left at a fire station that same day and brought to the hospital. The parents decide to adopt Randall, a Black child, and bring him home with Kevin and Kate—"The Big Three"—to start their lives together as a family. I think my friends believed this show would allow me to reminisce about my own family experience. I was doubtful.

It took all that downtime during the COVID-19 pandemic for me to finally start watching the first episode, ready for a completely uninformed take on interracial adoption. Hollywood has a way of taking what is important and turning it into something trivial for the sake of commercial viability. I was wary but curious about seeing the portrayal of a family that looked a little bit more like mine than most shown on television.

As adults, Kevin and Randall begin to talk more directly about their experiences growing up—especially Randall's experience around race, racism, and interracial adoption, and how Kevin had been oblivious to much of it. Although we see Kevin trying, in the past and present, to understand and be there for his brother, at times he committed significant microaggressions toward Randall, caused in part by Kevin's jealousy. Randall was smart and accomplished in ways that Kevin was not, and Kevin felt that his brother was treated as special because he was Black.

This brought up real emotions from my own past. There is something special about the love between brothers, a bond that is unique, in my experience, yet I had felt jealousy toward Kacey at times: when he grew taller than me even though I was the older brother and the one who loved basketball, or when girls would swoon over him and only see me as a way to get to him. As a young teenager, when I told Kacey about feeling jealous, he laughed and said he wished he was "book smart" like me. The idea that he could be at all envious of me was surprising, and he may have just been being kind, but it made me feel better anyway.

The parts of the show that were focused on the childhood of The Big Three didn't resonate much with me, but when they were shown as adults it made me wonder, as I often do, about what it would be like if Kacey were here today. Among many other things, I wish we could sit down today and discuss, as adults, how race and racism, and particularly his adoption and experience growing up, impacted him. Kacey and I used to talk about what it was like to be Black and to be adopted, and what it was like to be white and not adopted. That gave me a sense of how he felt, but we were both teens at the time. At the end of the day, I will never truly understand exactly why we lost Kacey or what exactly he was feeling. The white parents and siblings in *This Is Us* are often unaware of what Randall is experiencing, and when they do see it, they don't know how to handle it, so they tend to just ignore it or smooth things over. They do their best, but for the most part, they are unprepared.

While our parents were not ones to ignore racism when they saw it, there were times when they missed it. And as close as we brothers were, there were times I would call something out that Kacey would say was no big deal and other times when I missed painful microaggressions that he would mention later, and I have no doubt there was plenty that he never mentioned. There was certainly a lot that I kept inside, and still do.

Growing up together, Kacey, B-J, and I had a lot in common—we loved to laugh together, crack on our parents, and make everything into a competition—but we all knew that our experiences were different in ways that mattered. Some of it was due to birth order and our many natural differences with respect to interests, abilities, and disposition. Too much of it, though, was due to racism. One thing that I learned early on was that empathy only goes so far. I will never know what it was like to be Kacey, growing up Black in an otherwise white family, in the 1970s and '80s, in the towns we lived in.

This is an important point for white folks to understand.

Often, in an attempt to demonstrate empathy, we will say that we understand someone else's experience and give an example of something we have been through that we believe is comparable. When it comes to race, in particular, this can be problematic. White people often equate momentary inconveniences or losses of privilege to a lifelong experience of racial oppression, but the two are incomparable. Sure, we can empathize, but empathy is not a full understanding. And, to further complicate things, not every person of color's experience with white supremacy and racism is the same.

Makkie has made it clear to me and her mother that her experience as a "mixed" kid is different from Kecia's experience as a Black woman or mine as a white man. Of course, Mak also makes it clear that our experiences are different because her mom and I grew up in the "olden days." Even way back then, my growing-up experience was very different from most other white folks', and I often felt most different among those who looked like me. What I can understand about Makkie's experience is what it is like to feel different. That is a connection point but not a full understanding, so it is important to listen and believe her when she talks about what it is like being her in the world today.

Part of my experience since Kacey's passing has been taking responsibility for what I missed and the things I did not speak up about. It has also been about being intentional about how I live my life moving forward. After George Floyd's murder, when my little one challenged me to do more, I began to reflect, again, on all that I wished I'd done in the past and all the things that I have yet to accomplish.

One morning a few years ago, Makkie walked into my room, gave me a hug, and asked what I was thinking about while I happened to be looking at some old pictures.

"Uncle Kacey," I said, and she asked for a story.

I cannot remember which story I told Mak that morning—the one about how Kacey and I used to play catch with baby B-J as if he were a football, or the one about how we used to push B-J into Mom and Dad's room on Christmas morning to wake them up, or the time Kacey and I stole Mom's car in the middle of the night to go see some girls.

I cannot explain how much joy I get from hearing Makkie laugh when I share those memories. "Tell me the story about how you and Uncle Kacey got caught searching for all the Easter eggs in the middle of the night!" she demands, giggling. "Tell me how you and Uncle Kacey jumped off the roof with an umbrella like you had no sense!"

Sometimes I forget how much fun we had. The racism that seeped into our lives, and the loss of Kacey at age seventeen—these things cloud my memories. But I refuse to forget our childhood together, and Mak helps me embrace those joyous memories. Telling her stories helps me keep Kacey's spirit alive in a beautiful way—different from, but just as important as, the stories I share to encourage people to live antiracist lives.

I also wonder about the stories that never came to be, and all the good times we missed because we lost Kacey so young. When I dream, I see Kacey as an adult, telling our stories with the child he might have had on one knee and Makkie on the other, all three of them laughing at the funny parts.

Can you imagine all the stories their family and friends would have today if young people like Emmett Till, Tamir Rice, Aiyana Stanley-Jones, and so many others had not been lost at such a young age? It is painful to fathom how many stories never came to be because people were cut down in the name of white supremacy before they ever had a chance to live a full life or have their own children and grandchildren.

I believe that some of the greatest tragedies in life are the stories that are cut short. If nothing else, maybe that will give you pause about the impact of racism on the world and why it is so important that we do better. You and I might not be able to end systemic racism in our time, but we can absolutely make progress that could result in a few more happy stories being told.

> *Can you imagine all the stories their family and friends would have today if young people like Emmett Till, Tamir Rice, Aiyana Stanley-Jones, and so many others had not been lost at such a young age?*

Small, Brave Actions Build Momentum

As we have discussed, doing your part to oppose racism is not just about planning how you will address a particular issue or follow a particular antiracist path. When you value racial justice and endeavor to live an antiracist life, you *will* make a difference—never doubt that. The biggest challenge in this is not figuring out what to do; it is building your confidence so you will not be afraid to do what you can.

Making a difference is not always about the big, bold actions. Usually, it is about how we counter daily microaggressive behaviors with validation, support, compassion, and by simply doing our part in the moment as we go about our daily routines. These actions build momentum toward changes in families, friend groups, schools, communities, organizations, and beyond.

We also need a measure of confidence to be able to withstand the backlash and resistance that are common whenever we challenge microaggressions or racist norms. It has been my experience, from working with students over the past few decades, that establishing a solid base of knowledge is often a major factor in building confidence. This speaks to the need to educate ourselves—a lifelong endeavor—in order to feel like we have a grasp on relevant concepts, histories, and potential paths toward change.

Confidence also comes from practice. It is surprising how those challenging conversations with family, friends, and colleagues can help prepare us. So, embrace that debate with your uncle at your next holiday dinner or cookout. He may be a great sparring partner, and that could teach you something useful! Also, listen to experienced antiracist friends, colleagues, and elders; what they share about their experience can be helpful. Learn from their successes as well as their stories about how they have stumbled along the way.

Understanding Yourself and Your Gifts

I have been referred to in many ways over the years: Mike and Maxine's boy, Kacey's brother, Dr. Joe-Joe, Mak's dad. I have also been called not-so-loving names, plenty of times. Ultimately, of course, I am just Joe-Joe.

We are all complex individuals. We assume different roles and wear different hats. We change as we learn, grow, and take on new responsibilities. Through it all, our core values are there to guide us through life.

I have known people who have one set of values at home and another at work, or one set of values publicly and another in private. This value-switching enables people to express genuine support for racial justice at home, for example, but then shift to become a cog in a racist system at work or in the voting booth. This makes no sense to me. Our values are meaningless if we do not do our best to live by them.

It is not enough to tell yourself and others that you are opposed to systemic racism. Examining your own behavior, through the lens of values that you believe you hold, can be an enlightening process. You may find that you truly believe certain values to be right—such as racial justice—but that you are choosing not to live by them. Tackling these types of internal conflicts, and ultimately aligning your values and behaviors, is a critical step in knowing and valuing yourself for who you are.

I encourage you to take stock of your strengths. What are you good at? Which skills have you developed, and what knowledge base and experience do you bring to the table? Of course, knowing yourself, your social location, and gifts is foundational for being able to make your best contributions. Knowing who you are, and how you are perceived, will help you determine some of the ways you can best contribute as an antiracist. That understanding, along with recognizing your sphere of influence, will help you see some of the impact that you could have.

Most of us have no idea of the depth and breadth of our impact on others. Sometimes, modesty can keep us from seeing the potential range of our impact. Other times, we do not want to know, because then we might feel a heavy responsibility. Either way, I think it is safe to say that your influence is far greater than you think.

Kacey kept a card with him over the years that read "I may not always be perfect but I'm always me." He learned that lesson from Mom and Dad, who told us to just be ourselves, that we could do anything we set our minds to. Kacey personified those words, and I believe that is why he had such an extraordinary impact on people. He knew and loved himself, embracing all that made him uniquely Kacey, and that gave everyone around him permission to be themselves as well. He taught me that it's not possible to be the best version of yourself if you are trying to be like someone else. Learning this difficult lesson has been a lifelong process. My insecurities often get in the way—but they didn't when I was with him. I could just be myself, without worries about being judged or only seen for my flaws. I think that is why I took pride in being called "Kacey's brother." I knew that was the most honest version of who I was.

Over time, I have come to understand that each of us is able to make our unique mark in the world because of—not in spite of—what makes us a unique, quirky, or distinctive part of the human family. Spend time thinking about how you can use your unique attributes, the talents you were born with, and the skills you have developed to make a difference in the way that and in the spaces where only you can. In other words, use your superpowers for good!

I used to think that becoming an antiracist activist or an advocate for racial justice meant responding in a certain way to bigotry and learning the "right way" to challenge and replace racist systems. I wanted to be like people who I had seen do it well. But no matter how I tried, I could not be anything but a poor facsimile of any of them. I had to remind myself of the lesson Kacey modeled so well: I could never be any better than a wannabe version of someone else, but nobody could ever be a better version of Kacey's brother Joe-Joe than I could.

The fact that your voice is different from mine, or anyone else's, is exactly why it is so valuable.

No particular antiracist voice is the best kind. Once you solidify racial justice as a core value, your own unique voice will be the best way for you to live that value out loud. The fact that your voice is different from mine, or anyone else's, is exactly why it is so valuable.

Courage Can Be Contagious

Sometimes, the most powerful statements come from those who are speaking up for the first time. This is not beginner's luck. It is the combination of urgency, authenticity, and courage that is so impactful. When the circumstances are important enough for someone to take that chance for the first time, it is often unexpected and causes others to take note, and it can even help them locate their own courage moving forward.

As I was consulting with an organization's leadership team a few years ago, a white, male vice president of finance, who by all accounts had never taken a stance on an equity issue before, spoke up for the first time. We were discussing a common component of diversity plans—a hiring initiative—which they had implemented a couple of years prior. It looked good on paper but seemed to have produced no significant results. Predictably, everyone was placing blame on the pipeline and questioning whether people of color were even interested in applying.

I have learned to be comfortable with silence in these situations, so I remained quiet until they had worn themselves out with excuses. As I waited, most of them became visibly uncomfortable. Then, the vice president of finance said, "This didn't work because we didn't fund it." He went on to provide details supporting his claim, and his voice got through to the decision-makers in the room. They ended up agreeing to allocate funds and save the initiative. Measurable progress came about as a result of that vice president speaking up. His speaking up around racial justice also seemed to inspire others to speak up on equity and inclusion issues over time; it was like it was contagious.

More recently, while serving as an executive diversity officer at a university, I sat in on the first day of a particular class. The professor was introducing the syllabus for the semester, and I was curious about the course.

One student, an African American woman who was active on campus, raised her hand. "Why are all of the assigned authors white?" she asked.

The professor responded, not quite believably, that she had not realized this.

Others began to chime in, mostly Latinx and white students, asking the professor to update the curriculum and pointing out the importance of diverse perspectives. None of them backed down or seemed impressed by the professor's attempts to deflect.

A number of the students who knew my position on campus followed me out the door to express their concerns after class. I asked them to keep me posted and said I was hopeful that the professor would make substantive updates. I met with the faculty member privately a couple of times and provided resources. Later, I heard from the students that she had made significant changes to the syllabus but seemed uncomfortable with what she was teaching. That was the spark for a related PD initiative for faculty, which gained support and became a success—all because those students took a chance and spoke up, and the faculty member had the courage to make changes and engage around a curriculum that was largely new to her.

At some point, progress requires taking chances. Courage is required to speak up, possibly for the first time, because you feel nervous, concerned about retaliation, or afraid that you might not know enough. It also takes courage to make changes to your own approach. There is no getting around those challenges, but we can keep it all in context and put a better foot forward each day.

I love sci-fi, so I'll give another example of courage from the entertainment world—the original *Star Trek* series. Fans know that the Reverend Dr. Martin Luther King Jr. himself encouraged African American actor Nichelle Nichols to continue in her role as Lieutenant Uhuru when she was considering moving on. She decided to stay because Dr. King let her know how impactful her representation in that role was. The original series also included George Takei, a gay Japanese American actor who had lived through Japanese internment in California, as Lieutenant Sulu, and a major Russian character, Pavel Chekov (played by Walter Koenig) was notable because we were in the midst of the Cold War between the US and the Soviet Union at the time. *Star Trek*'s producers took chances to be inclusive from the beginning in their casting choices and with multiple storylines addressing racism in the context of a futuristic view of humanity. Many of the show's fans over the years have been white US Americans, who have internalized antiracism and the vision of a more inclusive future. The courage of the writers, producers, and actors made a difference for Trekkers, like me, all over the world.

Whichever chances you take to stand up against oppression—whether you choose to speak up at home, at work, or in a moment when something happens at the grocery store—each time will make you more confident and more resolute. Each brave step will contribute to your understanding of the important issues around race and racism and how you can best contribute to progress. Some efforts might land flat, and you will learn from them. Others will find success and fuel your commitment. Either way, these experiences are reminders that you do have the courage to step up, and that your voice matters.

Good Times with Good People

At some point after Kacey passed, Dad started encouraging us to have more fun. He had always made the most of our time playing ball together, chatting as he took us on meandering drives, and while we worked together. But after Kacey passed, he realized that he would have liked to have had even more fun with his boys. So, he stopped saying goodbye whenever we parted and replaced it with "Have fun!"

It was the fun we had while working together as a family that taught me how to have fun working with colleagues. Progress rarely comes overnight. That is why I have found it important to appreciate the time spent with colleagues as we do this difficult work together. Whether it has been at working retreats and conferences, doing our daily work in the classroom or office, or in video conference meetings, I have spent a great deal of time with some amazing colleagues. I have found great joy in these relationships.

As Dad always knew, we tend to do our best work in the company of those we love and respect.

Among the blessings that I appreciate daily are the late nights working, with music playing in the background, and sharing bad takeout. I love the deep conversations with brilliant colleagues between conference sessions, organizing, planning, and strategizing. And I have a lot of great memories of working with students who will take us all farther than we could ever expect. I could fill volumes with these powerful experiences. They are where my mind goes when I need to remember the beauty of what we are working toward. I see that future in the faces that shine bright in those memories.

Remembering good times with good people has helped keep me going when I feel like giving up. These memories remind me that I just need to pick up the phone and reminisce with friends who have become family through doing good work together. When I do that, without fail, I am lifted.

As I reflect on the people I have met through my work, and throughout life in general, I am convinced that we all have the potential to do far more than we imagine. We are amazingly good, deep, profound, and complicated, and we each have the potential for greatness in one way or another. Of course, among the many blessings of life, there are enormous challenges, and we also have a surprising potential for wrongdoing. Life is complicated, and too often we end up making it even more complicated for one another.

But I believe that we are improving—slowly, perhaps, and with far too many swings of the pendulum in the wrong direction, like the one we are experiencing politically right now. Nevertheless, as we find cures for everything from COVID-19 to cancer, I am hopeful that we will all be a little less callous and a bit more loving toward one another. I hope, for our children's sake, that we will overcome our bigotries and find better ways to live together. We have the capacity to love and to lead. We also have the capacity to hate and to harm. May we all aspire to the former and learn to rise above the latter.

The fight against racism and other intersecting oppressions continues to be my life's work. My determination has been fueled by the love of my family, including my chosen family, all around the world. I am driven by my desire to make the world better for Makkie and all her friends than it was for Kacey and ours, and better for our grandchildren than it was for our grandparents. I am holding on to the vision that our best days are ahead of us—knowing that is up to us.

In the end, it is love that matters—the love that we share, in struggle and in thanksgiving, and the love that we receive, which protects our hearts and feeds our souls. When things get difficult, living a purpose-driven life is what gets me out of bed every morning. My purpose is to be a good father, brother, friend, and colleague—and I can only be those things if I am also living my best antiracist life.

> *My purpose is to be a good father, brother, friend, and colleague—and I can only be those things if I am also living my best antiracist life.*

Hope for a New Normal

If I called my brother B-J right now and said I needed him, he would be on the next thing moving—no questions asked, ready for anything. And he knows that I would do the same. Likewise, Makkie knows that whenever she needs me, nothing could stop me from getting to her. I have been supported, loved, and saved in a variety of ways by aunts, uncles, and cousins, and by folks who have become family through critical experiences and over time. That is just what family does.

But being Kacey's brother has taught me that family is not defined by blood. Our collective ability to see family in one another may be the key to reconciliation and sustainable solidarity. Perhaps that is the new normal toward which we should be striving.

> *Being Kacey's brother has taught me that family is not defined by blood. Our collective ability to see family in one another may be the key to reconciliation and sustainable solidarity.*

It is not easy to define the connections I feel to people with whom I share a commitment to social, economic, and racial justice. Whether you like the term *ally*, or if you prefer *comrades*, *partners*, or *coconspirators*, I'm down. I don't have a problem with those terms, but for me, they fall a little short. This type of solidarity feels more like a familial relationship to me—one that extends across social constructs and borders. That bond is special, and I consider my extended family a blessing. We love each other through differences and are there for one another when it counts.

The relationships that make up these familial communities provide a glimpse into the future that we are fighting to secure for Makkie and her friends, those dream worlds that Kacey and I used to imagine out loud. We all need to begin seeing one another as family—as people who can disagree and still love one another, so long as our disagreement is not rooted in denial of the right to exist for any siblings in our human family. For now, though, we still live in a world where racism is entrenched in practically every system and institution, and Mak is still exposed to bigotry that she shouldn't have to endure. I try to remember that when we look at our children, we are seeing the before picture. The after picture is yet to come.

I remember after the memorials celebrating Kacey's life were over, and I went off to college, I began to feel like I needed to find a way to keep Kacey's story alive and continue to share the lessons I had learned. I was moved by how people had responded to the memorial events. I also felt like it made the most sense to work with young people.

I started by reaching out to teachers I knew and asking if I could speak to their classes. Among the first to say yes was a longtime family friend, Terri Fernandes, from our hometown of Carver, whose mom, Albertina, was the "Cake Lady"—a friend of Mom's who made the best cakes I have ever tasted. Terri, a high school math teacher, invited me to speak to her classes and at a school assembly.

Terri introduced me by talking about the connection between our families. I spoke about my brothers and me growing up in Carver, playing sports, and living behind the packie, and about the racism that Kacey experienced. Then I told the story about that little girl at the doctor's office. It was the first time I'd ever told that story publicly, and I could see the range of emotions on the faces of the students as they listened intently.

"Kacey was my hero," I said. "He made a difference in many lives, and I miss him every day."

It got quiet as I told them about losing my brother and asked them to help me keep his spirit alive by standing up against racism whenever they could.

"Speaking with you is part of my effort to make a difference," I continued, "and if I've convinced even one of you to reject racism, then it's worth everything to me."

Many of the students seemed touched by the stories I told, and some were visibly shaken. My delivery was raw, the experience of losing my brother was recent, and the students could see the pain on my face and in my tears.

Terri helped me wrap up the presentation with ideas for how the students could make a difference. After the bell rang for the next class, I was shocked to see how many students stayed behind. They lined up to speak with me, give me hugs, and offer condolences and promises that they would try to make a difference.

But one student did not line up. She just sat in the back and waited.

After the last of the other students had moved on, she approached and thanked me for sharing my stories about Kacey. Then she placed a marble in the palm of my hand, promised to always remember Kacey, and asked me to keep the marble as a reminder that I had made a difference that day.

I kept the marble, and it has done just that—reminded me that I am capable of making a difference. I remember that brilliant young woman fondly because of the gift she gave me, and for all of the marbles she has helped me to recognize since then: times I have made a difference in my own unique way.

Whenever I speak in public, I calm my nerves by reminding myself who I am: Kacey and B-J's brother, the eldest child of Mike and Maxine, and Mak's dad. I think of all that they have poured into me and all of the elders and siblings who are in my corner. They give me the courage to speak, to teach, and to write this book.

To live your best antiracist life in solidarity across all the social divides placed in our way, you must find the courage to make your own unique contributions. For my part, I will continue to offer myself as a brother to all who stand shoulder to shoulder in the ongoing movement to build a just world for us all. I hope to have the honor of standing next to you one day soon.

ACKNOWLEDGMENTS

I HAVE BEEN BLESSED TO have learned from and been guided and loved by more people than I could have ever hoped would take an interest. Some of their names are noted here and within the pages of *A Brother's Insight*, but many more are not. If you do not see your name, please charge it to my head, not my heart.

My learning and commitment to racial, social, and economic justice began at home, so first I want to thank my parents, Maxine and Mike; my brothers, Kacey and B-J; and my grandparents Amy and Joe. The best of me comes from them. I also want to thank Clive Anderson for protecting me from myself on the worst day of my life. And, of course, Makaila, my phenomenal daughter, who has inspired me since the moment she was born.

My family extends far and wide and has never been limited by blood. I am thankful for those who have guided me both personally and professionally. Russell Blake for showing me the importance of humility and perseverance. Ms. Audrey and Mr. Bennie Hopkins for being there when I needed a local family during college and beyond. Lenita and Ronald M. Joe for making me part of the family and for expecting me to lead.

For listening and providing words of wisdom and encouragement when it became difficult to remain hopeful, I thank Toni Battle, Francesca Lozada, Peter Lopes, Catherine Wong, Tasreen Khamisa, Julia Johnson, Mushim Ikeda, Kirindi Odindo, and LeShelle Woodard. Great appreciation for the feedback and wise counsel from Kristal T. Moore, Maya Cameron, Christy Trice, Jackie Reza, Patricia Lowrie, and Brother Yao Glover.

Thank you to Rheeda Walker for the encouragement and for agreeing to share a bit of her brilliance by writing the foreword. I am also grateful to Rheeda for connecting me with Gina Carroll, who I appreciate for very patiently guiding me through the writing process.

For always having my back, I have to thank more of the fam. I want to thank Stuart Lord and Michael Baston, who I consider brothers, for their friendship and guidance through the best and most challenging times. My sister, Elisha Fernandes; Kimberly Davis for the sunshine; Kerry Leary for fighting the good fight; Eurydice Stanley for all her strength; and Millie Okaro for her grace. Hollis Leary, a brother since our first fight; DeReef Jamison, because every conversation counts; Sheikh Sesay from Russia to Kenya; Sammy Bakali and the Malawi fam; Eddie Moore Jr. for his leadership; JuanCarlos Arauz because we've been there and get it; and Michael Benitez for always being real with me.

Deep appreciation for my DiCE family for the love, the D2K community for all the hugs and learning, my Rattler FAMUly for making me Dr. Joe-Joe, and the CLA/MLA team and alums for their ongoing inspiration. And, of course, all of the colleagues and students who have taught me along the way.

Finally, thank you to the friends and colleagues who provided such kind endorsements and all the editors and publishing professionals who have worked with me to bring this project to life.

NOTES

INTRODUCTION

1. I will use terminology in this text that refers to racial categories, including "Black" and "white," which are commonly used in the United States. This is not meant to further the myth of race but to speak to the social realities created by racism.

2. Rheeda Walker, *The Unapologetic Guide to Black Mental Health: Navigate an Unequal System, Learn Tools for Emotional Wellness, and Get the Help You Deserve* (Oakland, CA: New Harbinger Publications, 2020).

CHAPTER 1

1. Geraldine Heng, *The Invention of Race in the European Middle Ages* (Cambridge University Press, 2018).

2. Robert Sussman, *The Myth of Race* (Cambridge, MA: Harvard University Press, 2016), 12.

3. Sussman, *The Myth of Race*; Stephen Gould, *The Mismeasure of Man* (New York: W. W. Norton & Company, 1996).

4. Heather C. McGhee, "1674–1679 Bacon's Rebellion," in *Four Hundred Souls: A Community History of African America, 1619–2019*, eds. Ibram X. Kendi and Keisha N. Blain (New York: Random House, 2021), 53.

5. McGhee, "1674–1679 Bacon's Rebellion," 53.

6. Heather McGhee, *The Sum of Us: What Racism Costs Everyone and How We Can Prosper Together* (New York: One World, 2021), 222.

7. McGhee, *The Sum of Us*, 222.

8. Kimberlé Crenshaw, "Demarginalizing the Intersection of Race and Sex: A Black Feminist Critique of Antidiscrimination Doctrine, Feminist Theory, and Antiracist Politics," University of Chicago Legal Forum 1989, no. 1, Article 8, https://chicagounbound.uchicago.edu/cgi/viewcontent.cgi?article=1052&context=uclf.

9. McGhee, "1674–1679 Bacon's Rebellion," 54.

10. Jessica Naudziunas et al., "Trayvon Martin's Mom: 'We Are Never Going to Recover from This,'" ABC News, July 13, 2020, https://abcnews.go.com/GMA/News/trayvon-martins-mom-recover/story?id=71715637.

11. Mary-Frances Winters, *Black Fatigue: How Racism Erodes the Mind, Body, and Spirit* (Oakland, CA: Berrett-Koehler Publishers, 2000).

CHAPTER 2

1. Jenn Jackson, "ICYMI: Check Out This Video of Celebs Who Want You to Know James Baldwin's Legacy," Black Youth Project, March 15, 2017, https://blackyouthproject.com/icymi-check-out-this-video-of-celebs-who-want-you-to-know-james-baldwins-legacy/.
2. Jonathan Kozol, *Savage Inequalities* (New York: Crown Publishing, 1991).
3. Jon Schmieder, "One Bite at a Time," Huddle Up Group, February 19, 2024, https://www.huddleupgroup.com/post/one-bite-at-a-time.
4. Frans Johansson, *The Medici Effect: What Elephants and Epidemics Can Teach Us About Innovation* (Brighton, MA: Harvard Business Publishing, 2004).
5. "Herstory," Black Lives Matter, updated July 7, 2017, https://blacklivesmatter.com/herstory/.

CHAPTER 3

1. "PEN America Index of School Book Bans – Fall 2022," PEN America, https://pen.org/index-of-school-book-bans-2022/.
2. Alex Haley, *Roots: The Saga of an American Family* (Garden City, NY: Doubleday, 2000).
3. Charles W. Mills, "White Ignorance," in *Race and Epistemologies of Ignorance*, ed. Shannon Sullivan and Nancy Tuana (Albany, NY: SUNY Press, 2007), 11–38.
4. Ralph Hertwig and Christoph Engel, "Homo Ignorans: Deliberately Choosing Not to Know," *Perspectives on Psychological Science* 11, no. 3 (2016): 359–72.
5. Isabel Wilkerson, *Caste: The Origins of Our Discontent* (New York: Random House, 2020).

CHAPTER 4

1. "Protestors' Anger Justified Even If Actions May Not Be," Monmouth University, June 2, 2020, https://www.monmouth.edu/polling-institute/reports/monmouthpoll_us_060220/; Monmouth University, "National: Partisanship Drives Latest Shift in Race Relations Attitudes," news release, July 8, 2020, https://www.monmouth.edu/polling-institute/documents/monmouthpoll_us_070820.pdf/.
2. DEI Legislation Tracker, *The Chronicle of Higher Education*, https://www.chronicle.com/article/here-are-the-states-where-lawmakers-are-seeking-to-ban-colleges-dei-efforts.
3. The Constitution of the Confederate States of America, images 1–3, 1861, Library of Congress, Washington, DC, https://www.loc.gov/resource/rbc0001.2022pe57247/?sp=1&r=0.27,0.539,0.649,0.316,0.
4. The messages and papers of Jefferson Davis and the Confederacy, including diplomatic correspondence, 1861–1865, New York Public Library, 1966, https://archive.org/details/messagespapersof01conf/page/6/mode/2up.
5. Melanie Tervalon and Jann Murray-García, "Cultural Humility Versus Cultural Competence: A Critical Distinction in Defining Physician Training Outcomes in Multicultural Education," *Journal of Health Care for the Poor and Underserved* 9, no. 2 (May 1998): 117–25.

CHAPTER 5

1. G. W. Allport, *The Nature of Prejudice* (Cambridge, MA: Addison-Wesley, 1954).

CHAPTER 6

1. "Population and Housing Unit Estimates Datasets," US Census Bureau, August 2021, https://www.census.gov/programs-surveys/popest/data/data-sets.html.

2. "Characteristics of Public and Private Elementary and Secondary School Teachers in the United States: Results from the 2017–18 National Teacher and Principal Survey," Institute of Education Sciences, National Center for Education Statistics, US Department of Education, April 2020, https://nces.ed.gov/pubs2020/2020142.pdf.

3. Ruha Benjamin, *Race After Technology* (Cambridge, UK: Polity Press, 2019).

4. Cornel West, *Race Matters* (Boston: Beacon Press, 1993).

CHAPTER 7

1. *The West Wing*, season 2, episode 10, "Noël," directed by Thomas Schlamme, story by Peter Parnell, aired December 13, 2000, on NBC.

CHAPTER 8

1. Minda Harts, *The Memo: What Women of Color Need to Know to Secure a Seat at the Table* (New York: Seal Press, 2019).

2. Wikipedia, s.v. "List of companies involved in the Holocaust," last modified August 15, 2024, https://en.wikipedia.org/wiki/List_of_companies_involved_in_the_Holocaust.

3. Maria Santana and Chris Isidore, "Goya Board Silences Its CEO After He Tells Fox News the Election Was Rigged," CNN, January 26, 2021, https://edition.cnn.com/2021/01/26/business/goya-ceo-robert-unanue-silenced/index.html.

4. Martin Niemöller, "First They Came For . . ." United States Holocaust Memorial Museum, last updated April 11, 2023, https://encyclopedia.ushmm.org/content/en/article/martin-niemoeller-first-they-came-for-the-socialists.

CHAPTER 9

1. Ijeoma Oluo, *Mediocre: The Dangerous Legacy of White Male America* (New York: Basic Books, 2020), 49.

2. Louise Boyle, "'Here It Is Better Not to Be Born': Cobalt Mining for Big Tech Is Driving Child Labor, Deaths in the Congo," *The Independent*, February 23, 2023, https://www.independent.co.uk/climate-change/news/phone-electric-vehicle-congo-cobalt-mine-b2277665.html.

3. Walker, *The Unapologetic Guide to Black Mental Health*, 73.

4. "Clark, Septima Poinsette," The Martin Luther King, Jr. Research and Education Institute, Stanford University, https://kinginstitute.stanford.edu/clark-septima-poinsette.

5. Vanessa Romo, "NFL on Kneeling Players' Protests: 'We Were Wrong,' Commissioner Says," NPR, June 5, 2020, https://www.npr.org/sections/live-updates-protests-for-racial-justice/2020/06/05/871290906/nfl-on-kneeling-players-protests-we-were-wrong-commissioner-says.

6. Jemele Hill, *Uphill* (New York: Henry Holt & Company, 2022).

7. Matt Bloom, "Librarians, Who Lost Jobs for Not Banning Books, Are Fighting Back," NPR, January 3, 2024, https://portside.org/2024-01-03/librarians-who-lost-jobs-not-banning-books-are-fighting-back.

8. Monnica Williams et al., "Assessing Racial Trauma Within a DSM-5 Framework: The UConn Racial/Ethnic Stress & Trauma Survey," *Practice Innovations* 3, no. 4 (2018): 242–60, https://doi.org/10.1037/pri0000076.

9. Walker, *The Unapologetic Guide to Black Mental Health*, 73.

CHAPTER 10

1. Bellamy Shoffner, RevHum, https://revolutionaryhumans.com/.

2. Vu Le, "White Supremacy and the Problem with Centering Donors' Interests and Emotions," *Nonprofit AF* (blog), March 22, 2021, https://nonprofitaf.com/2021/03/white-supremacy-and-the-problem-with-centering-donors-interests-and-emotions/.

ABOUT THE AUTHOR

Dr. Joe-Joe McManus has held faculty, staff, and executive roles in higher education, including serving as executive diversity officer. He has served at an HBCU, an international university, an Ivy League institution, a religion-affiliated college, and at the public university system level. He has lectured, served on panels, presented, and consulted in the US and internationally for more than three decades.

His work has centered around how best to bring about and develop antiracist leadership and organizations actively engaged in inclusive excellence. Early childhood experiences provided the initial motivation for him to strive to live his best antiracist life. After receiving a challenge from his daughter to do more, Dr. McManus decided to write this book and return to public speaking after many years working behind the scenes.

Dr. Joe-Joe lives in Southern California with his daughter, Makaila, and continues his work as an advisor to leaders on antiracism and inclusive excellence.